Bad Sex

Bad Sex

*Truth, Pleasure,
and an Unfinished Revolution*

Nona Willis Aronowitz

PLUME

PLUME

An imprint of Penguin Random House LLC
penguinrandomhouse.com

Portions of this work were previously published by the author in a different form in the following:
"What Happened When the Mother of Non-Monogamy Fell Head Over Heels in Love," by Nona Willis Aronowitz on Elle.com, February 13, 2019.
"I Wish I Wasn't Married: In Defense of Domestic Partnerships for Straight Couples," by Nona Willis Aronowitz on GOOD.is, July 16, 2011.
"The First Time Women Shouted Their Abortions," by Nona Willis Aronowitz on NYTimes.com, March 23, 2019.
"Meet the Woke Misogynist," by Nona Willis Aronowitz on Splinternews.com, March 12, 2017.
"The Male Feminist Movement Time Forgot," by Nona Willis Aronowitz on Vice.com, March 18, 2019.
"Are Straight People OK? How We Can Improve Heterosexuality," by Nona Willis Aronowitz on TeenVogue.com © Condé Nast, November 10, 2020.

Grateful acknowledgment is made to the following for permission to reprint previously published material:
Stuart Bernstein Representation for Artists: Excerpts from "The Slow Dance" from *Loving in the War Years: Lo que nunca pasó por sus labios*, copyright © 1983 by Cherríe Moraga; and "Where Beauty Resides" from *The Last Generation: Prose & Poetry*, copyright © 1993 by Cherríe Moraga. The two volumes are to be reissued in a one volume edition by Haymarket Books in 2023. By permission of Stuart Bernstein Representation for Artists, New York, NY, and protected by the Copyright Laws of the United States. All rights reserved. The printing, copying, redistribution, or retransmission of this content without express permission is prohibited.

Cheryl Clarke: Except from the poem "great expectations" from *Living as a Lesbian: Poetry*, copyright © 1986 by Cheryl Clarke, published by Firebrand Books in 1986, and reissued by Sinister Wisdom in 2014. Reprinted by permission of the poet.

LIBRARY OF CONGRESS CATALOGING-IN-PUBLICATION DATA
has been applied for.

ISBN 9780593182765 (hardcover)
ISBN 9780593182772 (ebook)

Printed in the United States of America

1st Printing

BOOK DESIGN BY KRISTIN DEL ROSARIO

Some names and identifying characteristics have been changed to protect the privacy of the individuals involved.

For my parents

CONTENTS

Bad Sex

Introduction

In the last few days of 2016, everything in my life and in America was in extreme disarray. I was thirty-two years old. My marriage was falling apart. My father was a year out from a massive stroke that had changed both our lives. My forays into fresh pleasures had left my heart and libido suffering from overexposure. The country was reeling after that infamous election. I was constantly sniffling—from crying, and also from the sinus infection that had rudely shown up on top of everything else. I felt at sea, and not in the placid way, in the thrash-around way. I looked at the crumpled-up tissues piled on my coffee table and between the cushions of my couch, and I had a strong wish to put my former life back together again, even though some of this turmoil had been my own doing.

In more hopeful moments, I'd feel the elation of dispensing with fear and inhibition. I'd be grateful for this intervention and the chance to rewrite my story. But during those few days, when self-doubt filled up the lonely void between Christmas and New Year's, I wondered: Did I really blow up a relationship that lasted a quarter of my life, just because of bad sex?

What even is "bad sex"? It's a cruel descriptor, both lazy and below the belt, an indictment of everyone involved. When people heard the title of this book, they assumed I would be discussing the nuts and bolts of the sexual act: stale technique and sexual dysfunction, low libido and the orgasm gap. To me, the mechanics of sex are important but limited. I'm far more concerned with the broader question of what cultural forces interfere with our pleasure, desire, and relationship satisfaction. And I'm particularly concerned with a dilemma recognizable to many women who fuck men: sex has never been more normalized, feminism has never been more popular, romantic relationships have never been more malleable—yet we still haven't transcended the binds that make sex and love go bad.

We have not, for instance, succeeded in avoiding dudes who don't notice we're having a bad time, or notice but don't seem to care, or pretend to care but actually don't. We continue to deal with guys who cross our boundaries in some way, transforming bad sex (or even good sex) into something shitty and murky and scary. We still often end up indulging men's fantasies rather than our own. We're told that being vulnerable is the key to love and lust, and yet it's easier said than done.

Even the most sexually confident among us sometimes hesitate to talk about all this, because we don't want to hurt our partners' feelings or seem demanding, because we want to appear as horny as we initially advertised ourselves to be, because the length of time it takes us to orgasm will spoil the mood, because we're physically or emotionally afraid, because too much is at stake, because we're simply not sure what we want. We still seem to face unpleasant consequences, both blatant and insidious, when we do talk about certain things that, even in the most progressive circles, are still treated like TMI.

Of course, sometimes bad sex, or a bad relationship, isn't anybody's fault. It may be caused by incompatibility, a dearth of attraction, an absence of chemistry. For some, this kind of neutral, blameless bad sex is a relatively small thing, certainly nothing to end a marriage over. For me, though, bad sex was the gateway that revealed all kinds of other truths. It was the thing that eventually exposed the desires I was ignoring in favor of society's expectations, which led to a break in the hum of my life, which in turn forced the questions: What, exactly, do I want? And are my sexual and romantic desires even possible amid the horrors and bribes of patriarchy, capitalism, and white supremacy?

This book is about the necessity, but also the complexity and absurdity, of answering those questions. They're questions I ask myself many times throughout this story, which mostly unfolds between fall of 2015 and the end of 2020. Even with very little distance from them, I think we can all agree that these years were a wild time to be alive in America, and an even wilder time for one's life to take a sharp turn toward the unknown. This has been a time of fear and death, but also of reckoning and reimagining. It's made me curious about other times in history that vibrated with the same transformative energy. About what I could learn from revolutionaries of the past who lived through moments when the norms of sexuality changed.

Which is why, during that low point in winter, I turned to my mother for advice. Not literally, because she had died a decade before, a few months after my twenty-second birthday. My mom,

Ellen Willis, a writer and early radical pro-sex feminist, was deeply involved in both the sexual revolution and Second Wave feminism, movements that were at once in harmony and in conflict. Her specialty was documenting the collisions of the personal and political, particularly when it came to sex. So I thought her writing might contain . . . not answers, exactly, but empathy, or articulation, or some sort of guidance. I chose a 1989 essay called "Coming Down Again: After the Age of Excess."

"It was the best, the worst, the most enlightening, the most bewildering of times," she wrote in the essay, about the dawn of the women's movement. "Feminism intensified my utopian sexual imagination, made me desperate to get what I really wanted . . . even as it intensified my skepticism, chilling me with awareness of how deeply relations between the sexes were corrupted and, ultimately, calling into question the very nature of my images of desire."

The source of my own self-doubt, I have since realized, was precisely the double-edged sword of radicalization that my mother describes. Reconciling personal desire with political conviction is, frankly, a tall order. It's chaotic, maddening, grueling, confusing, and yet essential—an exquisite mess that propels this book's zigzag pursuit of sexual liberation. Alongside my own intimate history and my family history are other stories stretching back nearly two hundred years: those of ambivalent wives and unchill sluts, free lovers and radical lesbians, sensitive men and woke misogynists, women who risk everything for sex, who buy sex, reject sex, have bad sex and good sex. These are stories of pleasure, peril, safety, freedom, and the muddy paths that connect them all.

1. Bad Sex

We *had* to tell the truth; so much depended on it.
—ALIX KATES SHULMAN, ON CONSCIOUSNESS-RAISING

It was six months after we'd broken up when Aaron found the pros and cons list. It'd been ripped out of a yellow Moleskine notebook, presumably so I could stash it somewhere more discreet or maybe dispose of it altogether. Yet it was diligently dated "11/21/13," which apparently I couldn't help noting for posterity.

I'd written it during a five-day solo trip to France before I started a full-time reporting gig. The trip was conceptualized as a long weekend in upstate New York, but somehow I found myself on Airbnb browsing quaint French dwellings instead—the ultimate setting, I thought, for a romantical getaway with myself. During this search I learned the word *gîte* (cottage), and that I could not afford one in the places I'd heard of, like Provence, but could maybe swing one in this mountainous area in the south called the Cévennes. The place reasonably fit my fantasy of solitude against a medieval limestone backdrop, unchanged by the modern world. I booked a *gîte* and a plane ticket.

It took me a day and a half of navigating a Parisian train station, a car-rental kiosk, endless roundabouts, and a tense standoff with another driver on a supposedly two-way dirt road that, I swear, could not have been more than six feet wide. (He eventually took pity on me, reversing back up the mountain when he heard my panicked English.) I finally arrived at my *gîte* in the teensy, leafy hamlet of Monoblet.

The cottage's owner, Fabien, was a fortyish salt-and-pepper dad of two girls who recommended I call the town's restaurant to announce my plans to dine. The cobblestones were slick with rain when I arrived at the square. There was one tobacco store that doubled as a bar, emitting fluorescent light and some rather unwelcoming male energy. There was one bakery selling bottles of wine for three euros each. And there was the one restaurant, white-tableclothed and empty. I sat down and ordered a six-course meal, complete with a sorbet palate cleanser that the waiter had to pull away from me prematurely, à la Vivian from *Pretty Woman*.

After that night, the damp late-fall weather mostly left me tucked inside the cottage with my yellow notebook, consuming the bakery's three-euro wine and bread and soft cheese and various spreadable meats. Fabien only enhanced the appeal of hunkering. Every morning, he came to my cottage, which he'd built himself, to start a fire in the woodstove and bring me little treats like fresh eggs, fig jam, and homemade vinegar. I learned he was going through a divorce, that this Airbnb might not be long for this world. He was very sad and very hot, and while I was too shy to do anything more than flirt with him, I began to fantasize nightly about leaving my life in New York City with Aaron to roll around naked in front of the woodstove with Fabien, feeding him slices of Camembert as a postcoital snack.

I did start to wonder why I'd come all the way to Monoblet just to gorge and scribble and masturbate. I'd given people a lot of reasons for this trip—a last hurrah before a demanding job; a chance to write in peace—but why this random, far-flung, English-free place? The woodsy, misty landscape was, if I was very honest, not unlike my original destination of upstate New York, and so was its bone-chilling November weather. A higher salary was on the horizon, but at the moment I plainly could not afford this.

I think I knew that I just wanted to spend some uninterrupted time, far away, contemplating whether I should end my marriage.

Consider, for instance, the pros and cons list. I wrote it at the kitchen table on a gray afternoon, as naturally and casually as a shopping list. Transcribing the circular thoughts that had become fixtures in my brain, I put Aaron's good and bad qualities in two columns. They were around the same length. The pros lavished praise on his tender heart—"generous," "sensitive," "affectionate," "sense of comfort," "always on my side." The cons were mostly different ways of pointing out our incompatible interests: "we sometimes have nothing to talk about," "doesn't read." And then, one vague entry, covered over with scribbles: "bad place with sex."

Aaron found the list one day in our protracted post-breakup period, when, amid the rage and its rebound into knee-jerk intimacy, there was also a deluge of mundane tasks to do, like going through a bunch of boxes together and divvying up the items. When the paper fluttered out, he scanned the list, unsurprised by its content (we'd talked about all these issues to death), but flabbergasted by the date.

"Twenty thirteen?" he exclaimed. "You stayed with me for *three more years* after this?"

"There were just as many pros as cons," I replied weakly. But I knew what he was thinking: Why did this woman stay with me for so long if she was clearly miserable?

It's still a good question. It's one I've asked myself a million times. It's one best answered by that euphemistic crossed-out entry on the list. Thousands of miles away in France, alone, in a *gîte*, with no sunny days, no work, no friends, no parties, no chores, no Aaron, I wasn't ready yet to be honest, even on a list meant for nobody but myself.

I'd like to say that my divorce began with that one seed of doubt in France, which eventually blossomed into the clarity I needed to end our eight-year relationship. The truth was that the doubt seeds had been sowed for a long while, at least six of our eight years together, usually plowed over by the comforting, everyday marital routine one becomes used to and is convinced one cannot live without, or by more potent sensations like fear and the pleasure of acceptance. The pros and cons list might have been the starkest proof of the doubt seeds' existence; Fabien and his *gîte* might have been the most poetic instance of them taking root. But there were always one hundred seeds sowed every so often, with a pathetic germination rate of 15 percent, then 20, then up and up until finally the sprouts were clustered so close together they were impossible to ignore.

There were some doubt seeds in the very beginning, when Aaron and I were twentysomething hedonists who had incoherent late-night fights, ones that involved shoving each other and slamming doors. There were some doubt seeds later when I made him move from his hometown of Chicago to my hometown of New York: he hated the city and its seven-dollar beers and dirty screeching subways and tussles with aggressive strangers. Very understandably, he couldn't fathom why anyone would want this punishing life. And doubt seeds showered everywhere each time I craved an intellectual sparring partner but then remembered there were huge chunks of my brain I knew he didn't understand, and vice versa.

But the doubt seeds that turned into saplings, and then giant weeds, were the bad-sex seeds. I can now say with certainty that our sex was bad, and toward the end it got worse, metastasizing in a hideous way. It was bad in 2008, when it mostly took place drunk at six in the morning or hungover at noon. It was bad in 2010, at the tail end of the honeymoon period after moving in together, and a few years later when many of our attempts at fucking would snowball into an unclothed argument and end with him storming out of the bedroom, and with me curled into a fetal position. It was bad when I started to sleep with other people, at first adhering to but later breaking the rules of our already nonmonogamous relationship. It was bad up until the last time we fucked, August 19, 2016, two weeks before I moved out. It was bad!

Even when our sex was "good"—everyone's body parts were doing what they should; if you saw a video of us doing it, you'd be like, "hot"—I wasn't present, nor was I lost in bliss. Most of the time I was some putrid combination of bored, irritable, and dissociated. A couple of years in, when I requested an open relationship, I came up with all kinds of sexpert-approved reasons: because it creates and maintains healthy tension, because monogamy isn't sustainable, because to hell with patriarchy and the marriage industrial complex. But I knew deep, deep, deep down that the main reason I wanted to fuck other people was because I no longer wanted to fuck him.

So what, exactly, was so bad about our sex? During our harrowing mid-coitus fights, I'd fixate on technique and positions, not acknowledging that we simply didn't have that unlearnable spark, which could, of course, be enhanced with but not created by skills. I knew I'd had wonderful sexual encounters with other people where our chemistry transcended mechanics or traditional markers of success; one of my favorite sex partners, for instance, had never even witnessed me orgasm. I was also attracted to Aaron, and always had been. So it really boiled down to the fact that most of the time, sex with him felt physically, rhythmically, olfactorily wrong. And once in a while, when I was in the mood for self-honesty, I could see clearly that our "bad sex" was the symptom of a bigger problem—that I didn't love or understand him in the way I needed to. That our connection, though real, wasn't strong enough. I was scribbling out the one con that mattered most.

For a long time, I couldn't admit any of this to anyone. This was me, who had a reputation among my friends for being candid, dishy, horny, and emotionally indulgent. Me, who had thought and written about sexual politics for years. Me, who grew up with a radical feminist mother who never settled for an unsatisfying relationship and had taught me, through her writing, to value passion and intellectual chemistry.

It was partially because Aaron's good qualities routinely quelled these moments of misery. He was vibrating and alive, a well of empathy who wanted to absorb the world's beauty and pain. Aaron was my ravenous partner in consuming pleasures—beaches and bike rides and cocktails and all kinds of food—and he was also down for a depressive cry while listening to Cat Power or Explosions in the Sky. His soul was stripped bare for me: no guile, no shade, no contempt for me ever. Not once did I catch him in a lie. I felt like a sinister double agent in comparison.

Our lives became further intertwined when Aaron welcomed me into his giant midwestern family, while mine shrank before my eyes. My mother had died of lung cancer a year before we met, despite never having smoked. She'd been diagnosed my junior year of college, and by the time I graduated, it had gone into remission. But on Halloween 2006, when I was twenty-two, I found my mom on the couch at my parents' new house in Jackson Heights, Queens, with a bad cold. My parents revealed that the cancer was now in her lymph nodes. We hugged, and she told me that she might live for a few years, but probably not longer than that. Nine days later, she was dead.

The scariest day wasn't the one she died on but three nights before, when no one from the medical establishment yet had the balls to tell my father and me that she was definitely going to die. My dad sent me back to my apartment to rest after we'd spent two straight days feeding my mother Ensure, keeping Otis Redding and Janis Joplin in constant rotation, whispering softly that we were there, that we loved her. I spent the night in my tiny room with a knotted, caffeinated tummy, in and out of sleep, more hopeless and frightened than I'd ever felt in my life.

My close-knit nuclear unit of three broke off into just me and my dad—two floating, grieving, barely touching icebergs. It was Aaron who stepped in to re-create the dependable bond and familiarity everyone hopes to have with close family. He helped me care for my father (by that time in his mid-seventies), a job that would've normally fallen to my mother. Aaron took to these roles with a reassuring goodwill and a sense of shared purpose. This kind of loyalty wasn't easy to gamble away.

But there were other things holding me back, things that had little to do with the affection or emotional support I got from Aaron. The truth is I was secretly terrified of being single in my thirties, despite my feminist posturing about independence. Besides that, I worried about being a hypocrite. How would it look if I admitted I stayed with a person I didn't like to fuck, despite my almost religious devotion to the fruits of the sexual revolution, especially the pockets that focused on female pleasure? I couldn't see clearly whether this was just my problem, or if this was a common feeling among women like me, who outwardly had their sexuality all figured out but privately had doubts about their lives.

It hadn't yet occurred to me that if you keep your worries and fears and suspicions to yourself, if you travel halfway across the globe alone and still end up covering those fears and suspicions with scribbles, it's impossible to know which parts are personal and which parts are political—or whether there's a difference, or whether it matters. I hadn't yet asked myself: What happens when you say your darkest thoughts out loud?

• • •

In the fall of 1967, a small group of mostly white, mostly educated women in their twenties started meeting in the evenings in narrow, tenement-style apartments on the Lower East Side in New York City, the kind that still had bathtubs in the kitchens. They wore fitted paisley minidresses and tidy updos; long hair and jeans; billowy white linens and gingham clamdiggers. They'd sit on chairs or windowsills or cross-legged on the floor, chattering and taking notes. Later, when the meetings got crowded, they'd stand on the edges, craning their necks and moving their bags from one shoulder to the other.

Restless revolutionary energy was all around them. Some of these women had been active in the civil rights and antiwar movements, but many of them had caught a distinct sense of dismissal, even contempt, from the male activists for whom they'd been stuffing envelopes. They often struggled to gain political clout on the Left, especially if they declined to trade sexual favors—feminist Francine Silbar wrote that women were treated like "sexual garbage cans" by activist men.

The group was called New York Radical Women. Their idea was to talk about their daily lives and put them in the context of society. Though many of them had yet to consider how racism and sexism overlap and collaborate, they did draw inspiration from the civil rights movement. A couple of group members recalled their time in Mississippi working with the Student Nonviolent Coordinating Committee (SNCC), where they'd witnessed mass meetings at which Black people would stand up and "testify" about their own personal experiences with racism. A radical civil rights worker from Iowa, Carol Hanisch, connected the concept to Mao Tse-tung's slogan "Speak pain to recall pain."

Before women were encouraged to compare notes, slogans like "Sisterhood Is Powerful" had the force of shouting a taboo. These gatherings were more in the spirit of Betty Friedan's silence-breaking 1963 book, *The Feminine Mystique*, than her subsequent project, the National Organization for Women, which seemed hopelessly bourgeois to the women in these sessions. The young radicals were calling for women's liberation, not just the right of women to participate in the same oppressive societal structures as men did.

In the meetings, the women talked about all kinds of things that were previously considered private affairs, from pregnancy to abortion to harassment to rape to beauty standards to the tyranny of childcare and domestic chores. And sex—lots about sex. Entire sessions would be devoted to sexual pleasure and lack thereof. One workshop on sex at a 1968 radical feminist conference memorably lasted long into the night. In a 1980 essay, feminist writer Alix Kates Shulman remembered those early sessions: "Sex was a central and explosive subject to which we continually returned"; participants "used their sexual discontents to help them understand the power relations between men and women."

These meetings also gave women permission to expose intimate relationship details to the open air, often for the first time. Some admitted that their husbands hit them, talked down to them, or unapologetically swallowed up their identities. Some of these women came out as lesbians: "I had to keep it a secret when I made love to women," said a participant in one meeting, "even though I knew that if we had free choices that would be one of them." They revealed their most taboo sexual fantasies. They discussed shame and fear and also everyday affronts like partners who appeared to be decent humans but didn't even bother to feign interest in their pleasure, boundaries, or birth control methods. Shulman remembers a mass admission of faked orgasms, but "instead of feeling guilty about it, we saw faking as a response to pressures that had been put upon *us* by men." The point wasn't to solve everyone's private problems, but rather to understand the social basis of their complaints—and then change them.

Often, the women grappled with ambivalent feelings about the 1960s sexual revolution, which hadn't yet been analyzed through a feminist lens. For some, this new era had brought relief, a rush of freedom, a release of deep-seated shame. The advent of the birth control pill helped lift the albatross of pregnancy risk for women who slept with men, and, particularly in countercultural crowds, women were no longer considered "damaged goods" if they had sex before marriage. Longtime *Cosmopolitan* editor Helen Gurley Brown wrote *Sex and the Single Girl*, a perky 1962 guidebook that combined sexual liberation with makeup tips and packaged sexual freedom for mainstream America. A few years later, the burgeoning counterculture, and the rock 'n' roll era that preceded it, quivered with openly sexual energy.

But sexual liberation had also created new problems. Male icons of the movement like Hugh Hefner espoused the goal of more, widely accessible sex. This gave many young men (who seemingly had no inkling as to why women would have more reasons to fear the consequences of sex) a pass to pressure women to "put out." Women wanted to be able to pursue sex without forfeiting their right to say no. And because many men had seen the sex revolution as quantitative, not qualitative, a lot of this sex was bad: most men had no idea what they were doing. "The guys fucked like rabbits—in, out, in, out," recalled feminist sex pioneer Betty Dodson, who later issued a clarion call to encourage masturbation. "It was so boring you could die." Yet women were expected to writhe around in ecstasy, lest they be called "frigid" or "a drag."

In June 1968, New York Radical Women compiled some of these ideas into a twenty-nine-page journal called *Notes from the First Year*, selling it for fifty cents to women and one dollar to men. Much of the journal's format was dispatch-style: One article was an amalgamated "conversation" about women's liberation that provided a retort to any anti-feminist argument—about economic power, about man hating, about dishwashing, about whether female oppression even exists. Another, by Kathie Amatniek (who'd later change her last name to Sarachild), was a satirical "funeral oration" for "traditional womanhood." ("The grand old lady finally died today—her doctor said, of a bad case of shock.")

Sexuality was all over *Notes*. The piece that got the most attention was Anne Koedt's "The Myth of the Vaginal Orgasm." Koedt rejected Freudian ideas of frigidity, "defined by men as the failure of women to have vaginal orgasms." Advocating for the clitoris to be seen as essential, she called on women to "redefine our sexuality" and for "new guidelines which take into account mutual sexual enjoyment"—not just the penis-in-vagina friction that caused men to come.

Shulamith Firestone included a militant speech she'd given at an abortion rally protesting the jailing of abortion activist Bill Baird: "We refuse to be your passive vessels becoming impregnated for the greater good of society," she declared. "We are not just grease between men, links between generations, not just the mothers of sons and their future wives!"

Firestone also included a reconstruction of the group's meetings about sex. A participant in Firestone's re-created dialogue pinpointed the twisted new form of pressure that the sexual revolution had created: "If you don't want to sleep with him, he assumes you're hung-up and then you have to stay up the whole night anyway convincing him you're not!" Another woman in the piece wistfully called for a movement that centered female desire: "We've got to learn to sleep with people because WE want them, not because THEY want us," she said. "Not to prove anything to them, not to make them feel better about their masculinity, not out of weakness or inability to say no, but simply because we WANT to."

Some women couldn't enjoy sex unless they were in love;

others resented the lingering expectation of marriage. Some felt sexually rejected by their partners; others felt harangued by them. Still others didn't yet know what they wanted.

"I guess we're not going to get any conclusions from this session," one woman remarked in a small group meeting. "We're all saying completely different things."

"Beautiful!" another replied. "Maybe that's what liberation really is."

Soon after its publication in the summer of 1968, *Notes from the First Year* had been mimeographed all over the country, and women's groups in Chicago, Gainesville, Boston, and Seattle had created pamphlets of their own. New York Radical Women planned a September action at the Miss America pageant in Atlantic City to protest how women were judged as sex objects. They didn't burn bras, as the urban legend goes, but they did fling them into trash cans—along with girdles, copies of *Playboy* magazine, and other articles of oppression. "Ain't she sweet, making profit off her meat," one jingle went. Four of the women managed to hang a sign from the convention hall's balcony: WOMEN'S LIBERATION. The triumph was nationally televised.

• • •

In the fall of 1968, my then twenty-six-year-old mother, Ellen Willis, was on her way to San Francisco with her boyfriend to visit their mutual friends, Fred and Jenny. She read about the Miss America protest in the newspaper and was dubious: "Won't people think they're just ugly, jealous women?" she wrote in a diaristic chronicle of the early women's movement. Even so, she continued, "I remember what it's like to be examined and compared at a party. And I'm proud that women are in the papers for fighting."

When my mother arrived in California, Jenny gave her a copy of *Notes from the First Year*. "It disturbs me," she wrote at the time. "All our problems aren't caused by men—are they? The tone strikes me as frighteningly bitter, especially about sexual relationships. Either I've been remarkably lucky, or they've been unlucky . . . or maybe I let men who give me a hard time off the hook too easily." Though she was skeptical, she agreed to go to a women's meeting with Jenny. It was chaotic and unfocused, but she was impressed by the sheer fact of women organizing a meeting to talk. During earlier attempts at activism—she'd gone to a few Congress of Racial Equality (CORE) meetings and donned a SNCC button in the mid-sixties—she'd always detected aloof suspicion from the men, which in turn made her feel insecure. Here, she felt welcome. Like she didn't have to prove herself. She resolved to join the women's movement as soon as she got home to New York.

At the time, Ellen was working as a freelance writer and living in the East Village, a stone's throw from those women's meetings. The group was now convening every Thursday at the offices of the civil rights organization Southern Conference Educational Fund, where Carol Hanisch worked. Ellen had been in that neighborhood since 1966, shortly after she left her husband. She'd married him at twenty years old against her better judgment, in an era when getting married was still considered essential to being a woman.

Her cousin Judy, who was as close to her as a sister, remembers Ellen explaining her wedding as little more than an airline ticket: She was about to graduate from Barnard and was dating Henry, who at the time was a student at Columbia. The way Ellen saw it, marriage was the only socially acceptable way she could accompany him to Berkeley, California. At their wedding, she had a sullen look on her face. She gave it a good-faith effort with cooking and cleaning, doing what Judy called the "real wifely bit," but she hated it. One night, she was out to dinner with Judy, along with a married couple who were friends of Henry's. The conversation turned to domesticity, and at one point the wife leaned over to Ellen and said, "But don't you just love it?" Ellen didn't protest out loud—in 1962, no *real* woman would publicly admit they hated being a wife—but the look on her face was one of pure horror.

The couple had moved from New York to Berkeley to Washington, DC, where Henry was preparing for the Foreign Service. They were fighting all the time, and Henry was snubbing Ellen in the bedroom. Feeling miserable and stifled, she had a rapturous, short-lived affair with another Foreign Service trainee and immediately told Henry about it—her way of making a break. The marriage was over. She was free.

Ellen moved back to New York, rented a studio in the East Village, and got an editorial job at a quarterly magazine called *Fact*, famous for having been sued by Barry Goldwater. She presently began dating Bob, a journalist who'd gone to junior high school with her back in Queens. A "very cocky" guy who delighted in debating her, he served as a kind of countercultural spirit guide. He brought her around to his artsy friends. After turning down an assignment about Bob Dylan at *Commentary*, he suggested to his editor that Ellen write it instead. Her seven thousand words on Dylan's artistic transformation later turned heads at two publishing houses and *The New Yorker,* where she soon became the magazine's pop-music critic. Eventually, Ellen moved into a rent-controlled apartment downtown, and Bob moved in shortly afterward.

After her 1968 California trip with Bob, Ellen met the women behind *Notes*, who were "nothing like my fantasies of anti-sex fanatics," she wrote. "They seem no different from other women, except friendlier." In the first few months, she and Shulamith Firestone, who would publish the feminist classic *The Dialectic of Sex* less than two years later, formed a breakout group called Redstockings. They planned their first action in the spring of 1969: a three-hundred-person abortion speak-out at a church in Greenwich Village, inspired by a New York State legislative committee hearing on abortion the month before, whose "experts" had consisted of fourteen men and a nun.

By then, Ellen had fully crossed the Rubicon. "Consciousness-raising has one terrible result," she wrote in the same diaristic account of the period. "It makes you more conscious." Suddenly she was noticing every catcall on the street, every condescending "dear," every time men wouldn't clear their own plates at a dinner party. The women's movement also ended up affecting "what used to be called my private life." Certain things she'd taken for granted about her relationship with Bob—their mentor-neophyte dynamic; his displays of male aggression—were now bathed in the harsh light of her new awareness. She began to have her own doubt seeds about their conventional dyad, doubts that came to a head in the fall of 1969.

She planned to move to Colorado Springs with Bob for several months to help organize a GI coffeehouse project near the military base there. Because Bob had to travel for a reporting trip, she arrived a couple of weeks before he did. In that time Ellen had a magical, erotic acid trip in the mountains with a younger guy named Steve, a mellow hippie with long strawberry-blond hair who had been convicted of draft resistance that summer and was expecting to go to jail any day.

Upon arriving in Colorado Springs, Bob was hit with some discomfiting news: Ellen wanted to sleep with her crush, and she wanted to open up the relationship. He felt jealous as hell, but he tried to get in the spirit of things. He dropped acid with Ellen, Steve, and another hippie. At one point, they decided to search for the most beautiful thing they could find and bring it back to share with the group. My mother kept trying to transport a handful of silky, glinting water extracted from a mountain stream; every time, it slipped through her fingers. Bob would soon realize that she had slipped through his.

Only six days after arriving in Colorado, Bob left. Distraught over the seemingly sudden eruption of their three-year-old romance, he inundated Ellen with letters, convinced that "ten months of feminist nagging" had forever altered their relationship. He'd always appreciated her high sex drive; now he resented her need to explore sexually on her own terms. "I no longer dig your lust because I have come to perceive it as destructive," he wrote. At times, Bob diagnosed their breakup in terms of universal human betrayal: "I trusted you to be kind," he wrote, and she broke that trust. But while he believed in the project of women's liberation, he also thought himself a casualty of an incomplete, fledgling revolution. "The women's movement clearly needs a new kind of consciousness, one that somehow encompasses struggle and love, but it sure ain't found it yet," he wrote. "I am the victim of cultural lag. How poetic."

Bob was bitter and he was angry, but he wasn't entirely wrong. As he worked through his pain, he struggled to locate his role in the emotional truth of a woman whose politics had transformed so suddenly and dramatically in front of his eyes. While Ellen expressed ambivalence in almost every letter—writing things like, "I am beginning to doubt myself again and wonder if I am really crazy"—mostly she reinforced Bob's cultural-lag theory. His aggressiveness and tendency to dominate were "essentially male supremacist phenomena," she wrote, while gentle Steve was "more like what I think men should change into." On liberationist grounds, Ellen defended her right to follow the "supercharged emotional excitement" at the start of a relationship, a feeling she'd never felt with Bob: "I have had it with repression—had it with so many years of bottling myself up." She even attributed the dynamic of their split—Bob's explosions of self-righteousness and possessiveness, Ellen's impulse to give in so she'd stop hurting him—to deeply ingrained gender roles.

And yet they also reminded each other how facile it is to simply blame a movement, how impossible it is to separate the personal from the political, especially during a breakup. Bob, caustic as ever, wondered if the reason she was leaving went beyond her faith in freedom and autonomy: "Maybe it has to do with some missing sense of yourself, some center that just isn't there for you, and that you're not going to find in a man, or work, or feminism, or a community, or chemicals."

Meanwhile, Ellen blamed both their personalities. "Our relationship was in trouble in New York—perhaps external pressures were mostly responsible, but not entirely," she wrote. "The important thing is how we get along together in very specific ways." She was feeling dissatisfied for a long while, though she "didn't realize how unhappy I'd been till I got to Colorado and started to relax—like you don't realize how tight the shoe is till you take it off." She brought up specific sexual grievances beyond monogamy. "Part of it had to do with your determination to conquer my inhibition about being very matter of fact about sex, telling you exactly what I wanted, etc.," she wrote. "Maybe it's reactionary, but I am just not that way, and you were interfering with a very deep thing you're just not qualified to interfere with." The fact is, she felt bullied by him.

Was Ellen leaving Bob because the consciousness she'd gained had magnified the cracks in their pre-revolution union? Were there just parts of Bob's personality that were deal breakers, women's movement or no? Is it possible that she was in her twenties, just a few years out from an unsatisfying marriage, and she prioritized expansiveness? It could have been—almost definitely was—all three.

• • •

Ellen and Steve began living together in a big group house not too far from the Home Front Coffeehouse, a place with black lights and posters where GIs who were disenchanted with the war could talk, read, listen to music, and do drugs. (There were a *lot* of drugs.) The $150 a week from her monthly *New Yorker* contract—a significant sum at the time—covered rent and food for the entire group house.

By the winter, Steve had won his appeal. He wasn't going to jail. Despite their conversations about non-possessive love, she and Steve had become just as entrenched in claustrophobic coupledom as she and Bob had been. But they got along. They loved each other. For a handful of months, they organized the GIs, listened to Ellen's free review copies of records, and snuggled their cats, Molly and Boo. Then the coffeehouse project began to fizzle and sour. Ellen started suffering from sleeplessness and writer's block. The couple moved from Colorado to recuperate in upstate New York, where they had ups and downs of their own: "isolation, dependency, honeymoonisoverness," but also a closeness that comes from pushing through that initial infatuation. Eventually, they moved back to New York City, where they rented the basement of a house in Brooklyn for a couple hundred dollars a month.

And then, at the tail end of 1973, when she'd just turned thirty-two, Ellen initiated a breakup with Steve. He remembers it not as one defining incident—although their fights were at times acutely painful—but as a result of her amorphous desire for freedom and solitude. It wasn't a clean break. She and Steve felt like family to each other, and for years they would occasionally sleep together after a night out on the town. But partnership never felt quite right. As she said to Steve, miffed after discovering he'd gone on a few dates with another woman: "You know, we were always better friends than we were lovers." Looking back, Steve thinks she was probably right. "Ellen really did want to live on her own," he reflected years later on the phone to me. "She wanted to have other relationships. She wanted to be by herself."

And she *would* live alone, for six years after that, first in the place they once shared in Park Slope, then in a small apartment on Waverly Place in the West Village. Nostalgists might picture a modest but sunny studio, perhaps with dusty parquet floors and other prewar details. I certainly did as a young teen growing up with two professor parents in the nineties. By the time my mom got tenure at NYU and we moved into a university-owned apartment in 1995, Bleecker Street's musicians and artists had long ago been replaced by drunk tourists and college freshmen brandishing fake IDs.

Sadly, old photos confirm that my mom's place on Waverly did not fit my bohemian fantasy. It was shabby, without the chic. The floors were black-and-white-checkered linoleum, even in the bedroom; my mother's thousands of records were held up by plywood and cinder blocks; her bed was a frameless mattress and box spring covered with tattered floral sheets. Still, this apartment was hers. It became the place she'd hole up and write (or have writer's block) for days, eating marshmallow circus peanuts and blintzes from the Polish diner. It became a place she danced to Creedence Clearwater Revival, had affairs, gossiped with friends, and read books while chain-drinking coffee.

Through those years of being a single woman in her thirties—still rare, still considered pitiable, but becoming both more accepted and common—consciousness-raising remained part of her life. She attended meetings once a week with her women's group, which she sometimes called the Sex Fools. The group was started in the mid-seventies, when there was already backlash to radical feminism's most transformative ideas. The group met regularly for fifteen years. Perhaps it lasted so long because the Sex Fools expanded beyond just sharing; they'd pick a topic to focus on for several weeks, like class, and discuss it in a structured way. On the other hand, it could have endured because it remained small and didn't have as much of a revolving door as other groups. The personal details that fueled those meetings opened the door to everyday friendship. Raw honesty wasn't just a political strategy; it was also a new and exciting way to experience womanhood, one that would define the generations to come.

• • •

By the time I was a teenager, candor between women, especially about sex, was the norm. It certainly was among my groups of New York City friends, which were racially diverse, middle-class, and mostly straight (though fewer of us would be straight by the time we became adults). I looked to my high school and college diaries, at miles-long Gchat convos made possible by boring internships and entry-level desk jobs, in which my friends and I frequently shared bawdy sexual details. We spilled about our partners' embarrassing orgasm sounds and our first vibrators, then later about our lackluster sex with too-drunk Tinder matches and the first times we got our butts eaten. "Sometimes having sex on my period is good but then sometimes it just makes me feel all achey," I chatted to my college buddy Vanessa. "And then when guys say to you, 'well can i just fuck you in the ass instead?' at my MOST sensitive time? yeah RIGHT."

We were also blunt in our assessments of people we were having sex with, especially when they disappointed us. This bluntness continued for years, even two months into my then situationship with Aaron: "When we got into bed he just started talking crazy," reads a message I wrote to my friend Ruby in the spring of 2008. "Some things were mean and some things were just intensely romantic and some were just literally nonsense. Sometimes I think he's like the darkest person I've ever met."

But an unsettling thing started to happen when people around me paired off in more serious relationships. Many of us who were coupled up defaulted to a hermetically sealed bubble of "things are hard but everything is cool." My single friends still messaged me things like, "Finally got my brains fucked out by some neanderthal from Tinder, he bit my lip so hard I'm afraid it's gonna swell." Yet it suddenly felt inappropriate to complain about a person you'd already invested so much time in, whom you'd deemed different from those losers you dated when you were young and stupid.

Instead of providing every single unvarnished detail of every one of our dumbass melodramas, like I did in the beginning, now I'd give a sanitized version of Aaron's and my struggles. I'd gloss over whole leitmotifs of our daily lives. There were fleeting expressions of doubt about our future, and equally fleeting hints from my friends—kind and tactful—that they'd had the same thoughts about our relationship. It felt improprietous to go further. I never said what I really felt, never truly detailed the magnitude of my loneliness and dissatisfaction and sexual frustration.

I yearned for a structured way to talk about it, not in a therapy way (though I should have done that too), but to compare notes with my peers. *Did anyone else have similar doubt seeds, and if yes, did they nurture them or stamp them out?* I couldn't get it out of my head that I should be past the need for group feedback to put my problems in perspective. Modern women like us knew what we deserved, what we were looking for—which made it that much harder to admit when you were unhappy, especially if it was for a retrograde reason like not wanting to be single. The biggest shame of all was staying in a passionless partnership. If you knew you had a right to a fulfilling and stimulating relationship, intellectually and sexually, wouldn't you rather be single than stuck? Besides, wasn't it kind of pathetic to obsess over your relationship? What about your brain, your career, your friendships, your family?

For me, the result was the same as it had been for women in the pre-consciousness-raising days: a prevailing sense of isolation.

That's not to say that who we decided to love and date felt apolitical; to the contrary, we all expressed our sexual and societal ideologies through relationships that bent gender or scoffed at monogamy or blurred traditional roles. I was with a guy who did housework and supported my career and my desire for other sex partners; I had the freedom to go wherever I wanted, in any outfit I wanted; as a journalist, I constantly wrote about and criticized America's unhealthy relationship with sex.

Still, those markers of modern romance didn't allay my fears, some of which I detailed in an unusually candid 2011 email to my friend Kate, a writer ten years my senior whom I'd first befriended back when my mom had died. When I think about it now, it's obvious to me why I confided in her and no one else: I felt enough trust between us to divulge private thoughts, but the fact that she was well outside my everyday social circle created a space devoid of judgment and context. With Kate, there was no party line to be toed.

In the email, I expressed a growing desire to end my relationship because "something is missing," and my inability to do so because "1) no one will understand and 2) I'll never find anyone better. And cuddling is fun, and 'playing the field' has never come naturally to me. And we live together. And I really, really do want a kid." (Of course, I didn't mention the thing I couldn't yet admit to myself, much less write or say: our bad sex, our weak connection, was depressing the hell out of me.)

I mulled over the idea of settling: "There's definitely a chance I'll just 'go with it' and have a family with Aaron and be the fucking breadwinner for the rest of my life," I wrote, "because people assure me that dating deeply sucks in NYC and that Aaron is amazing. Which he is in so many ways, but ya know. Ugh."

In other words: better trapped than alone. Life is a series of trade-offs, I told myself, and an imperfect partnership might be a better choice than the social and emotional consequences of being a woman without a partner—feminist legacy be damned.

In an essay called "The Family: Love It or Leave It," from 1979, my mother characterized the six years she spent without a partner in her thirties as "neither an accident nor a deliberate choice," but rather evidence of feminism's success: "The sense of possibility, of hope for great changes, that pervaded those years affected all my aspirations; compromises that might once have seemed reasonable, or simply to be expected, felt stifling. . . . For me the issue was less the right to be alone, in itself, than the right to take as much time and room as I needed to decide what kind of life I wanted, what I could hold out for."

I reread those words shortly after I came back from France. It was one of countless times I'd consulted my mother's writing since she died. When she was still alive, I'd been half-assed about reading her work, but after she was gone I gorged on her books of essays and the endless stack of articles in her filing cabinet, some of which were deeply personal. I guarded my mom's public legacy, which felt like a proxy for guarding the legacy of her brand of radical feminism. I protected my mom's Wikipedia page from falsehoods. I set up a Google Alert on her name. I spent weeks in my dad's basement in Queens meticulously preparing her papers to be archived at the Radcliffe Institute, poring over every word on every sheet of paper she'd ever saved. I put together an anthology of her rock 'n' roll writing in 2011, and then compiled *The Essential Ellen Willis* in 2014. When a big political event happened, I'd put a prescient quote of hers on social media.

It was all a way to hear her voice again, even if her writing voice was so much more probing and impish than the woman I knew. As a mother, she was loyal, dependable, and kind of shy—nothing like the "cool mom" you might expect a feminist rock critic to be. She was awkward at parties, quiet around my friends, in the shade at the beach, the introverted counterpart to my boisterous dad. She made goofy jokes that only the closest people to her heard. She was the mother who packed nutritious lunches and bought educationally enriching Hanukkah gifts, like a kit for building your own erupting volcano. She'd given birth to me at forty-two, so she was older and less stylish than most of the moms I grew up around in middle-class Brooklyn in the eighties, then later when we lived in ultracosmopolitan Manhattan.

She was a very attentive mom in the ways that mattered. She always made time for me, a perpetually restless only child, by playing word games, telling me stories, and helping me bake cookies. She took me to Bloomingdale's for training bras and jeans. She answered my panicked late-night requests to edit a college essay that was due the next day. She told me all the time how proud of me she was. Still, despite her devotion, she believed in sharp boundaries between parent and child, and therefore shielded me from her full, manifold humanity. She remained a mystery in important ways. I knew some broad details about her pre-mom life, but not much about her inner thoughts or feelings. In retrospect, she might have known more about the lethality of her cancer than she let on.

Then, just as I graduated college, the chance to know her as an adult evaporated. Reading her words was partly a way to remember her, but it was also a way to discover new versions of her as the questions she grappled with applied to me more and more.

I often cringed at the thought of my dead mother knowing my fate. Staying in an unsatisfying partnership because of such a 1950s-era fear felt like a betrayal of the highest order. Even when I was going through smooth-sailing periods with Aaron, I felt uneasy that I'd "settled down" so early without experiencing another committed relationship, and now I felt I'd invested too many years to undo it. My perennial suspicion, back in full force after France, was that my self-interrogation stalled out when I met Aaron. I harbored shame that my life ended up by the book compared to my mother's and her friends', that I remained in arrested development, unimaginative and codependent. "Breaking up with Aaron is the ultimate risk that my mom would 100%-guaranteed tell me to take right now," I wrote in that same email to Kate.

Of course, I could guarantee nothing of the sort. Her boundaries went the other way too: My mom had never been the type to dole out lifestyle edicts. Part of her liberationist politics and generally humble disposition included refraining from regulating other people's lives. Her friends often told me she was the least judgmental person they'd ever met. She didn't flinch when I told her as a Disney-obsessed little girl that I planned to marry as soon as I turned eighteen, didn't tell me to go change when I wore push-up bras and miniskirts in high school. She wanted me to figure things out for myself.

At times, this quality made her hard to talk to. She listened when I felt like sharing about my crushes or friend drama, but she declined to offer solutions. I complained once in my tenth-grade diary that after venting to her about clique woes, "the conversation seemed one-sided and I got tired of talking to her." Much to my annoyance, she'd never give a definitive answer to a complex question. Instead she would massage her lip thoughtfully and say, "Well, it depends." If she had been alive during the Aaron years, I'm sure she would have been maddeningly hands-off if I'd asked her directly for romantic advice.

Still, it crushed me that the opportunity to ask was out of my reach: she was gone. The only thing I could do was consume her writing, again and again, clinging to decipherable morsels of counsel.

And during that particularly intense bout of post-France ennui, those morsels were steering me toward freedom. I flipped through the galleys of *The Essential Ellen Willis*, not yet out in the world. "Family morality regards sensual pleasure for its own sake as frivolous, sexual passion as dangerous and fundamentally anti-social," my mom wrote in "The Family: Love It or Leave It." "Since passion is by definition spontaneous—we can behave in ways that inhibit or nurture it, but finally we feel it or we don't—a marital arrangement based on legal, economic, or moral coercion is oppressive."

The marriages she saw around her seethed with unattractive compromises, emotional repression, and sexual boredom. Most partnerships she knew of were predicated on "a sexist detente: the husband had made it clear that he would not give up certain prerogatives and the wife pretended not to hate him for it." She inverted my calculation, turning it from feeble to hopeful: better alone than trapped.

2. Status Bump

I believe marriage to be the primary political experience in which most of us engage as adults.

—PHYLLIS ROSE, *PARALLEL LIVES*

We met at an eighties-themed birthday party. It was freezing and snowy that night, a week before Valentine's Day in 2008, when I was twenty-three and had lived in Chicago for only a month. After receiving an invite from a kindly coworker at my new restaurant job, I showed up to a house full of strangers with a bravery born out of new-city energy. Aaron was hard to miss—at six foot five, he towered over almost everyone at the party. He had a head full of wavy dark hair. His eyes were the color of Spanish olives, sleepy through his thick-framed glasses. He kept going out on the porch in the frigid Chicago cold to puff cigarettes and shoot the shit with his buds. I asked him for one even though I wasn't a smoker.

Our first conversation, slurring and confessional, revealed that he was a twenty-six-year-old bartender, a little aimless but trying, working toward his bachelor's after years of putting it off. He seemed genuine, hypersocial, frank, and bohemian. He wrote poetry. He hosted open mic nights. His friends at the party all seemed like Rob from *High Fidelity*. After sucking in a gulp of helium from a birthday balloon, he serenaded me with Neutral Milk Hotel's "King of Carrot Flowers Pt. 1," the first time I'd ever heard the song. We made out for two hours on a beanbag chair. I ended up hopping into his cab and passing out fully clothed in his bed.

The next few weeks were a mindfuck. He was hot and cold in that twenties-dude way. We shared an easy intimacy in private, but he ignored me at the parties happening nearly nightly at his house. The tail ends of our evenings—including when it was time for sex—were often ruined by coke and alcohol. Our fights were melodramatic, cinematic, entirely avoidable. I tried my hand at making "scenes," which felt liberating compared with the emotional suppression every Chill Girl of my era had practiced during the entirety of college. He'd abruptly swing from one mood vine to the other, as he employed lines that felt like they belonged in *Garden State*. "Do you *feel* what I mean?" he once asked me during an embrace.

Still, we kept hanging. Things gradually got smoother and less intense. The sex got more sober and therefore better. He initially resisted the boyfriend label, but one night, I tearfully gave him an ultimatum at a bar that served lychee martinis and played EDM. He started to reply with what I'd heard from sex partners for years: I was so casual and fun and sexual—was I really trying to have a relationship? *Yes*, I assured him. *I'm like every other girl you've heard about.* My declarations befitted the most treacly romantic comedies. "It's hurtful for someone to tell you that you're not worth being with," I told him.

The next morning, he turned to me in bed and said, "I changed my mind. You're completely right." (Clearly I wasn't the only one who'd seen those movies.) I met his parents within days of the ly-chee martini night. In May, we spent the night at their house in the suburbs, and kissed for a long time after we fooled around in the dark. I was frantically plotting how to tell him I loved him, when he took the words right out of my mouth, whispering, "I love you."

Shortly afterward, we moved into the first floor of a two-story greystone in northwest Chicago. I was surprised by how much Aaron embraced domesticity. He still partied, but he also loved to cook and cuddle and binge TV shows with me. We intertwined our lives in ways both abstract and logistical. We bought a used car. We shared a credit card. We became each other's emergency contacts. We talked about the future playfully, casually.

By the next winter I'd gotten a local reporting job that offered health insurance—which, in my pre-Obamacare bartending days, sort of felt like winning the lottery. During orientation, I learned I could cover my domestic partner too. Cook County issued certificates for that, but we wouldn't need it, a human resources manager told me: all I had to do was sign some internal papers. Aaron hadn't had health insurance for years. *He* didn't seem to care, but I lived in constant fear that he'd get in a car accident or require an urgent kidney transplant. The new insurance put my mind at ease.

He ended up having to go to the emergency room a few months later for bizarre chest pains that ended up being severe acid reflux. His seven-thousand-dollar hospital bill was covered by my plan. But the bill must have raised a red flag to my employer, because all of a sudden, corporate sent off a letter asking for an official affidavit to prove our partnership. You know, the one we didn't need.

Aaron and I put off going to city hall to get our domestic partnership until two days before the deadline, and when we got there, the clerk dropped a bomb: in Illinois, we could only get the certificate if we were gay. "If straight people could get them, no one would get married!" the city hall employee informed us. *Wouldn't that be nice*, I remember thinking. But once my self-righteousness wore off, I realized we had an infuriating choice to make: we could get married the next day, or Aaron could lose his health insurance and face seven grand in medical bills. On a Wednesday afternoon in July, over a slice of soggy Sbarro pizza, we decided to just sign the damn piece of paper.

It was all a big joke at first. I wore a stretchy black sundress and flip-flops; Aaron wore a red carnation behind his ear and an all-white linen outfit that invoked John Lennon's ashram days. We tied Pepsi cans and a JUST MARRIED sign to Aaron's bike and rode around the block in downtown Chicago. We posed for photos grinning outside city hall and clinked champagne glasses at a rooftop bar. The photos were snapped by his family, whom we'd invited at the last minute.

We mass-texted all our friends that hey, by the way, we got married, meet us at Gold Star, the dive bar Aaron worked at. Every friend I had in Chicago showed up. My coworkers came to take shots and tell me they'd fill in for me the next day. We drank Old Overholt for free all night and ate pulled-pork sandwiches crouching on the sidewalk. Too drunk to fuck, we fell into bed feeling happy and irreverent. I was nearly twenty-five years old. It was the best party I'd ever been to.

Everybody is tickled by this story, the broad strokes of which, I admit, are romantic and organic and quasi-unconventional. I told it for years after that 2009 summer, partly because it's a good conversation piece and partly because it was an opportunity to brag about how our insurance nuptials exposed the farce of traditional values.

After my initial flare of resistance at feeling practically forced into it, I framed my marriage of convenience as a defiant gesture, meant to make a mockery of outdated institutions—not only of sentimental matrimony, but of the cruelty of our failed healthcare system. It made it even better that I was bestowing benefits on my husband, and I relished correcting people who assumed that it was the other way around. It became key to shaping my identity as someone whose commitment was pure yet subject to change, un-related to a binding contract, uncontaminated by cynical things like registries or honeymoons or lifelong financial security. *No rings, no checks, no 'til death do us part,* I explained. *Just a gesture of love from one insured person to an uninsured one.*

Unfortunately, marriages—even marriages like mine—have never been that simple. I had assumed that since the institution meant absolutely nothing to me, I could bend it to my whims, re-jecting and using aspects of it as I saw fit. But no matter how blasé I thought I felt about our transactional union, it managed to take on a life of its own.

• • •

At a Christmas party in 1847, a black-eyed, dark-haired, pale-skinned thirtysomething woman named Mary Gove met a younger dandy called Thomas Low Nichols. They were both regulars of New York City's downtown literary scene; at that same party, Ed-gar Allan Poe recited "The Raven." After a number of dates, the two struck up a correspondence, falling hopelessly in love. "It is a rare thing to love with all the heart, might, mind, and strength, and it is as beautiful as rare," Mary wrote Thomas in those first few heady months.

Still, Mary was hesitant to start a full-blown affair. She had begun a new life in New York City's East Village, but her reputation was tenuous: six years before, she had escaped a marriage that she would later refer to as a "burning prairie," and she had been dealing with the stigma of being a fugitive wife ever since.

From the beginning, her husband, Hiram Gove, had been controlling and possessive. She endured what would now be considered marital rape (but was considered perfectly within a husband's right back then). The violations led to five excruciating pregnancies, only one of which resulted in a child. To cope with her suffering, Mary taught herself about anatomy and physiology. By the late 1830s, she'd become a successful lecturer on women's health and bodily autonomy, traveling across the Northeast and speaking on the dangers of corsets and a wife's right to say no to her husband's sexual demands. She was making unheard-of amounts of money for a woman, but Hiram was pocketing it—yet another privilege granted legally to a husband. One day, at a lecture, the audience voted to give her a purse full of thirty-five dollars in gold. She used it to escape.

The next few years were tumultuous for Mary and her young daughter, Elma. She took refuge from the irate Hiram at her childhood home with her father, and when he died, she bounced from boardinghouse to boardinghouse. She hoped that West Roxbury's Brook Farm, one of the utopian communities that sprang up in the mid-1800s, might welcome her; given its radical vision, it seemed like a potential haven for separated women. But Brook Farm rejected her application because it didn't want to be associated with a sexually disreputable woman. Finally, in 1845, she moved into a town house in New York with a group of like-minded bohemians. She started publishing fiction under a pseudonym and running a small medical practice. She hosted regular salons with the likes of Poe, Herman Melville, and Horace Greeley.

No matter how much she adored Thomas, she refused to risk her career in order to love him openly. But then she got lucky: after years of spreading lies that she was unfaithful and that she was running a brothel in New York City, Hiram wanted to get remarried and therefore finally gave her a divorce.

Being a divorced single woman might have been even more scandalous than being a runaway wife, so in 1848, less than a year after they met at the Christmas party, Thomas and Mary got married—albeit on their own terms. "In a marriage with you, I re-sign no right of my soul," read her vows. "I enter into no compact to be faithful to you. I only promise to be faithful to the deepest love of my heart. If that love is yours, it will bear fruit for you, and enrich your life—our life. If my love leads me from you, I must go."

Their wildly unconventional vows were an early inkling of a diffuse nineteenth-century movement known as free love. This movement was made up of Spiritualists, abolitionists, and nonconformists later labeled "sex radicals" by historians. Both "free love" and "sex radicals" sound lustier than they are. Their philosophy had little to do with promiscuity—in fact, many of these thinkers were disapproving of no-strings-attached sex. Rather, the free lovers believed in the idea that a legal agreement like marriage corrupts an untamed, transcendent force like love. Both women and men, they argued, should be free to conduct their love lives any way they chose without interference from the state.

At that point, the link between love and matrimony was

relatively new. For thousands of years, marriage was an unsenti-
mental contract that divided up a household's workload, which,
before washing machines and supermarkets, required a truly mind-
boggling amount of labor. It consolidated families and, in the elites'
case, their wealth and power. Up until a few hundred years ago
(and then only in the Western world), marriage was widely considered to be irrelevant to and in some cases expressly incompatible
with romance. At best, love between two spouses was a nice bonus
to an economically and politically beneficial union; at worst, love
was an unpredictable, disruptive force that belonged in the domain
of adultery or idolatry.

In the decades following the American Revolution, the script
changed. The idea of the "love match" spread from Europe to the
States; newly minted Americans extended the "pursuit of happiness" to romance too. People were now expected to freely choose
their partners, marry for love, and stay monogamous. With this
new type of marriage contract came the strict gender roles for
which the Victorians are infamous. Middle- and upper-class
women were now held up as bastions of morality, piety, and purity
who tended to hearth and home—which meant that they were not
to contaminate their holy souls by working or being in men's
spaces. Wives became even more dependent on their husbands,
who now had the shiny new moniker of "breadwinners," as labor
was increasingly outsourced from the home to work sites starting
in the 1830s.

Of course, since women had very little earning power and no
socially acceptable way to have sex outside wedlock, marriages of
convenience continued apace. The difference was, now it was crass
to acknowledge it.

This hypocrisy is precisely what inflamed the free lovers. While marriage masqueraded as the exclusive sphere of romantic affection and loyalty, the reality was that love's uncontrollable nature made the promise of lifelong commitment a cynical, often futile enterprise. Still, abolishing marriage was a scary thought, especially for women. Practicing free love in a culture where marriage remained supreme could lead to a woman facing abandonment from her husband, the loss of her children (custody of whom, in the first half of the nineteenth century, would be granted to her husband), and desperate poverty—not to mention social condemnation for divorce or spinsterhood. Mainstream women's rights reformers like Henry Blackwell worried that free lovers would "thrust their immoralities before the public in a 'Women's Rights' disguise." Even though one of the free love movement's central tenets was that marriage oppressed women, in the short term men stood to benefit from the era's rampant individualism a lot more than women did.

By 1871, suffragette and presidential candidate Victoria Woodhull would declare her "inalienable, constitutional and natural right to love whom I may, to love as long or as short a period as I can; to change that love every day if I please." But Mary Gove Nichols had begun turning over such ideas nearly twenty years before. In 1854, Mary and Thomas published a joint screed, a book called *Marriage: Its History, Character, and Results.* "Abolish all marriage this day," it read. "Leave all men and women free to have or to refuse the sexual embrace. . . . [Marriage] debauches, enervates, and pollutes society!"

The next year, Mary went further: she wrote a thinly fictionalized autobiography called *Mary Lyndon: Or, Revelations of a Life,* another blistering critique of marriage that advocated for women to have control over their own bodies. *The New York Times* ripped it to shreds in a review headlined A BAD BOOK GIBBETED. The reviewer called Mary a "shamelessly immoral person" and, despite the fact that she and other sex radicals condemned loveless promiscuity, a "slave of the coarsest lust." But married women across the country, recognizing their own lives and feelings, ate up the autobiography with a spoon. M. E. Lazarus's 1852 book, *Love vs. Marriage*, was seminal but stodgy; Mary's comparatively breezy voice likely appealed more to educated white ladies like herself.

With those two books, it was official: Mary Gove Nichols had established herself as the most prominent female free lover. And yet, even after her first harrowing experience with matrimony, Mary Gove Nichols got married. As did Victoria Woodhull—thrice. As did M. E. Lazarus, and pretty much all the well-known free lovers of the time.

There were a few purists like Francis Barry, leader of the Berlin Heights community in Ohio, who criticized married free lovers as spineless obstacles to change. Radicals "must move forward at greater or less peril of life, property, and social position, or society would forever remain in a changeless, stagnant condition," Barry wrote. But most of the sex radicals grasped for the privilege available to them using the same rationale as Aaron and me: they would be pragmatic and get married, but they would make a political point out of their concession.

The free lovers labeled their nuptials "free marriages" and bargained in various ways. Sex radicals Ezra and Angela Heywood, for instance, explicitly rejected the labels "husband" and "wife." Mary Gove Nichols wrote those ultramodern vows but tied the knot because she didn't want to be arrested for fornication or lewdness while traveling with Thomas. Defending their marriage, Thomas talked of the impossibility of political purity, how even the most ardent abolitionist is a "patron of slavery, by using its products, and in various ways." He likened their marriage certificate to protesting unjust taxes while still paying them in order to avoid jail: protective measures within an immoral system.

This defense makes sense on its face but also highlights the low stakes of the marriage debate compared with what else was going on in the 1850s. Abolitionists were getting arrested constantly for civil disobedience, but most activists weren't willing to do the same for free love. Undoubtedly this was partly because abolishing slavery was more of a life-or-death cause, but perhaps it was also because, even among progressive northerners, opposing marriage was an unbelievably fringe idea. In fact, many abolitionists identified depriving enslaved people of legal marriages, and depriving enslaved women of moral purity, as among slavery's worst offenses. The abolitionist movement actively recruited formerly enslaved people to speak about how enslavement had ripped their families apart.

Meanwhile, Southern defenders used marriage to *justify* the existence of the institution. They framed the dynamic between the enslaver and the enslaved as much like the supposedly benevolent paternalism of a husband toward his wife. Both enslaved people and wives were suited for subjugation according to God and nature, the logic went, so the inequality of both relationships was mutually beneficial.

It was precisely this comparison that inspired women's rights reformers like Elizabeth Cady Stanton. She and other feminists drew attention to how marriage, while less blatantly coercive, was institutionalized domestic dominance akin to enslavement. Most of these reformers took this metaphor way too far and conflated the starkly different realities of enslavement and white wifehood, seriously trivializing slavery as a result. Wives, after all, were at least considered to be human beings. But the legal and ideological parallels resonated, and not just with white women. Black abolitionist and author Frances Ellen Watkins Harper observed that some formerly enslaved husbands "positively beat their wives," whose "subjection has not ceased in freedom." (That said, she always made it clear that she deemed slavery the most extreme form of oppression.)

In any case, both abolitionists and the women's rights reformers stopped short of publicly attacking the existence of marriage itself. Suffragists like Stanton, Amelia Bloomer, and Lucy Stone (who had her own "free marriage" to Henry Blackwell) kept women of questionable morality, like Mary Gove Nichols, at arm's length. They weren't comfortable with their own metaphor's logical conclusion: Whether it's through marriage or enslavement, owning another person is morally wrong. A truly free society, free lovers argued, has no place for either institution.

The abolitionists won the moral and legal battle against slavery, but the free lovers hardly succeeded in dispensing with marriage. Instead—in a jagged way, through fits and starts—society improved it, slowed down its timeline, expanded its definition, and loosened women's dependence upon it.

• • •

The perfect image of the breadwinner-housewife marriage reached its pinnacle after World War II but started to crumble after just a couple of decades. Betty Friedan, Hugh Hefner, the Beats, and other anti-conformists critiqued the model, and then came the women's movement, which proposed an array of solutions. A few radicals committed to abolition—"marriage means rape and life-long slavery," political lesbian Ti-Grace Atkinson told a reporter in 1969, echoing the free lovers—but many more were interested in molding the institution in feminism's image. Alix Kates Shulman, fresh out of her consciousness-raising groups in New York, caused a sensation in 1970 when *Up from Under* published what she called her "marriage agreement" (which was reprinted in *Life*, *Redbook*, and *New York*). She and her husband had "decided to re-examine the patterns we had been living by," she wrote, "and, starting again from scratch, to define our roles for ourselves." What followed was a formal document outlining the egalitarian division of childcare and domestic chores.

Feminists also made it easier for women to escape an abusive or loveless marriage by easing divorce's legal restrictions and social consequences. Birth control, women's access to the workplace, and (thanks to feminist lawyers) a rash of legal decisions rendered women more self-sufficient and less dependent on marriage. The divorce rate more than doubled, from 9.2 to 22.6 divorces per 1,000 married women. One out of every three marriages that happened in the 1950s eventually ended. Singlehood, shacking up, childlessness, and having a baby out of wedlock didn't have nearly the same stigma anymore.

It was in the context of these cultural changes that my own mother left her husband in 1965 and became a radical feminist. But the parameters of what marriage could mean transformed so completely by the late 1970s that she experienced a period of fantasizing about getting married again. It wasn't a feeling of acquiescence so much as triumph: "Now that I was strong enough to love a man and preserve my identity . . . I would do it over again and do it right—I would get to talk, play rock-and-roll, wear what I pleased," she wrote. "By marrying I would beat the system, give the lie to all the old farts who insisted that women could not have autonomy and love too."

In the early eighties, not long after she wrote those words, my mom fell in love with my dad, Stanley Aronowitz, in precisely this beat-the-system way. A political organizer and socialist professor, Stanley had read a book review of Ellen's and was so impressed that he asked Rosalyn Baxandall, a radical feminist and a mutual friend, for her number. They had a tentative first lunch, and things went quickly from there. My mom's cousin Judy remembers the night when Ellen brought her new boyfriend over to Judy's house for dinner. She had never seen Ellen be so unapologetically immersed in someone else, like there was a "glass globe" over them. Throughout the evening, the couple fluttered their eyes at each other. He caressed her wrists; she pushed his black curly hair out of his denim-blue eyes. Around this time, Ellen remarked to Judy, "What a big fish I've pulled in."

Stanley was a husky hedonist who was often forgiven for his arrogance because of his formidable intellect and the twinkle in his eye and because, surprisingly, he was an excellent listener. He had a reputation as a bed hopper and had trouble managing his often concurrent love affairs. A prolific writer with working-class roots and a gift for public speaking, he was a larger-than-life figure within a certain socialist-leftist crowd. But I suspect Ellen wasn't referring to any of this when she called my dad a "big fish." Instead, she felt she had finally found a man with whom she could fuse commitment and passion, without that "stifling dependence or low-level static" she'd observed in others' partnerships.

For nearly twenty years, they pointedly avoided wedlock. Stanley had also had a couple of pre-feminism, pre–sexual revolution marriages that left him with an aversion to the institution. My parents referred to each other as "partner" or—much to my abject humiliation—"lover." They were proud that their relationship had stayed under the government's radar. "We've resisted marrying," my mother wrote, "partly in symbolic protest against the relentless drumbeat for 'family values,' partly because we feel no need to get the state involved in our relationship, and no irresistible economic or social pressure to do so." She published these words in New York *Newsday* in 1994, when conservatives like Charles Murray were cloaking racist Reagan-era critiques of "welfare queens" and unmarried mothers in the language of seemingly pragmatic social science. She acknowledged that unlike privileged women like her, low-income women bore the brunt of conservative anger, punished for their independence through "reform" (read: cuts) to public assistance. But she saw this as a broader campaign to exploit "middle-class distaste for welfare" in order to restore "women's dependence on marriage and submission to a sexual double standard."

My parents' protest quietly ended four years later for a reason free lovers like the Nicholses would understand: their property and assets needed to be protected in their wills. They invited me to the "wedding" at city hall, but I declined; I had a ninth-grade biology test that day, and it would have been a pain in the ass to miss it. Their marriage was incidental, reluctant, rarely mentioned by either one of them. The nuptials didn't warrant so much as a mention in my mom's vast published archive.

It was important privileges like my parents' property rights that kept marriage part of the civil rights conversation long after slavery was abolished. In 1967, the Supreme Court unanimously struck down laws banning interracial marriage in *Loving v. Virginia*, defining marriage as one of the "basic civil rights of man, fundamental to our very existence and survival." In 2015, a few years after Aaron and I city-halled it, the Supreme Court legalized gay marriage in *Obergefell v. Hodges*. It was a civil rights coup for the

LGBTQ community, but also a win for the cult of matrimony. "No union is more profound than marriage, for it embodies the highest ideals of love, fidelity, devotion, sacrifice, and family," wrote Justice Anthony Kennedy. Gay couples "respect it so deeply that they seek to find its fulfillment for themselves."

It was nearly drowned out by cheers across the nation, but Kennedy's ultrasentimental framing was a strike against alternative models of love—both platonic and non-platonic. "I'm glad gay marriage is now legal," wrote Briallen Hopper shortly after the *Obergefell v. Hodges* decision. Still, as a happily single woman, she acknowledged "an immeasurable debt to the intersecting groups of people who have historically been barred from the privileges of marriage by law and demography, and have learned to create intimate lives apart from it"—like, for instance, the enslaved women in Louisiana sugar country who enjoyed casual lovers due to the high male-to-female ratio, or pairs of live-in Victorian-era lesbians who got characterized as old maids. Marginalized groups "have done the hard work of loving and world-making in defiance of the powers that be, and all unmarried people benefit from their centuries of emotional and material labor."

Partnered people also voiced ambivalence about what the expansion of marriage would mean for queer couples. Domestic partnerships and civil unions were "an opportunity to order our lives in ways that have given us greater freedom than can be found in the one-size-fits-all rules of marriage," Katherine M. Franke wrote in *The New York Times* the day before gay marriage was passed in New York State. She told of a heterosexual colleague who married his girlfriend so they could get on the same health plan, "though they were politically and personally uninterested in doing so." Before gay marriage was legal, all Franke had to do was fill out a form saying that her partner lived in the same household, which allowed her relationship to exist outside the unimaginative dichotomy of "married" or "single." The way she saw it, "having our relationships sanctioned and regulated by the state is hardly something to celebrate."

Reading Kennedy's syrupy love letter to marriage, I had the same reaction the free lovers had to the abolitionists, who advocated granting enslaved people the right to become virtuous married citizens. Instead of correcting the wrongs of discrimination by granting access to an oppressive institution, why couldn't we get rid of both?

Here's why: Marriage has always been dangled in front of us as a social and financial aspiration, a sort of bribe for getting society's full benefits. It's remained that way even after all these years of tweaking it and dilating it to suit our modern world. It thrives on exclusion by promising entry into a certain club with seemingly endless benefits—the extent of which aren't fully obvious until you actually join.

• • •

I don't remember what I thought about marriage before my own, but it probably ranged somewhere between indifference and hostility. During my four years at Wesleyan University, I boned a lot but didn't have a steady boyfriend. I usually preferred it that way. Sure, I wished for more respect than I got from garden-variety fuckboys, and I intimately knew the pain of keeping it way too cool, but I didn't feel like any clock was ticking.

The average age of first marriage in America is now twenty-eight years old for women and thirty years old for men. Those ages are even higher for people with a college education. My Wesleyan classmates didn't seem at all pressed to run to the altar after we graduated. They were doing things like waiting tables while nursing their music careers or going to law school to avoid the recession. I diddled around New York City for a year after college, tending bar and doing journalism internships, then taught English in Brazil for a few months, then split to take a road trip with my friend Emma, where we photographed and interviewed our female peers about feminism.

By the time I ended up at Chicago's city hall marrying Aaron, the significance of a transactional wedding had come full circle: amid a sea of unencumbered peers, our marriage itself was the rebellion.

Then, starting in my late twenties, I began to receive wedding invites at an impressive clip from some of the same people whose jaws had dropped at my off-the-cuff wedding. Lots of those Wesleyan drifters "got serious" with well-paying careers and paired up, often with each other. Virtually nobody in my college circle opted for solo parenthood. These friends married for love, surely. Theirs were what writer Emily Witt called "neo-marriages": in most cases far from a "housewife-patriarch dynamic," these couples acknowledged that some level of autonomy was to be retained. But their weddings also marked a consolidation of their money, power, and social capital.

Aaron's social circles looked very different. He finally got his BA at twenty-nine, but his parents hadn't finished college, and neither had many of his friends from his middle-class suburb or his service industry jobs. For those friends, marriage was a distant goal they might consider once they started making good money or had a "real" job. A few who did get married got divorced within a few years. Some had kids and didn't stay with their partners. Among his crowd, ours was an example of a stable and upwardly mobile partnership.

Millennia before the free lovers, marriage was nakedly, unapologetically a way to secure your family's financial future. Even when that frank system of material gain was replaced by the Victorian cult of domesticity, matrimony was hopelessly tied to class. Middle- and upper-class women were expected to pour every bit of their morally pristine energy into tending to their homes and families. People who were enslaved, or poor people of any race, needed not apply to wedded bliss. In fact, it was their very existence as farmers, domestic servants, wet nurses, and sweatshop workers that allowed rich white women to set aside grueling household tasks and concentrate on "uplifting" their homes. By 1850, there were twice as many servants per white household as there were just fifty years before.

Lower-class workers and formerly enslaved people could get married, technically, but their marriages couldn't hope to approach the ideals of the day. Mary White Ovington, a suffragist and early member of the NAACP, wrote in her 1911 study *Half a Man* that a Black woman in New York who did manage to marry had to accept "the necessity of supplementing the husband's income," which rendered their union tenuous. "She has no fear of leaving him," Ovington wrote disapprovingly, "since her marital relations are not welded by economic dependence." And unwed women were financially on their own. As Jane Austen wrote in a letter to her niece while grudgingly defending marriage: "Single women have a dreadful propensity for being poor."

Nineteen fifties America was a veritable marriage propaganda machine, one that can't be separated from peak consumerism. After two decades of Depression and war, times were better than ever:

Many working-class Americans moved on up; by the mid-1950s almost 60 percent of the population was middle-class. By 1960, nearly two-thirds of American families owned their homes, which were being built in the suburbs at lightning speed. Meanwhile, less than 10 percent of Americans thought an unmarried person could be happy in 1955. Perhaps that was why the median age at first marriage was 22.6 and 20.2 for men and women, respectively—lower than it had been in the 1890s. This was the first time in American history when the romanticized ideal was actually attainable for people other than the rich.

Of course, the breadwinner-housewife nuclear family wasn't attainable for everyone. This perception of the "universal" norm put families who couldn't achieve it—namely, the working class and virtually every person of color, who couldn't afford to be a one-income household—in the position of having failed. Women who toiled at backbreaking jobs often envied housewives and viewed the home, not work, as the fulfilling aspect of their lives. The reaction of Black women to white feminists demanding to enter the workforce often was "We want to have more time to share with family," Black feminist bell hooks wrote in 1984. "We want to leave the world of alienated work." When you've spent years improving other women's domestic lives for little pay, inhabiting your own with a stable partner is a luxury.

By the time Aaron and I got together, marriage was much improved from a feminist perspective; it had gone from a male-dominated institution to one ostensibly built on partnership and mutual respect. But the class divide had gotten worse, not better. It was precisely this new focus on personal fulfillment that made marriage even more of a prohibitive luxury reserved for middle-class white people. Nowadays, the college educated are more likely to be married than people with only a high school degree, and their marriages last longer. Educated people also wait longer to get married and have children—which not only affects their earning power but also improves the prognosis of their marriage.

A 2013 study out of the University of Virginia and Harvard found that the shift from authoritarian marriage to "companionate" marriage among equals came at a price, literally. The couples who can throw money at their problems—from therapy to date night to babysitters—have a better chance of surviving. And for financially stable marrieds, "sharing resources with a partner is more likely to be an investment than a risk," as journalist Amanda Hess wrote in *Slate*. The researchers also found that economic instability had a direct correlation with mistrust and instability in one's relationships. Many of the working-class interviewees were focused on their own financial survival, not providing "materially and emotionally for others."

White, rich people have long used marriage's supposed virtues as a way to denigrate low-income Black families under the guise of concern. Mary White Ovington, in the same 1911 study, wrote that most Black women in New York were beset with "sexual immorality" and deprived of their "full status as a woman" because they were not properly courted by male suitors. "Slavery deprived her of family life, set her to daily toil in the field, or appropriated her mother's instincts for the white child," Ovington wrote. "She has today the difficult task of maintaining the integrity and purity of the home. Many times she has succeeded, often she has failed, sometimes she has not even tried."

It was evident in 1965 that attitudes like these had staying power when Daniel Patrick Moynihan, then a Labor Department official in the Lyndon Johnson administration, wrote in a much-criticized report that Black children with single mothers were doomed to fail. The government has continued to tout marriage *itself* as a cure-all for poverty. The George W. Bush administration's Healthy Marriage Initiative, which was still funding programs as of 2021, has poured hundreds of millions of dollars into promoting marriage rather than alleviating the poverty of families that already exist.

In 2003, Katherine Boo memorably profiled two Black women from Oklahoma who attended a state-sponsored marriage seminar. Kim, the younger and less jaded of the two, counted getting married as an integral part of the "healthy, wealthy, normal-lady life" she aspired to. The profile glances over the poorly attended, uninspiring seminar itself, and its stilted conflict-resolution video that features a middle-class couple squabbling over who should clean the guest bedroom. Instead, it lingers on the treadmill of poverty: a $114 penalty for writing a bounced $12.18 check; Kim's pangs of hunger after smelling the mall's cinnamon buns; the seven city buses that pass her by, threatening to make her miss a job interview.

By the end of the piece, Kim still hopes to be part of the one-third of Black women who marry before age forty. She's optimistic about her fledgling relationship with a soft-spoken man named Derrick. "This year," they tell each other, "we're going to make something of ourselves." It reminded me how my friend Sadye, who is Latina, had a big, traditional wedding because she wanted to "win at life." Years later, she had the clarity to realize the whole process was partly about reaching for "white American success" after a childhood of feeling ugly, undesired, and less than. "Assimilating was part of my survival," she said. Like that of many status symbols, marriage's power lies precisely in its exclusion: It's an institution that remains desirable, yet more and more out of reach, for millions of marginalized Americans.

Besides the tax breaks and the security of health insurance, marrying Aaron wasn't exactly an "investment." Our marriage occurred during the depths of the recession, when our bank accounts hovered in the mid–three figures on any given day. Even years later, we were still too young and broke—and, in my case, ambivalent—to have kids or save up to buy property. But the announcement of our nuptials unlocked something more inscrutable, and therefore more insidious, than financial gain: an alluring social acceptance that would prove hard to resist. The most iconoclastic among us think they're impervious to marriage's charms, so they consider it safe to buy in ironically, for the benefits and nothing else. But there's no easier way to defang a radical than the lure of a status bump.

● ● ●

Mary Gove Nichols's writings had made her a star among the literati, but her books about free love also made her life a living hell. In the manner of the *New York Times* reviewer who "gibbeted" her fictional autobiography, the press relentlessly talked smack about her. A hydropathy (or "water cure") school she opened with her husband had to close after her autobiography fanned the flames of scandal.* In 1856, Mary and Thomas moved to Yellow Springs, Ohio, and founded a commune-like "harmonic home" dedicated to what we'd probably now call wellness, irritating nearby Antioch College's president, Horace Mann. Her writing inched more and more toward endorsing chastity.

---

*The nineteenth-century practice of "hydropathy," sadly for Mary's legacy, has long been discredited as bullshit.

And then, in 1857, to the shock and consternation of their bohemian crowd back in New York, Mary and Thomas converted to Catholicism.

The conversion itself wasn't as big a leap as it might seem. Mary was a Quaker and a Spiritualist with a history of conversions, and the Second Great Awakening had made these sudden conversions very common. But in order to be accepted by the Catholic Church, Mary had to disavow her free love principles, even editing out her sex radicalism from her previous publications. For a few years after the conversion, the couple gave lectures all over the country touting the water cure and health reform. Biographer Jean Silver-Isenstadt described those years of traveling, during which the two were met with "universally warm acceptance," as a "soothing balm" after years of being abused and excoriated and misunderstood. The negative press and rebel fatigue might not have been the impetus for their conversion, Patricia Cline-Cohen, a history professor at UC Santa Barbara who is writing a biography of Mary Gove Nichols, told me. But, after they moved to England in 1861, "being Catholic did allow them to present as a couple who took marriage seriously."

Mary Gove Nichols was now a wife—for real this time.

• • •

During those first days after our vows, I walked around Chicago as an undercover bride. I was like any other ironic, adventurous, unattached twentysomething, only now I was technically married.

Then I posted some pictures online.

My world was divided by two reactions: "Amazing, you're *married*!" and, "Wait . . . are you *serious*?" My New York friends and family were perplexed, remembering my revelrous, non-tragic bouts of singlehood. Other friends were surprised I made the move given my outrage at California's upholding of Prop 8, its anti–gay marriage law, only weeks before. Aaron's bohemian friends seemed equally bemused. "I thought you were this big feminist," one teased me. "Isn't that, like, against the rules?"

But these comments were countered by other delighted reactions, the intensity of which belied another emotion: relief. My coworkers from the suburbs had been hard-pressed to find anything to talk to me about, but now they were fawning all over me. Buried in their generic "congratulations!" were little epiphanies— they'd finally found a way to relate to me, to pin me down as "normal." Meanwhile, Aaron's family started treating me . . . well, like family. His parents' friends sent cards and checks. I began to realize why people get so into weddings. Instantly, miraculously, everybody loves you!

I became a blank slate for others' fantasies and judgments, an unwitting recipient of advice and wedding proposal stories and even an object of palpable jealousy. I discovered the effectiveness of saying "husband" when dealing with bureaucrats. The word proved useful for my reporting job too: when I was interviewing senior citizens or Christians, using "husband" helped us find common ground. I now had an ironclad comeback for sleazy guys who wouldn't stop hitting on me. (It hadn't yet dawned on me how depressing it was that identifying myself as another man's property was more convincing to a harasser than "I'm not interested.")

But it wasn't just these little sparks of social capital that I could reach for dispassionately and only when necessary. To my horror, I started to *truly feel* self-satisfied. Even though my marriage was never meant to be a happily ever after, I felt "settled" in a way I hadn't before. Our partnership was perceived as validated, solidified.

Elders went from treating me like a child (or, depending on their leanings, a vaguely tragic tart who showed too much cleavage) to addressing me as an actual adult. Even in the privacy of our own home, Aaron and I talked about our relationship as a forward-moving entity that would eventually lead to children and a mortgage.

To be clear, a stable partnership isn't bad in itself; it was in many ways a beautiful, much-needed development in my life, especially in the wake of my mother's death. The devotion and acceptance Aaron gave me during our marriage was profound. It's more my own smugness that disturbs me in retrospect. For a woman, "the status marriage confers insulates her somewhat from rejection and humiliation," my mom wrote in 1969, recalling her first foray into wifehood. "At least one man has certified her Class A merchandise." Forty years later, marriage was still offering me a ticket to acceptance. It reminded me of my intrinsic desire as a middle school floater to be liked by the popular girls, even as I talked shit about them at sleepovers with my more offbeat friends.

Once it was obvious that Aaron's and my relationship was breaking down, the smugness turned into fear. That fear smothered my doubts when the early limerence of our Chicago romance started to fade. And when I realized Aaron was trying to impress me less and less, which meant he didn't even pretend to keep up with the news anymore. When he drank too much and I criticized him incessantly for it. When I started to dread our sex, because I knew it would lead to either open conflict or silent despair. When he struggled to make money as a filmmaker, putting financial pressure on me at the age of twenty-six and causing me to envy other people's partners with flourishing careers—which, in turn, stoked my self-recrimination for being bougie and conventional.

The fear won long after I knew that this was not a forever match. I'd gotten a taste of marital privilege, and I didn't want to let it go. I also worried that the love I got from Aaron wouldn't be easily replicated with my friends, who adored me but weren't *committed* to me in the same way. We all half joked about buying a big building and raising our children together, but each time one of us coupled off, it diluted that sense of communal responsibility. I certainly couldn't count on my dad, who became close with Aaron but reacted to my premature marriage with bemusement and even a whiff of derision.

Not all my friends were coupled up. A handful were single, either as a resting state or between less serious relationships. Most of them, both queer and straight, had to fend off irritating pressure to settle down. But whether or not they wanted to wed, their lives were full and busy and pleasurable. They also had an autonomy I did not, even with a live-and-let-live partner like mine. Just as Aaron's and my relationship became riddled with doubt seeds, a cultural celebration welled up in praise of the single woman. The narrative of "smug marrieds" talking down to singles like Bridget Jones and Carrie Bradshaw had been replaced by cultural touchstones like Rebecca Traister's *All the Single Ladies,* which made a convincing and exhaustive case for single women's rising political power, and Kate Bolick's *Spinster,* a paean that profiled modern-minded gentlewomen like Edna St. Vincent Millay and Charlotte Perkins Gilman. (Like most of the free lovers, all the "spinsters" featured in the book got married anyway.) A woman's earning power gets hurt the moment she gets married, studies discovered— even if she never has children. Especially if they were educated, single women were not only enviable; they were politically and often economically powerful.

Yet I seldom envied them, even though I publicly related to them more than to my married friends. Instead, I dreaded the uncertainty and the vulnerability of being an unpartnered woman in her thirties. In my head, I would ignore the joy of their spontaneous decisions and the blissful mornings they spent alone in bed, choosing to fixate on the moments when they'd explain what skin hunger and extreme loneliness felt like. My friend Samhita, a self-possessed woman several years older than me who made six figures at her editing job, kept it particularly real. She said the things affluent single women weren't supposed to say in the rah-rah Obama years. Things like: "I really want a boyfriend and I have for a long time. I'm tired of just having sex with guys and them disappearing." Or, about her immigrant parents: "I think if I had a boo, my parents would put less pressure on me. It's because I'm a single woman that they play me like that."

A lot of what she said affirmed my fears about being single in a marriage-supremacist society. She was vivid about loneliness and how confidence gets you only so far: I don't understand how we can literally be beauties, she messaged me in the summer of 2016, a few months before my marriage would end. Smart and cool and awesome and nice and give good hugs and still go home alone. Still, I was ashamed at my revulsion. What kind of self-sufficient feminist was *petrified* of being single? What woman of integrity applauds the concept of "single at heart" in public, then secretly pities unattached women? What supposedly class-conscious leftist clings to a privilege semi-accidentally afforded to her, at the expense of her own happiness? The only thing that would eventually prove stronger than the promise of societal approval, more compelling than the shivers of culturally endorsed dread about loneliness and abandonment, would be the courage of my desires.

3. I Want This

Desire so often feels like a punishment, especially if you're a woman.

—BRANDY JENSEN, "HOW TO POACH AN EGG AND LEAVE A MARRIAGE"

"I think we have two choices," he told me calmly. "You could leave with no hard feelings at all. Or you could stay, and I could try to help you feel better."

I'd gone from pacing back and forth in my living room, whimpering and panicking, straight to Rob's apartment. I was wearing the outfit I'd originally planned, a somewhat infantile black cotton dress from H&M that I hoped telegraphed a balance of sex appeal and nonchalance. At first I told him zero about what had transpired in the last few hours, trying to snuff out the pain by having wordless, sweaty sex, first in his black-sheet vortex of a bedroom, then on the avocado-colored velvet couch in his living room. The goal was to bathe my looping brain in a coat of white primer. The goal was to forget.

But that night, the balm wasn't working, and eventually it became obvious to him that my mind was somewhere else. "You okay?" Rob asked, in that unassuming voice, clement with a whiff of Louisville. I told him about the anxiety shitstorm I'd just thrashed my way out of, unsure how he'd react. Then he gave me that pair of choices. I was relieved. He'd handed me the reins to ride out this nightmare however I wanted.

· · ·

It all began four months earlier, on the Saturday after Thanksgiving. That morning, I was cuddling Aaron in a cabin in upstate New York. He'd woken up with a hard-on, and I'd stroked it briefly, but then all the feelings of dread came flooding back, as they had for years—dread that we wouldn't connect, that I wouldn't feel aroused, that he'd once again forget what I enjoyed, that I wouldn't be able to hide my exasperation. To avoid it all, I slipped out of bed on that chilly Saturday morning and announced I needed to go into town to find WiFi; I had an important email to write.

An hour later, Aaron and I were typing on our laptops at the Rensselaerville public library when I received a phone call from my father's best friend, Michael. "Stanley is in the hospital," he told me. "He might have had a stroke."

I was nervous during the drive back to New York City with Aaron, but calmer than I might have been if this feeling were brand-new. I'd experienced this same spike of panic a few years earlier when my dad had major back surgery, and even earlier during the falls to the ground that necessitated the back surgery. These were the kinds of falls that required scrubbing a bloody handprint off my father's kitchen wall because he lost his balance in the middle of the night and hit the floor so hard that his brow broke the tile. Ever since my mother died, a layer of worry had set up camp in my brain. When my dad ran twenty minutes late, my imagination ran wild: *Has he fallen or gotten into a car accident? Has he forgotten about our plans? Oh God, does he have Alzheimer's?* One snowy day in 2012, he was rushed to the ER because he was slurring his words. It turned out to be low blood sugar, but in the cab on my way to the hospital, I thought: *Fuck, did he have a stroke? Will I have to take care of him for the rest of his life?*

Three years had passed since then, and now the answers on that November evening were: "yes" and "yes." By the time I asked the hospital receptionist for Stanley Aronowitz's room, I knew a slice of my life's freedom had disappeared. Gone was the kind of idle, amorphous time that a newborn baby snatches from you when you decide to become a parent. Except my role as caretaker had been decided for me.

My life became a scrum of hospital going and stress crying and cat feeding and bill paying. Things got worse when Aaron got four long-planned nose and throat surgeries not long after. He left the hospital a swollen, druggy mess leaking viscera from his face and would remain that way for the better part of two weeks. Unlike my father, Aaron was actively in pain, which turned him into a touchy, impatient asshole. A few weeks before, my life had been chugging along. Now it was coughing, spewing, becoming a blur of errands and chores and emotional breakdowns.

Three weeks into this new scenario, I spent a Friday at a brand-new job, trapped in my office's phone booth arguing with my dad's insurance company about whether they would cover his physical therapy. At the tail end of the day, I got a text from Aaron that he was out of Percocet. I rushed home to get his ID (required for controlled substances), then booked it to Walgreens to pick up the painkillers before closing time, then sprinted back home to crush up the pills in applesauce and change the gauze on Aaron's bloody nose.

At ten o'clock at night, when he'd drifted off into a sludgy sleep, I stepped outside our Crown Heights, Brooklyn, apartment in the dead of winter. I sat on my stoop and wept hot tears. At thirty-one, I felt a million years old, mobbed by needy dependents but also utterly alone. Through the cumulous clouds of other people's needs, I couldn't yet clearly see my own.

• • •

One afternoon in the fall of 1951, Stanley wandered into the Thalia Theater uptown to watch a movie, a British dark comedy called *Kind Hearts and Coronets*. A girl he'd gone to high school with, Jane, was also sitting alone in the theater, killing time between a babysitting gig and her salesclerk job at the five-and-dime. She was seventeen and still in school; he was eighteen and had just gotten suspended from Brooklyn College for staging a sit-in to protest the suspension of the student newspaper. Young and newly radicalized, he figured factory work was better than enduring the "repressive rampages" of a bourgeois, McCarthy-era institution.

A week after Jane graduated in June, they were married—another rebellion, since she was Irish and Italian, not Jewish, and from a truly poor family, not born to working-class union members like Stanley. He'd been at a job drilling holes into flat pieces of metal during the night shift at Curtiss-Wright, a manufacturer of airplane engines in Wood-Ridge, New Jersey. Despite Jane's protests, the couple moved from New York City to an apartment with a coal-powered furnace in a rundown neighborhood of Newark, where Stanley had gotten a job at the Worthington Pump and

Machinery Corporation. Jane was shoveling coal into that furnace when her water broke. Michael, their son, was born in 1953. They had their daughter, Kim, four years after that.

Though Jane and Stanley were both devout socialists, the contours of their marriage "reproduced the prevailing relations between men and women," as Stanley recalled in his 1973 book about the labor movement, *False Promises*. Jane was forced to quit work after her pregnant belly prevented her from lifting TVs on the assembly line, so she stayed home with Michael while Stanley worked at a succession of New Jersey factories. He worked irregular hours and expected Jane to keep the kids from pestering him when he was home. He drank beer every Friday night after work and came home late to a cold dinner and his wife's bitterness. Isolated from her New York friends, Jane would walk miles with Michael in the carriage every day, sit with him in the park, then come back hours later without having spoken to a single other adult.

The couple fought constantly about finances and divergent priorities. "I heard myself yelling at my wife about money," he wrote, "and seemed unable to control much of my behavior generated by the pressures of bills, work, and alienated leisure." That behavior included angry outbursts, extended unexplained absences, and, on a few occasions, physical violence. His rage and avoidance were caused by a toxic blend of fifties-era misogyny and poverty, but also something Stanley didn't have words for until years later, when he wrote *False Promises*: his "fear and insecurity of being so young and having to support a family"—and, Kim and Mike surmise now, resentment toward a pre-countercultural domestic dynamic he never really wanted.

Almost from the start, he was much more interested in intellectual pursuits than in being a husband and father. Early in the marriage, as his night shift ended at the engine plant at eight a.m., he'd spend four hours at the local library reading books like Karl Marx's *Capital* and Joseph Schumpeter's *History of Economic Analysis*. Later, he became active in the neighborhood council and his job's union. Jane felt sidelined by Stanley's activist crowd; she had things to say in the council meetings too, but she didn't feel like Stanley and his friends wanted her there. Years later, during the women's movement, Jane would identify all this as sexism, but at the time she simply felt betrayed by other humans.

Once Stanley transitioned from factory work to professional union organizing and political activism, he was even less present. He volunteered on then New York State assemblyman Mark Lane's campaign, which kept him across the river. He started having affairs. He didn't come home for days on end. One affair in the early sixties functioned as a way to end his marriage. After the divorce, he spent the rest of his kids' childhood being an affable but forgetful weekend father, sometimes disappearing for weeks at a time for work. Through the years, Kim and Mike always made it clear that I'd received the better, more enlightened version of my dad.

Indeed, Stanley's gender analysis did evolve with the sixties and seventies. Whereas he'd underestimated Jane's intelligence during their marriage, he started viewing women more and more as intellectual equals. Female friends and lovers he met through organizing and academia schooled him on women's liberation. He read writers like Simone de Beauvoir and Shulamith Firestone and Angela Davis. The self-awareness displayed in *False Promises* could have been a result of Carol Lopate, a staunch feminist and Stanley's girlfriend at the time, who is thanked in the acknowledgments for her "valuable suggestions." By the time he fell in love with Ellen, at the start of the eighties, he was possessed of a robust feminist education, not to mention thirty more years of maturity. He seemed light-years away from that overwhelmed young hothead in Newark.

Ellen insisted that theirs should be a modern and egalitarian partnership, and Stanley was on board. He agreed to split the child-care fifty-fifty, and over the course of their relationship my dad would spend more time in the kitchen than she did. He was a warm and energetic father who played catch, helped me with social studies essays, picked me up from after-school, and toured colleges with me. Like many men, he was sentimental but not emotional. I told my dad even less about my personal life than my mom, but I did enjoy listening to him talk. "My dad can ramble on about nothing, yet it's interesting to hear," I wrote in a rare high school diary entry assessing my parents. I praised his laid-back approach: "He doesn't pressure me into anything and doesn't get mad at me for stupid things."

Unlike Jane, who had little say in the family's finances and household decisions, Ellen was an equal partner and in fact the dominant domestic arbiter in our household. As a child, I observed my parents' quirky, mutually respectful relationship. My assessment was that they were corny and embarrassing and ancient, but damn did they truly seem to love each other. Their warmth spilled over to our family rapport, which was full of inside jokes. After bedtime, through my bedroom door, I'd listen to them talk and laugh late into the night over way-too-peppery dinners cooked by my father.

My mother died with that idealized image still burnished in my head. But the instant she was gone, I got an inkling of just how much invisible work she did in our household. The apartments I grew up in had always been a blur of books and magazines and typewritten pages. Books by Antonio Gramsci and C. Wright Mills were stacked up on the toilet. My parents eschewed the black hole of domestic tasks for the absent-minded-professor aesthetic. My mother openly detested cooking and other housework; she once wrote that, as a girl, she admired her police lieutenant father, "who drew me diagrams of magnets and the digestive system," not her housewife mother, "who intruded on my life of the mind by making me dry the dishes." Yet our household was more or less in order: The books and magazines were in neat stacks. The bills got paid. Yellow legal pads filled up with crossed-off to-do lists in my mother's handwriting.

After her death in 2006, my dad's financial and logistical life went into free fall seemingly overnight. The regimented clutter of my childhood gave way to actual clutter. My dad would buy a rash of T-shirts, stuff them in a drawer, forget about them, and buy another pile three months later. Ominous letters about debt and default announcing themselves as the FINAL NOTICE got buried under newspapers. At first I thought it was the blindness of grief, but after a few years of the same, it became clear to me that my mom must have intercepted those impulses. I was unnerved, but instead of taking up the mantle of my mother's caretaking, I hightailed it to Chicago. I decided I was too young to concern myself with my father's tasks and errands.

I realized there had always been a way in which he delegated many little life concerns, even emotional engagement, to my mother so that he could write and work. I started to understand my dad's staggering productivity. He wrote a book every other year all throughout my childhood and had what appeared to be an unparalleled ability, perhaps honed during his library years in Newark, to tune out the world. It's not that my mom didn't get into writing holes too. Sometimes she'd stay up until two a.m. working and zombie through the next morning, valiantly fixing me some cereal in the six o'clock hour even when I was old enough to take the subway alone. But other times she'd be too distracted to write, instead obsessing over organizational domestic details, making doctor's appointments, looking into student loans, and ensuring I'd signed up for the SATs.

In the summer of 2010, right after I moved from Chicago back to New York and my dad was recovering from that first back operation, I witnessed a more intense kind of domestic dependence. He'd begun dating a reedy, silver-haired woman named Charlene, a retired big-shot lawyer who once represented the Church of Scientology but also worked on pro bono death penalty cases. She was managing his convalescence down to physical therapy appointments and the search for a sublet in a wheelchair-accessible building. She was the first woman my dad dated after my mom's death, but I eventually came around to the idea of meeting her. She sounded fascinating, no-nonsense, and self-sufficient. Unfortunately, we clashed from the moment we met. She could be spiteful and acid-tongued, but mostly she was domineering, which inflamed my own control-freak tendencies; at times her bossy outbursts felt like looking into one of those grotesque magnifying mirrors. By the fall, my dad was recovered, but Charlene and I reached an intractable boiling point that made being in the same room together excruciating.

My dad refused to engage in our dynamic. He viewed it as two broads having a catfight, not something he needed to mediate, much less acknowledge.

One day he and I were in the car together, and I couldn't help my twenty-five-year-old self: I started bawling. "Your girlfriend hates your daughter," I told him dramatically (albeit accurately) through snot and tears. "How can you ignore that?" He gave me a kind but distant smile and said, "The reason I've been able to get so much work done in my life is because I don't worry about these kinds of things. You have to let them roll off your back. You cannot get distracted by them. You cannot take them personally."

At the time I used these comments as an excuse to be self-flagellating: *I'll never produce classic and important writing because I'm ensnared in matters of the heart!* But when my father, single again, required my support in the aftermath of the stroke, those comments took on an unmistakably sexist tinge. What Charlene might have lacked in tact and tenderness, she'd made up for in domestic capability. I empathized with the resentment Jane must have felt when she was expected to tend to the children while my dad commenced an exciting career of political activism and scholarship. Meanwhile, I cursed the irony that comes with being born to a fifty-one-year-old dad: Although I benefited from those three extra decades that came before me, his later fatherhood also ensured that I would grow up faster than he ever had to, that I'd have less of the freedom he enjoyed because I'd be taking care of him.

Years later, while reading Gloria Steinem's introduction to male feminist Marc Feigen Fasteau's book, *The Male Machine*, I experienced a pang of recognition. Bemoaning Karl Marx's hypocrisy, Steinem pointed out that he acknowledged women's subordination as a result of oppression rather than nature, yet still demanded unreasonable sacrifice from his wife. Lots of powerful progressive men, she explained, ostensibly support feminism but have spent most of their lives saying some version of, "Shhh; Karl is working."

My dad is probably one of the very few people in history who managed to substantially self-improve, but even all those years of being partnered with a radical feminist couldn't cleanse him of certain sexist impulses ingrained during the oppressive era of his coming-of-age. It wasn't acceptable to sacrifice work or intellect for feelings, a feminine concern if there ever was one. In the months after my mom died, my dad revealed an unusual well of sentiment, sometimes bursting into tears at inappropriate moments. Still, even during that openhearted period, my dad seldom discussed personal details about my mom, preferring to praise what he called her "brilliant brain." It hurt me, this prioritization of scholarly pursuits over human emotions, the projection of a "who me?" disposition at all times. I couldn't imagine it was easy for my mom, one of the most emotional people I've ever known. I started to speculate that on some nights, even after those affectionate dinners, my mother would lie awake next to my father feeling lonely and engulfed in life's daily minutiae, wondering how to penetrate that kind but distant smile.

• • •

It's quite possible my mother sacrificed some of her own happiness because she loved an imperfect man. But it was also obvious that their relationship was actively good most of the time. That was a prerequisite for post-radicalized Ellen. Taking one's own desires seriously was practically her religion. "For me, for thousands of women," she wrote in an essay in 1989, "the explosion of radical feminism was a supremely sexy moment; we had the courage of our desires as we'd never had before." It was not *just* about sex, per se, but about "defining our fate, for once taking center stage and telling men how it was going to be."

My mother's contemporaries considered it a political necessity to identify what one truly wants. "You don't reach most women by toning yourself down, by lying about your needs and desires," wrote Kathie Sarachild in 1975. "The truth arouses people's imagination. . . . Lies are boring, lies are what women have heard a million times before." That included different models of horniness than what had previously been offered to women; rock music, for example, provided writer Karen Durbin, one of my mother's best friends, "with a channel for saying 'I want,' for asserting our sexuality without apologies and without having to pretty up every passion with the traditionally 'feminine' desire for true love and marriage."

Feminist thinkers began pointing out that, throughout Western society, male desire has largely been encouraged while female desire, in turn, has been suppressed in order to uphold the patriarchy—a truism now, but a revelatory statement then. In 1978, Black lesbian feminist Audre Lorde declared sexual pleasure an essential tool for fighting oppression. The erotic "offers a well of replenishing and provocative force to the woman who does not fear its revelation," she writes in her classic essay "Uses of the Erotic." We'd been raised to fear "our deepest cravings," but embracing our erotic impulse urges us "not to settle for the convenient, the shoddy, the conventionally expected, nor the merely safe. . . . In touch with the erotic, I become less willing to accept powerlessness, or those other supplied states of being which are not native to me, such as resignation, despair, self-effacement, depression, self-denial."

It hadn't occurred to me that this line of thinking had anything to do with me, a white, educated woman—I was liberated, sexual, certainly not oppressed!—until my dad's crisis pushed me to see how much I'd waved away desires of my own.

A couple of years after we met, I asked Aaron if we could have an open relationship. My knowledge of how to make nonmonogamy work was rudimentary, mostly culled from Dan Savage and a shady guy I hooked up with in college who supposedly had permission to fuck around on the side because his girlfriend's antidepressants had dampened her sex drive. At first the plan was that it would be temporary; I was moving to New York City six months before Aaron, and, well, we all had needs, et cetera. But then we just kept the relationship open, intermittently and tentatively. The rules often shifted: no exes; no one more than once; no more than three dates with the same person; don't ask, don't tell; must tell everything.

For years, I mostly followed the rules, mostly had one-night stands, mostly on work trips. I opted for my freedom way more than he did, which annoyed him. He claimed that the heterosexual marketplace was skewed in my favor: "It's not fair—any woman can have sex at any given time," he would say. "Men have to work harder." I maintained that this was bullshit. Sure, a lot of random men would probably sleep with me, but there were a lot more factors that could doom a good time. Not to mention that these sex partners weren't just appearing out of the blue: I was going out of my way to seek them out.

Not long before my dad's stroke, Aaron had told me he wanted to slow the open relationship way down—I was hooking up with too many people for his liking, he explained, and he wanted to be able to catch up to me. Again, I thought that was crap, but I suspected that if I said what I really wanted, we would have to break up, and breaking up brought on those familiar fears of lonely, regretful singledom. So I said okay. Once I was plunged into the post-stroke chaos, though, I began flirting with guys in bars and on apps behind Aaron's back, seeking a space that was all my own.

Eventually I made a date with Rob, a guy from Kentucky with a boring office job, an artsy streak, and a nonmonogamous relationship of his own. He was a good texter, a little older than me, demure and self-possessed. I remember being impressed that he, too, had read *The Other Hollywood*, a moderately obscure oral history of 1970s porn.

On the night I met Rob, I stuffed all the brutal chaos of the last few weeks into a stretchy jumpsuit with a diamond-shaped peephole under my sternum. We had a few beers and talked about our relationships, our childhoods, Justin Bieber, the fact that our moms were both dead. Then we went to go see a shockingly bad Francis Ford Coppola movie from 1981 called *One from the Heart*. We made out on the subway ride home and then fucked at his place, six blocks away from my house.

In the months that followed, I broke rule after rule to squeeze in weekly sex with Rob. Each encounter was baroque, circumscribed, and often planned out beforehand: Tomorrow I'd like to come over, silently blow you, and leave like it never happened, I would text him. Tuesday I'll bring the handcuffs and tie you up and come in your mouth, he would text me. Between dates, we texted incessantly about the hottest flashbacks, what we'd like to try, what we couldn't wait to do again. The surfeit of sexual energy sometimes spilled over to Aaron's and my bed. When we fucked, I was even more mentally far away than usual; he was blissfully unaware (or in denial?) about what was suddenly making me hornier.

Going over to Rob's house offered me a few precious minutes or hours of respite. It felt effortless and light, a completely levelheaded sex arrangement. We regularly patted each other on the back for being the world's chillest sidepieces. Of course, despite its lack of histrionics, my relationship with Rob ran roughshod over my own morals. I was lying to my partner and routinely ashamed of my selfishness. I knew somewhere deep in the recesses of my concupiscent mind that this cathartic sex was going to break any lingering bond I had with Aaron. In a certain way, that was precisely the appeal.

• • •

Until very recently, it's been difficult to explain why any woman in her right mind would contemplate having an affair, given the unimaginable risk it entailed. Women have been severely punished or even killed for their affairs throughout history. Hundreds of years of literature, from *The Scarlet Letter* to *Madame Bovary*, functioned as cautionary tales—for women—about infidelity. Even now, even in America, women are murdered by jealous partners, ostracized by friends and family, or subjected to online shame and harassment because they decided to have sex with someone outside their primary relationship. Even though Americans' views on most social issues are becoming increasingly liberal, "extramarital affairs" still ranks among the absolute lowest on the acceptability scale.

Nowadays, though, young women ages eighteen to twenty-nine are actually *more* likely to have affairs than men. The sexual revolution and feminism tamped down the material and social consequences of infidelity, especially for someone like me, who has independent income and rolls with a secular, nontraditional crowd. Though some people still judge adultery harshly, I wasn't worried about being stoned by my neighbors, or being abandoned with no way to earn a living, or becoming a victim of revenge porn. Feminist literature even framed affairs, in some cases, as righteous relief from a stifling marriage. Edna, the deeply lonely wife and mother of Kate Chopin's 1899 novel *The Awakening*, discovers the first whiffs of lust and passion through two different dalliances. Seventy-four years later, in Erica Jong's *Fear of Flying*, the protagonist's affair and subsequent romp across Europe are at the heart of her sexual and spiritual transformation.

Even outside the context of feminism, I'd seen lots of my friends cheat on their partners as a stepping-stone to easing their way out of a bad relationship. My own parents both employed this escape hatch in their first marriages. It's a testament to how a shot of illicit pleasure can underscore one's misery (and how easy it is to ride the wave of adultery out the door rather than acknowledge that misery). In any case, it's a well-worn narrative that, at first glance, I seemed on my way to being part of.

Still, I knew even while it was happening that my motivation wasn't mere boredom and unhappiness. If it was, I might have done it earlier. Throughout years of rebelling in small ways (seeing someone four times instead of three times, for instance), I'd never orchestrated a massive betrayal like this. I shocked myself every time I lied to Aaron by omission, which, during these months, was every single day. A consistent affair was a boundary I hadn't yet crossed, so it was worth asking myself why I was crossing it now.

Years later, I came up with a possible answer: Under normal circumstances, my caretaking responsibilities were virtually zero, which had been by design. Then, seemingly overnight, I was swallowed up by the needs of my dad and husband—and with my dad it looked like there would be no relief ahead. His stroke put me in the shoes of a much more conventional caretaker figure, with my needs shoved way, way down into the bottom of the priority bin. Aaron's diminished state, while temporary, just compounded the feeling. I didn't fear societal consequences for infidelity, but I *was* reacting to an archaic societal role for which I was ill-suited. It was magnifying a feeling of dissatisfaction I'd long had.

After interviewing hundreds of women for her 1992 book, *The Erotic Silence of the American Wife*, journalist Dalma Heyn identifies one function of an affair for married mothers. It was a way to get away from "selflessness and obligations to fill others' needs" and represented an opportunity to step into the role of a "sexually joyous and self-interested person." Heyn's argument recasts selfishness as a quality that can be positive or, at the very least, one that can combat deep-seated dissatisfaction. "Finding at home the kind of self-absorption that is essential to erotic pleasure proves a challenge," sex and relationship therapist Esther Perel would write two years after my affair with Rob. "When you have an affair, you know for a fact that you're not doing it to take care of anyone else."

Seeing Rob became a way to assert the autonomy I didn't consciously understand I wanted. I did, however, consciously want to keep having amazing sex with him. At that time my inner self-righteousness was louder than my moral standards: *Why shouldn't I listen to my own desires, rather than the desires of two needy men and the social mandates that tie me to them?*

My cravings to see Rob were straightforward and devoid of outside expectation. *I want this*, I thought, when I met him on a Sunday at work in his giant corporate office building, where he led me by the hand to various empty rooms, pulled my hair as he pressed me against the wall, then fucked me on a random colleague's filing cabinet. *I want this*, every time I stopped by his place for an eight a.m. sex session on my way to my office, where I would try to squeeze in actual editing work between phone calls about bedsores and stroke-specific reflexology. *I want this*, when I sexted with him while I waited for my dad to come out of speech therapy.

I want this, the time we had a sweet, stoned make-out hours after I uncovered yet another unpaid five-figure debt my dad had lurking in his financial history.

I want this, I told myself, a couple of hours after I found out that my dad's home health aide had stolen from him. I was going through his American Express statement, which gives you every last detail about each transaction, and there it was: a JetBlue ticket purchase with the caregiver's name on it. There was a flurry of phone calls, moral dilemmas, and logistical emergencies, which provoked, yet again, a flood of frustrated tears. It was the crisis that sent me into *I want this* overdrive and steered me directly to Rob's apartment, where he'd given me those two choices: I could go home, remaining in my current life of drudgery. Or I could choose the effortless pleasure bubble and leave that life behind, just for a moment.

I chose option B. We smoked a joint. He cuffed my wrists and ankles and hooked them together. He instructed me to lie down on the couch on my stomach. He warned me not to move, not to struggle—or else. Then, firmly doling out commands as he went, using his fingers and a Hitachi Magic Wand, he made me come for many minutes on end. It was archetypical BDSM: the rush of surrender, the act of trusting someone to take over and deliver pleasure.

In Lorde's "Uses of the Erotic," she describes how, as a child living through World War II, she'd buy packets of white margarine with a "tiny, intense pellet of yellow coloring perched like a topaz" tucked inside. She'd pinch the pellet in the bag until it penetrated the pale goop by releasing an ecstatic rush of hue. During previous encounters with Rob, my mind was mercifully blank, as if someone had wrapped my brain in a sugary, benzo-laced gauze. But this time was different. As the panic wafting out of my body was replaced by pleasure, I felt like that bag of margarine slowly turning golden. When the erotic is released from its concentrated capsule, Lorde writes, "it flows through and colors my life with a kind of energy that heightens and sensitizes and strengthens all my experience."

Lying on that green couch misted with sweat and the scent of a spliff, the same crisp revelation: *I want this*. Like the wives Heyn interviewed for her study, I was jolted with "a sense of competence and satisfaction," like I had "emerged from a trance." Through all those postcoital chemicals, I saw myself clearly. The topaz had burst.

• • •

Let's be real. It's not like I went right home from Rob's house and broke up with Aaron. Instead, I began to live in an alternate reality of sexual and intellectual stimulation that pushed me further and further from him. My sex appointments with Rob, fueled by weed and soft-spoken BDSM, grew in length and intensity. Our text conversations stretched for hours. I began to envy the autonomy and respect he and his girlfriend, who didn't live with him, seemed to give each other. A real connection was born—not love, exactly, but an expansive spark that had the ability to disintegrate tunnel vision.

The turning point came in March 2016, four months after Aaron and I had cut short our upstate weekend to tend to my dad, when Rob texted a long, fumbling explanation of why he really appreciated those mock-anonymous drive-by blow jobs (besides the obvious). "It's what you want, and you get it, and never once have I felt like I'm getting one over on you," he texted. "Which is pretty great."

My cheeks burned. It was one of the most cherished texts I'd ever received. This plain admiration of my most unvarnished desires, which up until this moment I'd seen as evidence of depravity and cowardice, reminded me of a Velvet Underground song that frequently played in my house as a kid. In "I'll Be Your Mirror," Nico sings that she can detect her lover's goodness, even through their self-hating cynicism: "Please put down your hands / 'Cause I see you."

Not long after this compliment, Rob told me he was moving in with his girlfriend and that they'd decided to put the nonmonogamy on hold for a little while. I sent him the least chill text of our whole relationship: that he and this had been special to me, that I was really glad I met him, that he was a sweet and thoughtful person in addition to being a great lay. His response was caring but noticeably more detached—a reminder that, unlike me, Rob wasn't having an affair. I was not his escape hatch, and he was considering his partner's needs in a way that I was not. For the duration of that exchange, my heart was open and he gently, politely sealed it.

It was over. I had "gotten away with it." I filed away the Rob era and resumed my relationship with Aaron. It could have easily stayed that way, my desire and restlessness confined to those final feelsy texts and that fusty velvet couch, but my subconscious trembled and teetered, urging me to jump.

By that summer, Aaron was long recovered and my dad's caretaking needs had ratcheted down from a primal scream to an irritating but manageable whine. Still, Aaron and I were no more connected than we had been earlier that year, and the universe had served up a whole new set of upheavals. America had plunged headfirst into political turmoil, provoking an apocalyptic release of collective id. The election results that fall are so indelible that few seem to remember the summer right before it, when the news was exploding with some of the most bloody tragedies in recent memory, tragedies that seemed to tap into marginalized Americans' ceaseless suffering. Elders were comparing it to the uprisings during the "long, hot summer" of 1967, touched off by the brutal beating of a Black cab driver in Newark by two white police officers.

First there were the hundreds of gunshots that rang through the Orlando nightclub Pulse on a warm June night, killing forty-nine people, many of them Latino and queer. Later that month, seven people were stabbed at a neo-Nazi rally. Less than a month later, police shot and killed two Black men: First Alton Sterling, a CD salesman with five kids, was wrestled to the ground and shot at close range. The next day, Philando Castile, a school cafeteria worker who had been pulled over for a traffic stop, lay in his car bleeding to death in front of his girlfriend, her child, and millions more on a Facebook livestream. Then one day after that, a sniper killed five police officers and wounded nine other people at an otherwise peaceful anti–police violence protest. Three more officers were killed in Baton Rouge less than two weeks later.

One might think all this bloodshed and bigotry would have distracted me from my comparatively trivial relationship problems, and in the short term, they did. They consumed my thoughts and filled up my work hours. But the very fact that none of it seemed to faze Aaron proved to be the last snip that severed our connection. His apparent indifference to the world around us made me feel profoundly lonely in a moment when all I wanted to do was hold my loved ones close. On the eve of the Dallas shooting, I worked well into the night, alternating between editing an op-ed and pep-talking one of our reporters in Castile's Minnesota hometown. Aaron had been out drinking; when I texted him about the shooting, he hadn't yet heard a thing about it. By the time I was done with work, he was passed out in our bed, too deep in sleep to detect my puttering and pacing.

What happened next didn't feel like liberation so much as demolition. After midnight, I started texting with a sweet, respectful software engineer I'd seen a few times before, aboveboard, within the parameters of Aaron's and my rules. Eventually it became clear that I was, at that moment, again going to break those rules. I slipped out wearing nothing but a sundress to go meet the guy while Aaron was dead to the world. When I walked through my own door at four a.m., knees buckling and hair a mess, there was a large part of me that wished Aaron would wake up and demand to know where I'd been—not just because the despair was starting to creep back and an angry confrontation would have been more satisfying than nothingness, but because I knew it was over, and I wanted him to do the honors.

He didn't. *I don't want this*, I thought: not this relationship, not an affair, not a life devoid of the erotic. A few weeks later, I moved out.

4. The Vulnerability Paradox

Sex never feels casual. It's basically either great or pointless.

—RANDOM MALE SEXTER, CIRCA 2015

On the last day of August in 2016, I stuffed a few garbage bags full of clothes into a closet-size room at Dane's place in Brooklyn. I barely knew Dane, only the fact that they were a buddy of Ruby's and Vivian's, two friends who'd initiated breakups of their own in the last year. Ruby and Vivian understood that I was about to be inducted into a club of people who'd willingly stepped off the heterosexual conveyer belt at an age when they were "supposed" to be settling down and were about to be in the throes of a soul-searching trampage. I needed to be housed and nurtured by someone who was frequently in their feelings. *Dane is always down for intimacy,* Ruby assured me.

She was right. Elfin, smiley Dane was an ideal doula for those first frenzied weeks of singledom. Over damiana-laced joints on the couch, Dane regaled me with stories of their white-hot, often short-lived flings with people of all genders, backgrounds, and temperaments. (Our friendship—which burned bright then faded away quickly—followed a similar trajectory.) They used a short-hand for people who fully immersed themselves in the overwhelm that was inherent in love and sex, as well as for people who did not: Team Intense versus Team Chill. They were an evangelist for be-coming a member of the former. They were currently ensnared in an obsessive long-distance entanglement with Tina, yet another friend of mine in the "club" who'd recently broken it off with her longtime partner. Dane would nest in their bedroom in a Tina bubble, then emerge to masticate every little detail with me on the couch. One night, they spontaneously booked a flight to LA to surprise Tina. "I just couldn't wait to see her!" Dane told me. "Think a plane ticket was too much?"

I wasn't sure anymore. A few months ago, I would have said, "Yikes, yes!" Apart from some crucial defections like the lychee martini night with Aaron, I'd been a lifelong member of Team Chill. Besides that long-term relationship, I usually erred on the side of casual and sex-forward. It's not that I didn't want emotional intimacy with the people I was having sex with, but I hoped that the sex itself, rather than ultimatums or grand gestures, would cre-ate it naturally. Throughout the years, it only sort of worked. Now here was unapologetically all-in Dane, who didn't demand cultur-ally prescribed benchmarks of devotion, but also did not feign non-chalance. Dane led with their desires for pleasure, both sexual and emotional. Their life seemed filled with passion, if not in the least bit peaceful. I was inspired.

I had to be careful, though, because I did *not* want another seri-ous relationship. I wanted fun, respectful sexual encounters while still being able to protect my heart and independence. In fact, I wanted a lot of things: the freedom I didn't get in the aftermath of my dad's stroke, the sexual abundance I couldn't have during my marriage, the fulfillment of existing fantasies and the discovery of new ones. "You can have all that!" Dane said. "Just don't close yourself off to anything." Sensing my opportunity for a redo of my Chill years, I set out to have casual, enjoyable sex.

On Labor Day weekend, I hooked up with three people in three days. On Friday I fucked an Israeli guy with whom I'd matched on Bumble at midnight and met in the depths of Brooklyn an hour after we began chatting. I observed his nervous, off-putting energy while we downed a few glasses of nondescript white wine, but decided I didn't mind it—he was a neurotic New York Jew like me, even if he looked like Gael García Bernal with an undercut. I tried not to be grossed out by his messy apartment or the fact that his mattress had been placed unceremoniously on the bare floor. He didn't have a job and, judging by the marmalade-colored pill bottles everywhere, appeared to be heavily medicated. I didn't ask what for. I just knew he was wide-eyed and gorgeous, his olive skin clustered with tattoos of varying quality and originality. We ended up executing an impressive romp until the sun glowed through his taupe shades.

The next day, I had a dance-floor make-out at a huge, impersonal party at the local surf club in Far Rockaway, with a winsome guy of very few words. The day after that, I went to my summer-camp reunion and hooked up with an old faithful, someone I'd been fucking off and on for years. The pace remained relentless for weeks afterward. I'd spend hours lying on Dane's guest futon in a libidinous fog, swiping on the apps, thinking of clever texts, and recalling hot details from previous encounters. I'd regularly come back to Dane's at seven a.m. on a workday, sore and rumpled and infused with adrenaline from a sleepover the night before.

These hookups dominated my conversations with friends. I felt freer than ever to express not only my misgivings about my marriage, but the pleasure I was searching for instead. Some of my friends were all too happy to go down the rabbit hole with me. The ones fresh off their own breakups—Ruby, Vivian, Tina, and all the rest—knew well how horniness could fold itself into that kind of abrupt life decision, and how fresh new flings provided the perfect potion of escape and connection. Other friends were jarred by the sudden disappearance of Aaron, perhaps nervous at the fragility of a seemingly settled union. My friend Sadye, who was one of the first ones in our circle to get married and was nursing a small baby during this time, had no bandwidth to hear about my sexcapades. One time she cut me off in mid-sentence, informing me: "Listen, I got four hours of sleep last night. I just can't do this." It occurred to me that our reasons for sleeping less than normal were quite different. The gulf between me and the people who'd chosen a more linear route never felt bigger.

Even without a baby, I might have been annoyed at my one-track mind too. Some of my friends harbored no moral judgments but could feel my energy veering into mania. I wasn't just pursuing pleasure; I was also engaging in a form of self-medicating to avoid the crash of the breakup, and sex was my drug of choice. The only problem was that the highs of the hookups were short-lived, though that's not to say they weren't worth it. A few fuckbuddies during that fall bestowed upon me very hot memories to fantasize about later. Sometimes I was just horny and would have sex that was perfectly serviceable. Usually, these encounters provided a shot of ego boost and much-needed escapism. Though I'd learned to manage them, the stress bursts of my dad's ceaseless medical needs still weighed on me heavily, and having a bright, airy time with a nice guy always made me feel better. We were doing the bare minimum of recognizing each other's humanity, so no one left feeling disrespected, objectified, or misled (at least, not to my knowledge).

But after a handful of hangs, these connections would fizzle out, even when there was good physical chemistry. Most guys didn't make it beyond the monikers I offered my friends: "the normie with the perfect penis," "the minimalist carpenter," "the Donald Glover look-alike." We were all performing best-case-scenario booty calls, yet I hadn't totally joined Dane on Team Intense. I wasn't having the life-changing sex I'd hoped for.

I thought back to the best sex I'd had in recent memory: the topaz pellet, my sweaty face on Rob's couch, limbs tied up, lava lake of desire completely exposed. I was so disarmed, so trusting. That wasn't the kind of sex you had with a one-night stand. Despite our best efforts, Rob and I had failed to keep it "casual," and that was with our respective partners acting as emotional buffers. The high stakes of seeing Rob had also heightened the hotness. It wasn't just sex but forbidden sex—a classic trope, of course, a source of eroticism that depended on dishonesty and the risk of negative consequences. That kind of thrill felt both inaccessible and antithetical to a slut with integrity. I wanted my hookups to be both fulfilling *and* morally sound.

Almost right away, I was confronted with a dilemma that has long complicated the success rate of casual sex, even between two upstanding humans. How could I have satisfying sex while feeling safe but not bored, cared for but not smothered in sentimentality? How could I stay true to my feelings but not be "too much"?

• • •

Vulnerability is inevitably a part of sexual pleasure and intimacy, from the very first second of a date; to the grimaces, guttural sounds, and literal nakedness of the act; to postcoital rituals like cigarettes and breakfast and follow-up texts. Even if an encounter is fetishy and finite, letting someone know your innermost fantasies is essentially allowing them to peer into your brain. As writer Katherine Angel puts it: "Letting things in, being porous"—being available, welcoming—"is what makes one tender to the feelings of others, and what puts one at their mercy."

Yet this vulnerable state of being is the precise thing that makes sex so risky, particularly if you're a woman wanting to have no-strings-attached sex with a man. The traditionally feminine trait of emotional openness exposes you to the pain and confusion of romantic feelings and rejection, neither of which is desirable when you're only trying to have "fun," a word that quickly becomes meaningless in this universe. And the dangers posed by physical vulnerability—pressure, boundary crossing, sexual assault, unwanted pregnancy—have long been the cudgels that sexual conservatives have wielded over a woman (and any marginalized person) who pursues sex outside marriage.

The tension between pleasure and vulnerability has hung over the heads of anybody negotiating sex without commitment for at least the last hundred years. Depending on the context, sex philosophers have called "vulnerability" different things, some positive—love, tenderness, humanity, honesty—and some negative—naivete, sentimentality, "emotional problems." The conundrum of how much of your soul to expose has always been there, threatening to ruin the tidy boundaries of casual sex. For women, there's the classic fear of rape and unwanted domination. This same fear hovers over queer people of any gender, people with disabilities, and other marginalized groups. But there are other fears to consider too: the possibility of becoming codependent and losing yourself inside someone else, or unleashing your worst, socially unacceptable instincts and cravings. Sexuality is unpredictable, prone to fueling existential dilemmas without warning. As Carole Vance puts it in the classic 1984 anthology she edited, *Pleasure and Danger*, "Having been told that pleasure threatens civilization, we wonder: what if there is no end to desire?"

While early revolutionaries like the free lovers did not believe in marriage, casual sex was hardly the goal. But by the time the mid-century sexual revolution rolled around, there was finally some agreement that sex for its own sake could be gratifying, even for women. Helen Gurley Brown's controversial 1962 blockbuster, *Sex and the Single Girl*, designated horniness as the number one reason for a single woman to have sex: "Her body wants to," she writes. "For weird and wonderful reasons that she will never really understand, some lucky special man 'has it' for her." Brown pushes back on the idea that women are powerless against their ooey-gooey feelings. Some women are capable of enjoying affairs "unwracked by guilt, anxiety or unrealistic hopes."

Given the cultural and physical baggage women were saddled with, Brown deemed a degree of self-protection essential. She's merciless about the fact that casual sex isn't for the faint of heart: "There is no question that an affair adds to the emotional problems of many women; however, the ones who suffer most are probably the ones who have the most emotional problems to begin with." Brown had an equally withering assessment of the "nymphomaniac," whom she regarded as insecure and desperate, someone who isn't vulnerable enough to check in with her own needs. "Far from being the sexpot many people think she is, having fun fun fun, she is frigid, technically," she writes of this type of woman. This "pseudo-wildcat" will "spend the entire evening in selfless concentration doing what makes a man happy."

So what made women happy? It wasn't necessarily love, but for some women, it *was* perhaps vulnerability. In 1972, a few years after radical feminists began discussing sexual dilemmas in consciousness-raising sessions, writer Karen Durbin wondered what had become of "a movement that in its early years spoke out strongly for preserving that humanistic sensibility which has traditionally been attributed to the so-called weaker sex." Instead, she described dispassionate hookups between "a pair of glorified vibrators," a sexual atmosphere that "seems bleak and a little dead."

And it wasn't just feminists who felt this way. A few years later, researcher Shere Hite asked mainstream American women about the aftermath of the sexual revolution. Her massive national study on female sexuality, released in 1976, was full of women theoretically supporting sexual freedom, who were grateful to have escaped the harsh consequences of being a "tramp." But many wished there was more connection and affection involved—even if it was just because it made the sex better. One woman spelled it out clearly:

I like sex a lot. But it can only supplement a warm, affectionate, mutually respecting, full personhood relationship. . . . I have found sex with people I don't really like, or who I'm not certain will really like me, or with people I don't feel I know well, to be very shallow and uncomfortable and physically unsatisfying. I don't believe you have to be "in love" and married "till death do us part." But mind and body are one organism and all tied up together, and it isn't even physically fun unless the people involved really like each other!

Another woman described sex as an intimate yet ephemeral experience, "like being in a world with just you and your partner, everything else becomes unimportant at that moment. Then comes the moment when it must stop and after a while, after he goes home, then the total separation [thing] sets in." A third woman condemned the men who played it too cool: "What gives me *least* pleasure is people who are emotionally inadequate." Most of these women were not yearning to revert to chivalry; they simply wanted to be treated like human beings. Reflecting on this stage of the sexual revolution, my mother wrote that the "conventionally masculine dream of pure lust"—unemotional sensation for sensation's sake—is "as conservative in its way as the conventionally feminine romanticism that converts lust to pure emotion. . . . All are attempts to tame sex, to make it safe by holding something back."

Many women in *The Hite Report* also discussed how consent lines got blurred amid the explosion of casual sex, reporting an exhausting pressure that made them hesitant to say no. "I was afraid I was overreacting if I just left, and he kept subtly making further and further advances after persuading me to stay over and promising me my own bed," went one woman's story, about a dynamic familiar to anyone who remembers the accusations against Aziz Ansari. "Eventually I got tired of listlessly fighting him off in bits and pieces and thought okay, let him have his stupid orgasm and leave me alone." In this case, her protective instincts kicked in, the sheer opposite of vulnerability: "I had *no* feeling at all."

These stories are painful to read, but not surprising. In a society with loosened sexual restrictions but still-pervasive misogyny, it's just a fact that having more sex poses some risk to women. Around the same time as *The Hite Report*'s publication, Susan Brownmiller's book *Against Our Will* popularized the crucial concept of rape as power. "Man's discovery that his genitalia could serve as a weapon to generate fear must rank as one of the most important discoveries of prehistoric times," Brownmiller writes. Rape is a "conscious process of intimidation by which *all* men keep *all* women in a state of fear." Outright rape and more subtle forms of socially sanctioned coercion weren't separate concepts: they were part of the same model men use to dominate women. Some feminists believed that the cultural paradigm of rape was so inherent and pervasive that the only thing the so-called sexual revolution accomplished was to cast the violation of women in a hip, countercultural light.

By the late 1970s, in certain circles, protection from sexual violence became the prevailing definition of feminist sexual politics. And for radical feminists like Brownmiller, Catharine MacKinnon, and Robin Morgan, nothing promoted sexual violence more conspicuously than pornography. With the formation of a new and politically potent group, Women Against Pornography, or WAP (not to be confused with 2020's ebullient pussy anthem courtesy of Cardi B and Megan Thee Stallion), anti-porn feminism became an all-encompassing rallying cry—and a legislative frontier.

Andrea Dworkin is probably the most infamous feminist from this crowd, a woman whose work I wouldn't exactly call "anti-sex" (she described it often in lush, filthy-mouthed detail) but who certainly held the hardest line when it came to protecting women from their own vulnerability. A foe of nuance, Dworkin argued again and again that yes, a woman's physical and emotional rawness is necessary for good sex, but no, men cannot be trusted with it. Indeed, sexual violence is baked into sex between men and women. She wrote that all intercourse, while not literally rape, violates the integrity of a woman's body; that men need to forgo their "precious erections" and "make love as women do together";

that women who enjoy penetration are "experiencing pleasure in their own inferiority." Physical danger was a constant threat: "We are very close to death," she said in a speech about rape. "All women are." She called women who craved sexual freedom but contorted themselves into male models of sexiness "left-wing whores" and "collectivized cunts." What women want, she argued, is "a more diffuse and tender sensuality"—a sexuality that simply isn't compatible with male aggression.

The anti-porn feminists' push for protection over freedom and their narrow vision of female-friendly lovemaking dismayed many feminists like Carole Vance, Gayle Rubin, and my own mother.* They insisted it was possible to condemn rape, harassment, and double standards without denouncing the progress of the sexual revolution. Lots of women had been radicalized by the discovery (or at least the possibility) of their own erotic freedom. Not only were groups like Women Against Pornography attempting to legislate sexuality and effectively promoting censorship; they were also shaming women for their turn-ons in a world that so often already muzzled female desire. Subjective judgments of what sex "should" be did nothing to acknowledge women's realities, these feminists argued, and only added to women's internal self-doubt machines. "In this culture, where women are still supposed to be less sexual than men, sexual inhibition is as integral to the 'normal' women's identity as sexual aggression is to a man's," my mom wrote in a 1981 essay that coined the term "pro-sex" feminism. It is "'excessive' genital desires that often make women feel 'unfeminine' and unworthy."

---

*The anthology Carole Vance edited, *Pleasure and Danger: Exploring Female Sexuality*, is largely based on the presentations at the 1982 Barnard Conference on Sexuality and is essential reading while exploring this tension.

With books like Nancy Friday's *My Secret Garden* in 1973—which collected hundreds of female fantasies ranging from incest to gang bangs to bestiality—it became clear that expecting anyone's sexual turn-ons to be politically coherent was a fool's errand.

Besides, pro-sex feminists asked, was the complete eradication of risk from sexuality really the goal of feminism? The threat of danger, and therefore vulnerability, can be an integral part of erotic tension. The promise of protection from danger was a lie, anyway, just a bribe to keep women's sexuality in line. In 1979, my mom called this sinister negotiation a "good cop–bad cop" routine: "The good cops are marriage, motherhood, and that courtly old gentleman, chivalry," she wrote. "Just cooperate, they say (crossing their fingers), and we'll go easy on you. . . . But you'd better not get stubborn, or you'll have to deal with our friend rape, and he's a real terror; we just can't control him." Anti-porn feminists were falling into an antiquated trap of assuming that the bad cop of pornography was the problem. The real problems, my mother argued, were cops and the law.

The "good cop" of chastity or marriage available to white women was a deal with the devil, but it did offer *some* level of protection and acceptance. Black and brown women were seldom offered ways to be safe from sexual violence at all. As Toni Morrison wrote in 1971, Black women "had nothing to fall back on: not maleness, not whiteness, not ladyhood, not anything." During the eighties feminist sex wars, women of color didn't easily fit into the pro-sex versus pro-protection dichotomy laid out by white women. Some Black writers like Audre Lorde, Patricia Hill Collins, Luisah Teish, and Alice Walker sympathized with white anti-porn activists but pointed out Black women's position in the crosshairs of racism and sexism. "Where white women are depicted in pornography as 'objects,' Black women are depicted as animals," wrote Walker in the 1980 anthology *Take Back the Night: Women on Pornography*. "Where white women are at least depicted as human bodies if not beings, Black women are depicted as shit."

Other women of color believed in fighting against sexual shame but still felt that their specific realities were often transposed onto white-specific ideas. At the famous Barnard Conference on Sexuality in 1982, which gathered key players to discuss pro-sex feminism, these tensions came to a head. Black scholar Hortense Spillers criticized white feminists for flattening the female experience: "Whatever my mother, niece, and I might say and do about our sexuality," she said, "remains an unarticulated nuance in various forms of public discourse as though we were figments of the great invisible empire of womankind." At a speak-out later that day, women of color in attendance urged their white counterparts to consider how their sexuality interacted with other sites of historical exploitation. "I am a Chicana, Catholic-raised lesbian," Cherríe Moraga told the crowd. "I can't keep looking to white folks to explain my sexuality."

Nobody could accuse Moraga of ignoring the power of pleasure—she had read some of her poetry in the closing session, describing "hungry longing" and "the memory of your passion dark & starving," among other vivid images of sexual desire. But to her, the stark terms of the sex wars debate seemed like "a white woman's thing." Later, in a letter to the editor in the feminist magazine *off our backs*, headlined "Played Between White Hands," Moraga took aim at both the "reductive" fear of the anti-porn feminists *and* the libertarians, who didn't seem to grasp why it might be harder for women of color to just proudly embrace sexual freedom. "I'm tired of this mess," Moraga declared. "Is it any wonder under these conditions that a deeper analysis has been slow to appear?"

• • •

In a broad sense, despite the mess and the blind spots, the vision of the pro-sex feminists ultimately prevailed over that of the anti-porn feminists. Women did not trade in their freedom for an illusory sense of protection, porn did not get banned, and casual sex came with fewer and fewer societal consequences. They won because people rarely respond positively to moralistic finger-wagging, especially if the taboo in question can be fun, transformative, and thrilling.

But pretty soon, like most popular ideas, there was a mainstream version of female sexual freedom with the radicalism sucked out. "Pro-sex feminism" had an uncanny valley that drowned out a complex conversation about pleasure and female desire: a particular strain of superslut "empowerment" symbolized by hot pink vibrators, stripper poles, tramp stamps, and Girls Gone Wild. Suddenly, any and all sex was good, as long as it was consensual. Much more nuanced slut theory lived on through the nineties and the aughts in the work of writers like Susie Bright, Candida Royalle, and Annie Sprinkle, who advocated for women to be able to pursue sex on their own terms and through the prism of their own fantasies. But screaming much louder were the girlbosses of sexual freedom—modern-day versions of Helen Gurley Brown's "pseudo-wildcats," or what Ariel Levy later called "female chauvinist pigs," women whose sexuality hewed closely to the pillars of what men supposedly thought was hot.

Sensitive souls who wanted some semblance of emotional intimacy despite their support of sexual freedom were often relegated to the side as unhip nuisances. Paula Kamen's *Her Way*, an ethnography billed as a 2000 update to *The Hite Report*, encountered many women who felt like this. If women "feel the basic and rational human need of wanting an emotional connection with sex, potentially the most intimate physical act between two people," Kamen concluded, "then they feel as though they must be weak."

The demand for fortitude went double for Black women. Lil' Kim and Foxy Brown, whose first albums were released a week apart in the fall of 1996, were definitely pleasure seeking, but it was the most invulnerable version of pleasure seeking there could possibly be, and whether it was on their own terms was an open question. Hip-hop writer and feminist Joan Morgan didn't feel liberated by Lil' Kim's sex-drenched lyrics, because they were centered so much in maleness. She felt the specter of Biggie and the Bad Boy crew looming over Kim, and the pressures of a commercial market that insisted she be both hypersexual and unflappable. As Clover Hope writes of Kim in her book *The Motherlode*: she used her voice as a tool of liberation as best she could, but "if being any other way than sexy wasn't a viable choice, she couldn't have a complete sense of power."

As a teenager who came of age during the height of the super-slut, I remember Kim and Foxy as the first sexual idols I had. I was twelve when their albums were released, when I was just barely in the throes of puberty and had never kissed anyone outside of a game of spin the bottle. I heard about them from my precocious best friend, Sarah, whose views on both sex and pop culture I considered gospel. We spent hours in her bedroom listening to *Hard Core* and *Ill Na Na* in tandem. We squealed over Foxy's "ta-tas perkin'," her "sex drive all night like a trucker." We could scarcely imagine what oral sex felt like, but we learned from Kim that it's something we should demand: "I don't want dick tonight / Eat my pussy right," she declared.

I belted out these lyrics within earshot of my mom, who

seemed to prefer them to the misogyny in the male hip-hop I listened to. But I'm not quite sure about that, because she never commented either way. I didn't often seek her counsel on things like puberty and sex, and she didn't pry or even offer. This often perplexes people, even the ones who knew her parenting was in some ways hands-off—*why didn't one of the preeminent pro-sex feminists pass along her wisdom to her daughter?*

I recently found a possible answer in an early, unpublished draft of a 1989 piece of hers on teen sex. "Teenagers *do* need adult support," she wrote, especially girls, who face enormous pressure from both their peers and the dominant culture. "Yet there's also something positive, something loving, even, about a parent's determination 'not to know': given all the contradictions, it's a way of respecting kids' privacy, and therefore their dignity." She recounted an anecdote about five-year-old me, who would shoo her out of my room and say, "I'm going to shut my door now, mama." She anxiously wondered what mischief I was getting up to but, she wrote, "I force myself not to peek."

In one sense I'm grateful that she never tried to police my sexuality. I never had to worry whether she was going to ransack my room in search of my diary, like other friends' moms had done. Yet sometimes I wonder if she erred on the side of giving me *too* much privacy. She might not have realized that in the absence of her guidance, I fully let my peers educate me instead.

I'd reread *Are You There God? It's Me, Margaret* dozens of times before I finally, *finally* got my period just before my thirteenth birthday. When my boobs and curves arrived shortly afterward, I immediately had a handful of kiss-and-touches with boys, each kind of jarring, but exciting nonetheless. Some girls tried to call me and my friend Sarah sluts, but it didn't hurt our feelings or social standing. We learned early that appearing savvy and in control while going out and "getting play" would help guard against sexual judgment. Researcher Laina Bay-Cheng would later recognize this logic as hewing to a new, third axis cutting across the "virgin-slut continuum": an additional metric modern girls need to navigate called the "agency line." We weren't sluts, because we were following what Bay-Cheng calls a neoliberal script of self-interest and independence (a script most readily available to white, straight girls like me and Sarah). We were participating in the sexual equivalent of a free market. Women who were getting "used" acted as our foils—we, unlike them, wanted it.

By fifteen, I was having genuinely good sex with a kid named Noah, sex that I initiated. He wasn't exactly my boyfriend, but we had strong sexual chemistry. "I think people are wrong when they say that sex and love HAVE to be together," I wrote in my diary, channeling the "agency" of Kim and Foxy and probably Samantha from *Sex and the City*, which had just premiered a few months before. "Physically, we're in love. Our bodies are perfect for each other, we satisfy each other's sexual urges like we were born for one another. And we're not really like that personality-wise. But that's okay!"

It wasn't always okay. Like many teen girls, I wanted more attention and affection than this guy was willing to give. This wasn't necessarily because we had a natural connection—our conversations were often stilted; I found myself getting along better with his friends—but because I'd been socialized to think that if a boy respected you, he would want to full-on date you. Besides, he hurt my feelings by being inconsiderate in that teen-boy way, by not calling when he said he would or ignoring me on AOL Instant Messenger.

Still, it's clear from my rapturous reports that I loved to fuck him, not only because of the physical sensations but because it created a temporarily cracked-open version of him, or at least the illusion of one. "When all of me is touching all of him it feels perfect and it's his most honest moment and there's physical sparks and that is how I know that deep down (even though he won't say it) he cares about me cause he's trying to make me happy, trying to make me scream, calling me baby, making me wet from his slightest touch."

That description is just as explicit as Kim's and Foxy's (sorry, Noah!) but doesn't quite mirror my idols' bravado. My experience was closer to the sex-as-ephemeral-intimacy theory that the woman had described in *The Hite Report*. I admitted (to myself, if nobody else) that the best sex involves some amount of vulnerability, that it needs an "honest moment" when a person, aided by a cocktail of orgasmic neurochemicals, was most present and open and exposed. I wanted some reassurance that my sex partner took me into consideration. Still, there was something that sincerely irked me about traditional, hand-holding coupledom. Despite the panic in the press about casual sex, it was more common in my high school to have an old-fashioned boyfriend-girlfriend arrangement. The possessiveness, chivalry, and gifting of corny teddy bears I observed around me was not appealing either. There didn't seem to be a good answer.

Then, in the beginning of senior year, a longtime guy friend, Derek, turned into my boyfriend. It was a relationship that required neither emotional suppression nor outdated gendered norms. "I love his personality and we just click together and it's so nice," I wrote. I was one of his first girlfriends, he explained, who really seemed to enjoy hooking up. "You're just a big ball of sex, you make me think of sex, you make me want to have sex," he told me one night. "When we hook up, it feels good but it's also fun, and loose, like we can joke around with each other," I recounted in my journal.

I was on the verge of telling him I loved him when he broke up with me three months before prom for a blond ballet dancer virgin who was only a junior, which, at the time, seemed insultingly young. This savage teenage rejection spurred a circumstantial but excruciating depression. He probably just liked the new girl better than me—her intact hymen likely had little to do with his decision to dump me, and I had not yet been clued into the fact that the very term "virgin" was reductive and arbitrary. Still, for the first time in my life, I felt slut-shamed, like an innocent girl had more credibility and leverage to be "girlfriend material." Luckily I seemed to know that paradigm was bullshit. If that's really how he felt, he'd be giving up "someone to share real intimacy with him . . . sex and playfulness," in exchange for "just a fantasy person," I wrote. However, this knowledge did not make me feel any better. I felt exposed. Chastened. Out of control. Like I'd been "too much."

And so I doubled down on Team Chill. All through college, I got into situationships with men who were at a remove, publicly toeing that "agency line," and privately chasing that same "honest moment" so the encounters wouldn't feel empty and pointless. In these relationships, I asked for very little. I tried to be a fun, engaging hang. No matter how inconsiderate they were, I never let on that I was offended. I was often a dude's "special friend" whom he'd confess things to in late-night DMs, have high-energy sex with whenever the stars aligned, and often move on from without much fanfare. Some of these guys caught feelings for me and I pretended not to notice, suddenly turned off by their availability. Other times I was the one getting attached, but I seldom came out and admitted a crush.

I wrote pining diary entries about the latter scenario. I got in the habit of putting those tender feelings into letters I'd never send.

"When the games stop and you can see the hurt/restrained look on my face sometimes, I feel like you know," I wrote to a guy I hooked up with maybe a dozen times over two years of college. "It just hurts me so much that I'm nobody you could EVER see yourself with." Of course, I wasn't sure about that, but I talked myself out of being up-front, which I was convinced "would scare [him] off from even being friends with me." A couple of years later, I wrote to another guy with whom I had unbeatable sexual chemistry, and who had cheated on multiple girlfriends with me: "I'm a romantic but nobody knows it."

Perceptive friends, of course, knew it—or at least could tell that my feelings were more nuanced than my schtick as a woman who boldly and fearlessly fucks while rejecting cheesy romance. Like most schticks, it wasn't a total lie, just a flattened truth. Laina Bay-Cheng makes a distinction between sexual agency that's "authentic" and "pantomimed," and mine was a mix of both. I *did* get joy out of sex, and I *was* turned off by the whole heterosexual dance of women demanding commitment, men acquiescing. I just also was searching for something else, something more that I couldn't name. And I couldn't yet admit that some of these hookups were a result of what writer Angela Chen calls "a funny reversal of the importance of sexual purity"—the pursuit of sex solely to show that I was rejecting traditional expectations, thereby proving the resilience of those expectations' influence.

Still, despite all this, I didn't feel permanently damaged by these experiences, even the painful parts. I considered them part of growing up and determining one's emotional bottom lines. Perhaps this is why I was miffed and bored by 2005's *Female Chauvinist Pigs*, as well as the critiques of college hookup culture that started popping up perennially in the mid-aughts. "I'm 22, went through it all, and came out fine," I sniffed in *The New York Observer* in 2007. Every couple of years, there'd be a wave of hand-wringing articles that worried whether casual sex was bad for young women. Some came from conservatives like Laura Sessions Stepp, Dawn Eden, and Wendy Shalit, all of whom were nostalgic for a time when men took women out on dates and brought them flowers. Other critiques came from sympathetic feminists, often ones who got to observe teen girls' agony up close, like Rachel Simmons and Peggy Orenstein. "It's become antifeminist to want a guy to buy you dinner and hold the door for you," Simmons wrote on her website in 2010. "Yet—picture me ducking behind bullet proof glass as I type this—wasn't there something about that framework that made more space for a young woman's feelings and needs?"

I felt grateful that I wasn't one of the women who'd grown up with abstinence-only education and slut-shaming. By that time, I'd openly acknowledged the twinge a lot of us felt when we suppressed swelling feelings or pored over text messages to try to get inside some guy's head: "Feminist or not, that shit sucks," I wrote in a 2010 blog post responding to Simmons. But like the pro-sex feminists of the eighties, I found the endless concern on all sides to be fundamentally conservative, caving to the demands of the "good cop" that felt the need to guard women's sexual honor so as to fend off men's uncontrollable aggression or heartlessness. "Girls deserve to discover themselves sexually at their own pace, to be neither rushed into having sex nor shamed into not having it," I wrote.

I was with Aaron by the time I wrote that post, still riding the high of our commitment, so it had an air of wistfulness, as if the "hookup culture" was some sort of compulsory obstacle course and the finish line was the type of long-term partnership I'd achieved. I was getting further and further away from casual dating and the insecurity that came with it. In retrospect, my ambivalence about casual sex was yet another deterrent to breaking up with Aaron— not just the societal stigma of being single, but the sexual dynamics that straight single women have to navigate too. I didn't want to go back to the days of pretending it was fine if a guy failed to firm up plans until the very last minute, or treated me like a stranger outside his sweaty sheets.

What I didn't realize, though, is that I was still clinging to the philosophy of Team Chill. The hookups I did have within my non-monogamous relationship felt safe. For me, having a primary partner was a shield against the sting of rejection, and for my sex partners, it was built-in assurance that I wouldn't try to tie them down. Though this method wouldn't work in the mainstream dating scene, it was in line with my longtime schtick, just in more countercultural clothing.

In the mid-2010s, two things happened that cut to the bone of this dilemma and seemed to illuminate a way out. One was the publication of Alana Massey's now classic Medium essay, "Against Chill," a magical manifesto that neither negated my belief in sexual freedom nor waved away my desire to have meaningful connections. Massey described Chill, a byproduct of the nineties superslut, as the posture of emotional vacancy that had "forced those among us who would like to exchange feelings and accountability to compete in the Blasé Olympics with whomever we are dating." Chill, she wrote, did not deserve its reputation for being a *good* thing:

> But Chill is not the opposite of uptight. It is the opposite of demanding accountability. Chill is a sinister refashioning of "Calm down!" from an enraging and highly gendered command into an admirable attitude. Chill suggests that young

love is best expressed as competitive ambivalence. Chill demands that you see a Read receipt followed by a "Hey, was asleep" text three hours later and not proceed to throw your phone into the nearest volcano. Chill asks you to be like, "LOL, what volcano?" Chill presides over the funeral of reasonable expectations. Chill takes and never gives. Chill is pathologically unfeeling but not even interesting enough to kill anyone. Chill is a garbage virtue that will destroy the species. Fuck Chill.

"Fuck Chill." It was a revelation. A drumbeat. A way to set some standards without leaning on the splintered crutch of traditional relationships. Though I couldn't yet dispense with Chill in my extracurricular hookups, I sensed that figuring out a way to do so was the only viable path. I sent a link to the essay to every one of my friends.

The other thing that happened was a national conversation about consent and sexual assault on campus, one that felt different from the sex wars of the eighties. The principle behind much of this activism, a clear precursor to #MeToo, was "yes means yes," a concept popularized by a 2008 anthology edited by Jaclyn Friedman and Jessica Valenti called *Yes Means Yes: Visions of Female Sexual Power and a World without Rape*. In 2014, the California legislature passed SB 967—the "yes means yes" law—which required all colleges and universities that receive state funding to adopt the standard of "affirmative, conscious, and voluntary agreement to engage in sexual activity" in their sexual assault policies. The context was preventing sexual assault, but to me the message was far-reaching: Consent was just the bare-minimum requirement for pleasurable sex. Going beyond that required communication and a true consideration of one's desires.

Facetious critiques of the theory and its resulting law expressed concern that enthusiastic consent would make sex artificial and sterile, requiring awkward checklists. Others gave the false impression that fishing for one "yes" and moving on was good enough, rather than interpreting consent as a fluid, ongoing process. Friedman would later clarify that enthusiastic consent is a more active process than just following rules or waiting for a green light; it's "a humanizing ethic of sex." Truly internalizing the values of consent, she wrote, must include "emotional literacy"—the ability to be vulnerable, and to be trusted with others' vulnerability.

At a "yes means yes" workshop I reported on at Colgate around this time, I witnessed this "humanizing ethic" in action. Students of all types were calmly discussing what sex acts they'd like to try: a threesome, a bathroom quickie, sex on the kitchen counter. And what they found most attractive in a person of their same gender, regardless of their own sexual orientation: tans, collarbones, confidence, big butts. They talked about their fears and insecurities too—about their bodies, about their sex skills, about not knowing what to say the morning after a hookup. "If you both care about each other's pleasure, that means you have to like each other a certain amount," the facilitator remarked at one point.

As students detailed their preferences and fantasies, the room was thick with sexual tension—and a gentle openness I'd *never* witnessed in my college days. There was a reverence not only for knowing one's desires, but also for mutual exploration, for tuning in and checking in during sex sessions, which inevitably shift shape as they go on. For those few minutes we were in the classroom, there were no prescriptions, no bravado, no bragging, no fixed sexual identities, no performed agency, no games of any kind. No Chill.

• • •

I thought a lot about those twin revelations, in the weeks after my marriage was over, when I was having lots of pleasant but ultimately shallow encounters. When "the Israeli guy," otherwise known as Mor, resurfaced and asked if I wanted to hang again, I told myself to commit more to Team Intense, if only for pure pleasure's sake.

That resolution kicked off long chains of texts, impulsive last-minute meet-ups, and eventually an all-consuming, sex-forward obsession. By our third encounter, I was outrageously attracted to him. I started appreciating his body's balance of masculine and feminine, equally comfortable being the big spoon and the small. It was the first time I'd really lavished attention on a man's beauty, noticing and worshipping every centimeter of his pouty lips framed by a thicket of beard, his delicate-yet-muscular body, his caramel skin, his long lashes, his curling happy trail. I marveled at how glowing and healthy he looked despite all the obvious demons roiling inside, like a petite fountain of life whose apparent anxiety did not interfere with his ability to succumb to the present, to either dominate or be dominated. He could fuck my mouth with authority and then moan with abandon when I fingered his ass and then suck my clit for a hundred years and then burrow his face in my breasts sweetly, lazily.

Without the emotional hygiene that came with having a primary relationship, my sip of vulnerability quickly became a chug. We spent night after night caught in an endless intimacy loop between his sheets, fucking, then talking about fucking, expressing our feelings, then talking about feelings. I constantly relayed to him fresh insights about my breakup with Aaron, the attention to detail of which he appreciated and encouraged. He'd been through years of therapy, so he never tired of talking about the inner child and the mind-body connection. And he, too, bemoaned the formulaic hookups he had on the apps, assuring me I was the one person who was sympathetic to his insecurities about not having finished college yet, to his debilitating mood disorder, to his generally jittery demeanor. Unlike all the young and frivolous women he matched with night after night, he told me, I treated him like a real person.

Isn't this better than eggshells? he texted after we'd mutually acknowledged that whoa, this was *intense*. I responded by sending him a link to "Against Chill." He kvelled: Every dumb hipster in Bushwick needs to read this and become a little more human.

And yet, at the same time, Mor was proving himself to be an unworthy recipient of my newfound openness. I started catching him in lies big and small. He wasn't actually at that bar the other night, he didn't actually use a condom with that twenty-two-year-old he slept with, his phone didn't actually die for seventeen hours. Eventually he'd confess these indiscretions—in the name of vulnerability, of course. He'd express a frightened innocence that, next to his deception, felt like a privilege to witness. "I'm not used to being this honest," he'd plead. "It takes some time to get used to. It's scary."

We weren't exclusive but we weren't quite nonmonogamous, either. He preferred to live in melodramatic purgatory, where somehow he was allowed to act possessive while still eschewing commitment. I got the feeling I wasn't the only one tangled up in this kind of web with him. Once, I sat next to Mor in bed while he scrolled back through his texts to give a timestamp to a funny anecdote he was telling. A few furtive glances revealed a teeming sea of random numbers never stored, snippets of eerily intimate language. It took no time at all for my mind to fill with speculative

scenarios of Mor toggling between these once and future sex partners while jerking off or whimpering or blowing off his to-do list
to go lose himself in sex. I wondered how many years he'd been
living this way.

A couple of days before Halloween, we broke it off abruptly,
blaming our mutual off-the-rails intensity. But a week later, on
Election Night 2016, after I pressed publish at 3:13 a.m. on a piece
I'd written with the headline NEVER UNDERESTIMATE HOW MUCH
AMERICA HATES WOMEN, I took a very expensive Lyft to his squalid
apartment. The sex was quick but ardent, caveperson-like, full of
grunts and intuitive grabs. As we cuddled afterward, silent and
stroking each other's skin, we both heard his downstairs neighbor—
an older, politically active lesbian—sobbing loudly. It was an excruciating female wail of despair that intruded on our private,
transhistorical moment.

Our bond now felt impermanent, flimsy. Mor became hot and
cold, hard to figure out. We were still "broken up," yet keeping a
constant link. Our hours-long phone calls would still result in sex,
but only half the time. My phone's photo library was littered with
screenshots of ambiguous texts, dispatched to friends so they could
offer their insight. The thing I dreaded most was still the thing I
dreaded back in high school and college: pushing him too far, being "too much." I was terrified of the switch that sometimes happens in fast-moving relationships, when the person with whom
you were once entangled in a bubble world of inside jokes and
cuddle-fucking now feels pity for your unkempt feelings and tact-
lessly severs the connection forever.

Two weeks before the year was over, the switch happened. In
a final bout of whiplash, Mor insisted we become exclusive, then
acted squirrelly for ten days, then ended it with me so he could be

with a former flame, a woman who sounded more Team Intense than I could ever hope to be. The day he broke it off was interminable, filled with crying, bargaining, and, of course, one last fuck, during which I slapped him across the face while he repeated, "I'm sorry, I'm sorry."

After that came the searing chokes of pain in my throat and the sink in my stomach. The pain was there day after day, blurring my eyes while I tried to work, keeping me awake hours after I'd retired to bed. Eventually, heartsickness turned into actual sickness, in the form of a fevered sinus infection. I took several days off work and camped out crying on my blue couch. I binge-listened to John Mayer, a favorite of Mor's, which should have been the only red flag I needed. "We're slow dancing in a buuuurning roooom," I sang through my stuffy nose. The Tuesday night before Christmas, aided by a bottle of wine to the face, I wrote what could only be described as song lyrics of my own. Strings of accusations like "You made me crazy / got me naked / made me cry / then said never mind." I was angry because my risk taking hadn't been rewarded like I'd hoped. I wasn't "too much," but I was also not, ultimately, what Mor desired.

And then, simultaneously, I finally crashed from the initial high of separating from Aaron. This kind of pain was less acute than the Mor wreckage, which felt so unfair, so nonsensical, so out of my control! Self-administered heartbreak was more wistful, achy. For the first time since I'd moved out, I craved the domesticity I left behind. I was back in our apartment by then, a privilege I'd fought Aaron for but was now regretting. Artifacts taunted me everywhere: the earring rack he made me out of wood and red lace, a stool we bought in a Chicago junk shop, absinthe from the Sazeracs we loved to make.

Going to holiday parties solo that winter, fielding questions from acquaintances about Aaron's whereabouts, I felt the long-feared loss of societal approval. But it was more than that. I wanted to be wrapped in a blanket of our stability, his kindness and honesty. I yearned to collapse in his arms after a stressful day at work or navigating bureaucratic nightmares with my dad. When it came to vulnerably expressing the need for security, he had made it easy. Now I felt alone in the world.

It got so bad that on Christmas Day, when I would normally be stuffing my face with artichoke dip and cheesy potatoes at his parents' cozy midwestern house, I texted him: Not gonna lie, spending the holidays without you has been painful. It'll always be really special to me that you all treated me like true family 🖤

That's because you were, Aaron replied.

I considered asking him to take me back on the spot, and later hinted as much during a couple of drink dates I had with him at the height of the January frost. Aaron took me at my word and pressed for a final answer. *Let's go to therapy*, he said. *Let's see if there's something worth saving.*

I told him there wasn't. I was hurting, destroyed by two break-ups at once, but I also sensed I'd gotten closer to what I truly wanted by choosing to get off the conveyer belt. This instinct mirrored my mother's as she waffled in her letters to Bob. In them, she frequently questioned her own sanity, but she ultimately stuck to her guns, despite the chaos she'd caused.

I went back and read my journal from October, at the height of my affair with Mor. There were nights of missing Aaron then too, parts of me that wanted to "go back and try, to stop this upheaval and put everything back the way it was." But then I pulled myself back and reasoned that "even if Aaron somehow repaired all that was missing, even if he became the best lover ever overnight, that I would still want to be single and free and experience something else. Someone else." I'd surely achieved that, albeit at significant personal cost. I just couldn't decide if it had been worth it. It turned out that when someone gave me everything I ever wanted sexually—endless orgasms, gallons of oxytocin, an intuitive understanding of the contours of my naked body—I would trade anything for those feelings, so willingly that I ignored the hemorrhage from the center of my bloody emotional core. I felt drained and alive at the same time.

• • •

In the wake of my post-Mor wound licking, I arrived at a bleak conclusion: sex with no emotion was a pyrrhic victory, and so was lighting a match to my boundaries. The herculean amount of emotional calibration needed in order to have satisfying sex deflated and overwhelmed me. What the hell was I supposed to do?

Then, months later, something awful and edifying took place. It reminded me that sometimes, vulnerability is not up to you in the slightest.

There was one day when I felt an urge to fuck a younger guy. Looking back on it now, the appeal must have been the power imbalance itself. After being blindsided by the winter's emotional upheaval, I wanted the chance to experience the unassailable safety that sleazy older guys must feel when they pursue much younger women. I was acting out of not only sexual desire, but also the desire for complete control. I set the age range on my apps to twenty-three and under. I was startled by how many young guys were absolutely fine playing the role of naïf.

James was a college student who was just shy of twenty. He was sweet, eager, and even a little bit smart. Didn't send any unsolicited dick pics. Told me he'd never fucked anyone older than him. Showed up at the café wearing a short-sleeved button-down with clusters of yellow tulips on it, and two pierced ears. He appeared nervous. I liked that.

After an hour of surprisingly engaging conversation, I asked in my best direct-candid-jaded voice: *Did he want to go to my house and have a whiskey and listen to vinyl?* He did. I made him a drink and let him select a record; he chose Fiona Apple. He undoubtedly knew these were my Sexy Older Woman Moves, but he didn't care. He seemed excited to fuck a curvy, confident woman who had more than a decade on him. After our drink, we boned twice in quick succession. His kisses were awkward, his chest was shaved, his maneuverings needed work, his dirty talk was . . . strange, but it was exactly what I was looking for. Not only did he do whatever I told him to, he also clearly was going to remember this forever. During our pillow talk, he told me it was even better than he had imagined.

I was pretty much done with him after the second time, but when he initiated a third round, I privately conceded that this would make the story better. I decided on a blow job. I was giving it my all. When I stopped for a second to look up, I realized he was filming me.

I was too stunned to yell and scream. I just gave him my best Very Disappointed in You look, made him erase the video in front of me, and kicked him out. As I lay in bed for hours after he was gone, the glass of whiskey souring my empty stomach, I felt embarrassed and kink-shamed by the universe. I was angry that my self-assured, all-knowing vibe hadn't protected me, even from a person who, in some ways, really was more vulnerable than me.

If you're a human fucking anybody, but especially if you're a woman fucking a man, invulnerability is an illusion. Yes, I was older and wiser, but even though he was bashful and indie and unassuming, even though I deftly engineered our power imbalance with my nineties records and mood lighting and adult Brooklyn apartment, no matter how much he wanted me and how little I gave a shit about him, he could still shatter my superslut power into a million pieces just by lifting an iPhone to my face when I was blowing him, and pressing record.

If I was only willing to engage in sex I enthusiastically want, the theory goes, it would become that much easier for my gut to identify a crossed boundary. But until a "humanizing ethic of sex" was pervasive, my desires wouldn't always be in safe hands, and expressing them wouldn't always protect me from violation or deception. In order to discover my desires in the first place, I must prepare for the unknown, which may very well end in pain or disappointment. When two people decide to have sex, even under the best and most controlled of circumstances, surprise vulnerabilities may lie in wait—for either partner.

Ultimately, the incident was liberating. I decided it wouldn't be worth it to chasten myself because of this, to retreat into the anti-porn feminists' protectionism, to shield myself from potential danger at the expense of my desires. I came to feel the same way about Mor: Even though he did not catch me at the bottom, that didn't mean I should have stayed on the edge of the cliff. To avoid a complete free fall, there would always be a need for *some* sort of parachute, and yet I would continue to jump. Because although the power of Team Intense may end up gutting me, life with Team Chill had also been a gamble, and with far less payoff. If I waited until I felt in utter control to have the kind of transcendent sex or love that could happen only by taking risks, I'd be waiting around forever.

5. The Vulnerability Gradient

Pleasure warred with common sense, even with
self-preservation.

—SAIDIYA HARTMAN, *WAYWARD LIVES, BEAUTIFUL
EXPERIMENTS*

Somewhere between Dane's futon and my own blue couch, I took
my bags full of clothes and stayed with my friend Selah for a few
weeks. She had a giant rent-stabilized apartment uptown, the second bedroom of which she frequently offered to friends at tough
spots in their lives. Selah gave me the opposite kind of support that
Dane did: instead of egging on my emotional intensity, she offered
a bit of calm in the storm. We'd meet for a dozen Wellfleets at the
Grand Central Oyster Bar before taking the 4 train uptown together. We watched Netflix on the couch, her sweet tabby cat
nudging our knees with her nose. We cooked, smoked cigarettes
on her roof, and went to bed early.

The past year had been transformative and tumultuous for her
too. She knew a little something about stepping off the heterosexual conveyer belt. In fact, she'd pretty much snapped it in two:
she'd fallen in love, come out as queer, and gotten her heart broken

all in the span of a few months. We all nursed her through the summer, in the form of tearful phone calls and cozy nights in. Though a manic post-breakup sex spree was not her style, Selah's heart was splayed open during that time, a state I now recognized in myself. It was the same kind of raw, exhilarating pain I felt. She was hurting in the short term, yet was clearly reaching toward happiness in the long term.

But in many ways, our routes to sexual and romantic self-discovery diverged considerably. When you trace the progress of the feminist sexual revolution, the people who have most easily and readily participated (and written about their participation) have been white, hetero, privileged women like me—and it didn't hurt that I had a mother who encouraged it all. Selah was a Black queer woman. She grew up in a family where respectability was of the utmost importance. Because of those things, she would always have a very different relationship to vulnerability.

Around the time I was staying with Selah, I began to think of sexual vulnerability as a gradient, from most to fewest shades of gray. Cis, straight, white men are on the lightest end, best equipped to be sexually invulnerable because they're trained for it. They're taught from the very beginning of their lives to avoid vulnerability, even at the cost of their own happiness and satisfaction, because there are social consequences when they don't. No matter who they fuck, it could never be considered rebellion or revolution. When they are raped or sexually abused, it's most likely at the hands of another man. Their pursuit of sexual pleasure isn't just unremarkable; it's still the original blueprint after all these years.

And yet, some of my male partners had other identities that did make them sexually vulnerable. After the sting of anger wore off, I thought about James, whose violation didn't erase the fact that he was more than a decade younger than me, his brain's impulse control not even fully developed. I thought about Mor: Yes, he had perfected the male skill of emotional vampirism. But also, his brown skin and Sephardic features had once subjected him to the racism of a white girlfriend's War on Terror–loving father. I thought about the Black men I've dated, who knew very well that one misunderstanding with a white woman could result in a fatal call to the cops. There was Simon, a pansexual guy I dated whose effeminate manner and pink sequined shirt were not unusual on the streets of Bushwick, Brooklyn, but were dangerous liabilities in his rural hometown. There was Diego, a Chilean guy I had a few hookups with when I studied abroad in Santiago. He displayed over-the-top machismo, once drunkenly criticizing how I wasn't enthused enough about going down on him while not acknowledging that he'd never once even seen my pussy. Still, as a much richer white American woman, I had a power I couldn't yet fathom at the age of twenty.

Then there are women of color, who have other interlocking vulnerabilities on the way to finding their authentic sexual selves, who have to face more danger, more stereotypes, and often more rejection than white women. Throughout history, they've faced a heightened threat of shame, sexual violence, arrest, imprisonment, sterilization, denial of abortion, and poverty. The three paradigms of Jezebel, sexless mammy, and Sapphire have been dehumanizing Black women since slavery. The origins of the "spicy," oversexed Latina stretch back to the Mexican-American War, when popular books and films portrayed Mexican women as both an object of desire and a sinister foil to "wholesome" American girls. The cliché of the meek-but-horny East Asian woman arose out of the US military's ubiquitous, dominating presence in Asian countries. Western men have fetishized the Muslim woman as an *odalisque* or a veiled belly dancer—erotic yet unattainable—for centuries. They're all subject to what critic and novelist Fariha Roisin calls "the brown girl's paradox": even as Black and brown women are sexualized and fetishized, they're seldom held up as examples of prevailing beauty standards.

And if you're queer or trans or disabled or fat or old or any combination of any of these, sexual freedom requires untangling even more still. Because the more layers of marginalization one faces, the scarier and riskier sexual vulnerability becomes.

• • •

Selah's grandmother, Irene, was born smack in the middle of the Great Depression. She and her five younger siblings grew up in a shotgun house in the Northern Liberties, a working-class neighborhood in Philadelphia with a sizable number of Black folks who'd migrated north to escape segregation, violence, and a sinkhole of economic dead ends. Irene's family had come up from the South and were strict church people. The most vivid childhood memories she has are spending every waking hour of Sunday at a storefront church run by her grandmother. They'd spend the morning praying and singing, eat church-lady-made fried chicken at around three p.m., then resume worship till the sun went down.

Irene retained her spirituality, but her true religion was education. After high school, she married at nineteen and had her two girls, Mona and Renee. But she wanted more. She went back for her bachelor's degree, then for her master's in teaching. When both of her girls met men they wanted to marry while they were still in college, Irene told them, "That's nice. I'm happy for you. But you are going to finish your degree."

Mona, a gorgeous serial monogamist with a small seventies 'fro, got engaged to a charismatic man-about-town who was studying to be a pastor. In the eyes of many people around her, this guy was the ultimate catch, a major rung on the ladder to the upper echelons of Black society. Their wedding was a tightly scripted affair with hundreds of guests at a historic Philly church. Mona wasn't allowed to pick her bridesmaids. It was her first clue that perhaps the role of being a pastor's wife was not for her.

The marriage was traditional, claustrophobic, and over after a few years. In the aftermath, the heretofore ultrastable Mona rebelled. She held on to her teaching job, but she also played the keyboard in a reggae band and hung out with Black nationalists. In the early eighties, she started dating Russell, a man twenty years her senior. By all accounts he was a hustler—an affable but capricious traveling vendor and autodidact whose money source was inscrutable. Irene wasn't exactly thrilled about Russell, but when Mona announced her pregnancy, she was all in.

When she grasped the reality of her impending motherhood, Mona's middle-class upbringing snapped back like a rubber band. From then on, she decided there would be no more risks, no more shenanigans. Mona and her mother cut off ties with Russell—she couldn't rely on someone who was patently unreliable. *It's now all about this child*, she thought. *I have to protect her, give her the absolute best of the best.* Her daughter, whom she named Selah, arrived in September 1983.

Mona never tried to fool Selah with mythical stories about storks. By the time the girl was six, Mona had taught her the proper names for her body parts and where babies really came from. But like many other Black mothers Selah knew growing up, Mona never, ever talked about pleasure. Instead, Mona was laser focused on consequences: If you have sex, you *will* get pregnant. If you have sex, you *will* get AIDS. Purity and chastity were paramount. Selah's stepfather, whom Mona met when Selah was still very young, had older children, including two daughters who had kids as teenagers. Mona made it clear to Selah that she was *not* to get herself pregnant. She was *not* going to go down the wrong path. She was going to grow up, educate herself, and get married. Period.

• • •

From its origins, slavery was a system inextricable from sexual violence, or as sociologist Joane Nagel puts it, a racial conflict "planted early in American history in sexual soil." White fear of Black men's sexuality justified lynching and castration, while the myth of Black women's heightened sex drive was a justification for rape by enslavers. Unlike the virtuous white woman, enslavers painted Black women as sexually available yet impervious to physical or emotional threat. They were placed in direct opposition to the Southern belle, who was "hoisted on a pedestal so high that she was beyond the sensual reach of her own husband," writes historian Paula Giddings. Enslaved women were "consigned to the other end of the scale, as mistresses, whores, or breeders." These stereotypes endured far past slavery's expiration date and thrived even among progressive social reformers like Jane Addams, who argued in 1911 that due to what she called the "lack of inherited control" in Black social culture, "Black women yield more easily to the temptations of a city than any other girls."

In other words, Black women could never hope to reach sexual purity no matter what they did. But that didn't preclude them from feeling shame anyway. In Harriet Jacobs's 1861 slave narrative, for instance, she blames herself for having sex and bearing children outside of wedlock. "I know I did wrong," she writes. "No one can feel it more sensibly than I do." She begs the "virtuous reader" not to judge her too harshly. "There is a definite note here of unnecessary agony," writes Michele Wallace in 1978's *Black Macho and the Myth of the Superwoman*, "the agony of measuring herself against a standard which was not designed to fit her circumstances, and which could only work to destroy her image of herself." The archetype of the callous, invulnerable Black woman—propagated by enslavers, internalized by enslaved people and their descendants, perpetuated by white people—had endured for centuries by the time Wallace's book became one of the first texts to criticize it head-on.

Given these minefields, it's understandable why Irene told her daughters, "Good little girls don't talk about that kind of thing," and why Mona told *her* daughter that she'd better protect herself. The policing of Black women's sexuality by both white and Black people has been a part of respectability politics ever since abolition; after the Great Migration, middle-class authority figures like W.E.B. Du Bois feared that armies of Black prostitutes were overtaking the race, excusing the "utter disregard of a black woman's virtue and self-respect, both in law court and custom."

Later, many Black women encouraged one another to suppress or deny sexuality, especially casual sex, in order to sidestep racial stereotypes. Nell Painter, who grew up middle-class in Oakland and attended UC Berkeley, remembers fiercely guarding her reputation. "I was brought up with a race and class identity that was sexed," she told historian David Allyn in 1997. "You weren't sexually loose. I knew about the sexual stereotypes of black women. I disdained black women who got pregnant." In Mya Baker's documentary *Silence: In Search of Black Female Sexuality in America*, several interviewees recounted not hearing much about sex growing up, except to "keep their panties up, dresses down, and legs closed." Despite the stereotypes of loose morality, many studies have found that Black women are less likely to hook up on college campuses and less likely to have oral sex than their white counterparts. Black girls often have less access to sex education, despite being perceived by adults as *more* knowledgeable about sex than white girls.

Because of this dynamic, most Black women didn't feel safe being part of feminist discussions about sexual liberation (if white women even asked, which they often didn't). Many scholars emphasized their historical exposure to sexual abuse and danger, but rare were mentions of pleasure. For years, Audre Lorde's 1978 essay "Uses of the Erotic" stood virtually alone in a sea of scholarship that either detailed Black women's trauma and sexual violence or avoided the topic of sex entirely. Even if white women had been more welcoming, it would have been impossible to have an interracial discussion about sex without confronting the long, painful history of white and Black women pitted against each other as sexual competition, including over Black men. Precious few were willing to do that.

Of course, there had always been visible pleasure narratives from Black women in pop culture and literature, from blues singer Lucille Bogan urging her lover to "grind me until I cry" to Shug teaching Celie about the "little button that gits real hot" in Alice Walker's *The Color Purple*. And there were those essential interventions during the eighties feminist sex wars, when queer women of color like Lorde, Cherríe Moraga, Barbara Smith, and Gloria Anzaldúa pointed out how their sexuality intersected with other kinds of oppression. But when it came to the politics of pleasure, the voices of women of color were few and far between. Black women certainly participated in the superslut nineties, but those who publicly talked about pursuing pleasure had very little space to express pain or doubt. Not to mention that they were pitted against Strong Black Women who were expected to disapprove. These two personas had something in common: They were un-fuck-with-able. Not allowed to be vulnerable in the slightest.

Writer Joan Morgan vividly remembers this impossible choice. She calls herself a Strong Black Woman "in recovery" in her 1999 book, *When Chickenheads Come Home to Roost: A Hip Hop Feminist Breaks It Down*. She admits to being envious of Black women who unapologetically traded on their erotic power, because they were the ones ending up with Black men. Independent feminists like her and "chickenheads" like Lil' Kim both "want the same thing— someone to love us, shower us with attention," Morgan writes. "In our loneliest and most vulnerable moments, we look at you and wonder . . . Is being alone the price we will ultimately pay for do-ing it the 'right way'?" The Strong Black Woman was a stubborn albatross; when it came to love and sex, "Fear will make ya front like Superwoman every time," she wrote. "Pretending to be totally self-sufficient is a helluva lot easier than handing your vulnerability over to a man who might drop the ball."

Since then, there's been Beyoncé and Nicki Minaj and Rihanna and Megan Thee Stallion and many other Black and brown female sex symbols. Though none have totally escaped the expectations of the past, there's more room than ever for moments of softness and self-doubt. Cardi can brag about her wet-ass pussy while still ad-mitting that her "heart is like a package with a fragile label on it." Audre Lorde now has welcome company: Black writers and activists like adrienne maree brown, Sonya Renee Taylor, and Ericka Hart prioritize harnessing the power of erotic desire and self-love.

But this reach toward sexual authenticity didn't come out of nowhere. Impervious sexual confidence and chaste respectability have never been the only two choices. Constant repression and censure—from both inside and out—often result in an explosive imperative to be oneself, no matter the consequences. Living at the peak of the vulnerability gradient means you are risking the most, but you also have the most to gain.

• • •

Selah had always been surrounded by beautiful Black women, and she always felt comfortable in her thick body. Still, it was confusing to be out in the world. She felt simultaneously invisible and hypersexualized. The white boys ignored her at her Quaker high school (and frankly, she ignored them), but on the streets of Philadelphia, older men were always making graphic comments about her body, which developed early. Even though she wasn't allowed to go to parties or have sleepovers like her white classmates were, she was curious about sex. So she found ways to test the waters. She felt safest with the church friends she'd known since she was young; a group of them all started to kiss and rub on each other whenever they could. One thrilling night, one of the boys fingered her under the table at a church function.

Counting the days until she could bust free from her mom's house, Selah continued to push the boundaries all through high school, unwittingly mirroring her dad Russell's sense of adventure. At times, Selah found herself in sticky situations. Some, in retrospect, were predatory—the first man she had sex with was an older authority figure—but some ended badly for other reasons. During the summer between tenth and eleventh grade, while she was working as an assistant at a summer camp program, she gave a blow job to a guy in the locker room. The sensation was electrifying. It felt so powerful to be in total control of someone else's orgasm. Her rush didn't last long, though: she got caught, the boy blamed it all on her, and she lost her job. Having to explain to her mother that she got fired for sucking dick was one of the scariest moments of her teenhood. Mona was so filled with a rageful worry that she popped her daughter right in the mouth.

A few years later, when Selah arrived at a mostly white liberal arts school in the Midwest, she was thrown for a loop. Seemingly everyone was some combination of queer, nudist, or polyamorous. Something about that don't-give-a-fuck attitude intrigued her—she even went on a couple of dates and fooled around with a girl—but, as in high school, Selah and these fancy-free white people just weren't attracted to each other. And anyway, what she desired most was the thing she hadn't gotten back then: a nice, normal boyfriend.

Finally, when Selah came back to Philly in the summer of freshman year, it happened. She met kind, sensitive Will while she was folding clothes at Express and he was selling sneakers at the Foot Locker across the street. He appreciated how bookish she was. They made each other laugh. They had A-plus sex. They stayed together through the next summer—until he broke up with her because he liked someone else. "I love you and I'm really sorry," he said gently, but the heave of first heartbreak clobbered her self-esteem. *What now?* Selah asked herself. *I just go back to this college in the middle of the country, where no one sees me?*

Sitting on the El in a morass of self-pity, Selah met the person she never, ever names—even to me, even during the many hours I interviewed her for this chapter. This guy was a middle-class nightmare, and therefore an ideal vehicle for defying her mother: a jobless drifter who was living in a squat house, a father of several children he didn't take care of, a bad boy with a staggering sex appeal. The beginning was a whirlwind, an avalanche of *I love yous*. Their first fuck felt literally magical; by the end, they were both speaking in tongues, and Selah swears they levitated off the bed. He would go down on her for hours, wringing her out like a rag. The sex was so good that it unnerved her. She remembers thinking, *This can't be real. There's something nefarious about this person.*

She turned out to be right. Instead of going abroad to Brazil as planned, Selah enrolled in an independent study program in Philly for a semester. It was during that time that this man started flying off the handle about small things. He'd push her a little too roughly, then apologize profusely. He'd brutalize her with hands and words, then crawl in her lap to cry. He'd put a gun to her head during a fight, then they'd have trauma-fueled makeup sex. She'd threaten to leave, and he'd threaten to kill her and her family. Selah was in way over her head, overwhelmed with shame and disbelief that she—she!—would let this happen. She couldn't square it: *How could someone who'd given her such unbelievable pleasure be hurting her so much?*

When he flushed her birth control pills and slammed her hand in a car door, she knew she had to cut it off for good. She succeeded, but then spent two full years in a post-traumatic, dissociative state. She was scared of her own shadow, rattled by sounds, noises, people, shapes, colors. At first, she lived in an echo chamber, not talking to anyone about her abuse, just wanting to move on. She had bouts of rage, then would stuff it down again. She wasn't feeling sexy. She couldn't even think about being around new men.

Finally, a friend urged her to get help. She went to counseling and acupuncture. She cut off her dreadlocks and got braids instead. By the fall of 2009, she felt ready to resume her life. She encouraged herself to get into the mix. She briefly felt herself veering back into darkness, having risky sex with strangers, just so she could feel a connection, feel *something*. One guy took off the condom without asking. Another guy started having sex with her while she was sleeping. Her natural instinct to be open was leaving her too susceptible to pain.

So, again, she flung back to the other extreme. She scrutinized every potential partner: *Are you a harmful person? Are you going to hurt me emotionally?* She frequently concluded that the person was not worth the risk. The negotiation of danger versus numbness, discernment versus hypervigilance—it was an exhausting balancing act. She felt like she was punishing herself. She didn't feel any better than before.

At one point, she had a fling with a transmasculine person, which she mentioned to her mother. "You know I'm kinda gay, right, Mom?" she said. "No, you're not," Mona replied. It was a mindfuck. Selah knew she at least had some bi leanings, but by that time, a lot of women around her were knee-deep in the progression of dating a guy, getting engaged, having a wedding, getting pregnant. Many of Selah's good friends, even ambivalently partnered women like me, made her feel like a failure. *Why is this so hard for me?* she wondered. *What's wrong with me?!?* She recommitted to finding an upstanding, gainfully employed man who would make her family proud. She didn't want to let anyone down.

Yet she knew in the back of her mind that searching for a perfect Black man with a master's degree was not going to solve all her problems. She knew the conveyer belt wasn't quite right for her, that she wanted something more, something different. Something that rewarded her capacity for reciprocated, delicious, full-throated love and vulnerability. To be sure, her sweet, hopeful pursuit of pleasure had been met with deception or abuse too many times. But that didn't mean the desire was wrong.

• • •

A couple of miles south and more than one hundred years before Selah was a teen in Philly, nineteen-year-old Mamie Sharp and her husband, James Shephard, lived together in a room in a cramped tenement on Saint Mary Street, the heart of Philly's worst Black slum. James worked outside the city. Mamie was lonely but made the most of her time when he was gone: window-shopped, drank beer at the saloons, went to the theater. One day, her landlady, Helen Parrish, knocked on her door and accused her of going around town with other men. "Yes, I like to go about as I please," she said. She didn't flinch, apologize, or explain. And yes, she and James weren't technically married, either; she'd fled an abusive marriage two years earlier. "Maybe I have been bad," she said. "But you can't understand what I need."

The landlady lectured the couple about morality and insisted that James leave right away. He protested to Helen, who fancied herself Mamie's rescuer: "Have you ever been married? Then you do not know what you ask," he said to Miss Parrish. "I love that woman as I love myself." In the end, the separation never happened. James got shot in the neck shortly afterward, and rather than abandon him, Mamie went to the hospital every day for two weeks to sit by his side. After he was discharged, they disappeared. To the landlady, this was all despicable, but others might call it brave. Mamie "didn't want to be saved" by this landlady's moral code. Mamie "refused to be governed."

The story of Mamie and James appears in *Wayward Lives, Beautiful Experiments*, a book of speculative history by Saidiya Hartman that reconstructs Black women's pursuit of pleasure and sexual authenticity at the turn of the century in Philadelphia and New York City. Before Hartman's book, their story likely would have remained embedded in a few of Helen Parrish's outraged diary entries. Mamie and James are victims of what Hartman has called "the violence of the archive," also known as "archival silence": the destruction and erasure of stories from people judged unimportant by the writers of history.

Hartman seeks to correct the record of America's sexual revolutions. She calls the flapper a "pale imitation of the ghetto girl" and lovingly injects agency, joy, and defiance into the stories of women who were criminalized, pitied, or ignored by white people and shamed by middle-class Black people, simply for existing outside their strict standards of virtue. For a Black woman, Hartman writes, "the mere willingness to have a good time with a stranger was sufficient evidence of wrongdoing." Harriet Powell, whose arrest for staying too late on the dance floor under New York's "wayward minor laws" was a deliberate protest, "has been credited with nothing: she remains a surplus woman of no significance, a nobody deemed unfit for history and destined to be a minor figure." A lesbian chorus girl's visit to an interracial sex party during the Harlem renaissance provokes quivering transcendence: The "choked breath of orgasm shattered the boundaries of the self, effaced the lines of social division, unmade men and women."

These women were not sexually liberated, Hartman insisted in a 2020 *Art Forum* interview—true freedom was aspirational, still so out of reach for them. But they were nevertheless in "open rebellion," reaching for better lives on their own terms. "[I] really wanted to think about sensory experience and inhabiting the body in a way that is not exhausted by the condition of vulnerability and abuse," which is "so definitive of the lives of Black femmes," Hartman said in the same interview. "And so, what does it mean to want to imagine and to experience something else?"

Hartman's book, published in 2019, joined other scholarship that has pushed back on respectability politics and reinserted pleasure into the story of Black women's collective sexual history. The replacement of archival silence with humanizing vulnerability is the backbone of what Black feminist writer and activist adrienne maree brown has dubbed "pleasure activism." Expressions of pleasure are all the more important for women of color, queer people, and other marginalized groups not despite but precisely *because* of the overwhelming shadow of sexual violence. "Witnessing an embodied yes in the body of a historically oppressed person is irresistible to me," brown writes. It's a concept that can be traced back to Lorde's "Uses of the Erotic," which rejected "the false belief that only by the suppression of the erotic within our lives and consciousness can women be truly strong." That strength, that lack of vulnerability, "is illusory, for it is fashioned within the context of male models of power."

There were historians of Black feminism here and there, like Stephanie Camp, who wrote that enslaved women attended secret parties, wearing stylish hoop skirts they'd fashioned with grapevines and tree limbs, to "make their bodies spaces of personal expression and pleasure." But most scholarship had focused on Black women's bodies as a site of suffering and violation. It was a necessary corrective, Joan Morgan wrote in her 2015 essay, "Why

We Get Off," but the downside was a "mulish inattentiveness to black women's engagements with pleasure—the complex, messy, sticky, and even joyous negotiations of agency and desire that are irrevocably twinned with our pain." Black feminists had become "overly reliant" on Lorde, Kimberlé Crenshaw, and a few others, Morgan wrote, "bequeathing them the sanctity of dogma." It was time for explicit, fresh conversations about sexual pleasure.

"Why We Get Off" was written two years after Morgan founded the Pleasure Ninjas, a small brain trust of Black female scholars she assembled to fill this intellectual vacuum. The women spent several days of 2013 engaging with pleasure as both philosophy and praxis. Stanford University, where Morgan was a visiting lecturer, put them up in a beautiful house in Berkeley. The women got massages, went salsa dancing, plucked lemons from the trees in the front yard to make lemonade. In between, they spent hours, sometimes all night, analyzing and plotting.

After that heady week, the Pleasure Ninjas and other like-minded writers sought to reinject the concept of desire into Black women's historical and pop culture narratives. Isn't it possible, Ariane Cruz asked, that highly ritualized BDSM can be a powerful mode of pleasure even (and maybe especially) for people who've been historically dominated? Shouldn't it matter, Brittney Cooper posited, that "respectable" civil rights activist Mary Church Terrell wrote in her 1940 autobiography that she loved dancing and, along with a female friend, would sneak out of her dorm room to "trip the light fantastic to our heart's content"? At a time when dancing was considered hypersexual and therefore forbidden, the inclusion of this detail, Cooper writes, is intentional and subversive.

Scholars Treva B. Lindsey and Jessica Marie Johnson *really* took it there: they mentioned slavery and orgasms in the same breath. A paper they cowrote side-eyed the widespread condemnation of a 2013 YouTube video called "The Harriet Tubman Sextape," a parody that depicted Tubman using sex to blackmail a plantation owner into freeing the people he had enslaved. The video wasn't very funny, the authors conceded, but it was worth asking why an eroticized version of Tubman was considered such a desecration.

Even though slavery was rife with sexual violence, reimagining Tubman and other enslaved women as having their own "sexual interiority," as "erotic subject[s] with desires and intimate needs," was essential to granting them humanity and agency. So was emphasizing the fact that sex *can* be liberatory and a tool of resistance, even the sex between enslavers and the enslaved that blurred the boundaries of consent and power. "Political goals of the moment do not rewrite the sexual lives, desires, and choices of enslaved and free women of color," wrote Lindsey and Johnson. "But they can obscure those lives to our detriment."

If we can instead "imagine ecstatic moments for slaves, if only brief and painfully ephemeral," they wrote, then "radical histories of black community can be created." It's a way to restore humanity, and in turn vulnerability, to the Strong Black Woman stereotype, to *any* harmful stereotype—even if we have to fill in the gaps with our imaginations, or dig through a white landlady's diary, or simply tune in to flickers of pleasure nestled in the pages of Black women's own memoirs. "Owning nothing and subsisting on so little, they let the heart decide everything," Hartman writes of Mamie and James. "Love was their only anchor. It was clear to [the landlady] that the sole thing that mattered to James Shepherd was: Do I want Mamie? Does she want me? Damn the law and Miss Parrish."

• • •

In April 2016, Selah flew to Atlanta for a long weekend to visit two college friends. The first night she was there, they all went to a screening of a Nina Simone documentary. The event was meant to protest the new biopic with Zoe Saldana, who'd darkened her skin for the role. The screening later turned into a giant party, a who's who of queer Black Atlanta, where Selah met a confident butch named Alexis. There was instant electricity. Alexis took Selah home to her apartment. They spent the whole weekend talking and eventually fucking. Selah came home to New York City on Monday night feeling a surprising gust of expansiveness. The weekend hadn't been an anomaly. She couldn't stop thinking about Alexis and the undeniable truth that meeting her had spurred: she was fully, extremely queer.

She called Mona and said, "I met someone. And I *am* gay. I'm not pussyfooting around this time." It was scary, and it was risky— Mona was not shy about her disapproval—but it also felt unbelievably freeing. She didn't have to comply with hetero-supremacist standards for one more second. The feelings of inadequacy just melted away. Instead of feeling like a failure, she suddenly felt like her life had gotten an imagination injection. Unlike me and the other straight people she knew who could choose how much they wanted to rebel, Selah broke the rules just by being herself, honestly and remorselessly.

She kept in touch with Alexis, for whom she was quickly falling. They talked on the phone for hours. Selah flew back to Atlanta for a weekend. Alexis took Selah to a sex store to buy a dildo, and Selah's first impulse was to sexily ask, "What toy do you want to use on me?" Alexis stopped her and said, "Baby. What do *you* want?" No one had ever asked Selah that before.

Alexis steered Selah's manic, rapidly developing consciousness toward sustained exploration, gifting her a language and a voice and a space for being her Black queer self. And then, not long after they met, Alexis went a different way. Her departure hurt. It was wild how much it hurt. Alexis couldn't be Selah's love savior; in fact, her rejection exposed such a concept for the farce it always was. *Fuck the happily ever after*, she told Selah. *Just live.*

6. An Old Male Revolt in a New Disguise

That neat, angel-devil theory was no longer useful.
—LORETTA ROSS

In January 1969, leftists of all stripes descended on Washington to protest Richard Nixon's inauguration. Organized by the National Mobilization Committee to End the War in Vietnam (Mobe), it was a three-day spectacle that was by all accounts urgent, absurdist, and sometimes violent. A few feminists with ties to Mobe sensed an opportunity—thus far, the New Left had yet to formally acknowledge women's liberation. Marilyn Webb, a local activist who'd been organizing consciousness-raising sessions with other DC women, secured a space for herself and Shulamith Firestone on the speaker program, and feminists in New York and DC started to plan an action. The theme was Give Back the Vote, and the idea was to destroy their voter registration cards as a comment on how little political power women still had, nearly fifty years after they gained suffrage.

Mobe suspiciously left out the women's action on the event's program, and when antiwar leader David Dellinger began the rally with a spirited denunciation of the evils of war and racism, he made no mention of the feminists.

"What about women, you schmuck?" my mother shouted.

"And, uh, a special message from women's liberation," he added. When he invited Webb up to speak, he said, "The women have asked all the men to leave the stage."

They hadn't actually singled out the men—just anyone outside their group, because the stage was too shaky to hold everyone—but Webb was too thrown by the instantaneous hostility to clarify. As soon as she began giving what she characterized, decades later, as "the mildest speech you can imagine," the men in the crowd booed and jeered. "Take her off the stage and fuck her!" one shouted. "Fuck her down a dark alley!" They guffawed at her accidental double entendres, like "We must take to the streets." Firestone's planned speech now came across as an impromptu act of defiance. She shouted over the leftist men, who grew more and more feral: "We women often have to wonder if you mean what you say about revolution or whether you just want more power for yourselves." Instead of telling the men to shut up, Dellinger pleaded with Firestone and Webb to get off the stage.

That night, when the women regrouped at Webb's apartment to figure out what to do next, Webb remembers a female Students for a Democratic Society member calling them and threatening to beat the shit out of them if they ever orchestrated a spectacle like that again. (For the record, the woman Webb thought was on the other line has denied threatening the group.) The whole ordeal was a clarifying trauma. In her chronicle of the incident, my mother remarked that the event made obvious how "a genuine alliance with male radicals will not be possible until sexism sickens them as much as racism. This will not be accomplished through persuasion, conciliation, or love, but through independence and solidarity."

This debacle, which was lore in my family, was not isolated. My mother often reminded me that in the sixties, it was perfectly commonplace for male antiwar activists and civil rights leaders to ridicule or ignore women, sexualizing them in order to dismiss them. Around the same time, an SDS pamphlet stated: "The system is like a woman; you've got to fuck it to make it change." In 1964, Stokely Carmichael made a tasteless, now infamous joke about how "the only position for women in SNCC is prone."

After the incident in DC, Firestone continued to rail against male leftists' failure to consider women's issues. In her 1970 book *The Dialectic of Sex*, she skewers Karl Marx and Friedrich Engels, who "acknowledged the sexual class system only where it overlapped and illuminated [their] economic construct." In the late seventies, Michele Wallace called out civil rights and Black Power activists' sexism in *Black Macho and the Myth of the Superwoman*, arguing that their rhetoric of revolutionary manhood pitted them against Black women and eroded the two groups' chances for solidarity. "Could you imagine Che Guevara with breasts? Mao with a vagina? [The Black woman] was just going to have to get out of the way," she wrote. To these male activists, "womanhood was not essential to revolution." Again and again, feminists shone a light on a searing truth: Men fighting for freedom in other ways tended to display serious cognitive dissonance when it came to the women in their lives.

I thought a lot about this tendency during the period right after the 2016 election. Like most people I knew, I was extra-indignant and extra-attuned to injustice and violence during that politically charged winter. This included the men in my life, who were horrified that our new president was, among other awful things, a proud male chauvinist who'd been accused of rape. But I didn't know whom to trust. Mor, for instance, had been firmly to the left on paper: he was pro-choice, pro-union, and pro–Medicare for all. Yet he also slut-shamed his ex and bristled at my attempts to pay for three-dollar beers. He mercilessly judged women on their looks and admitted that his feminine eyebrows made him feel like a "pussy." Not to mention that our relationship and its demise were classically gendered: an emotionally manipulative dude, tortured by the confines of his own masculinity and unsure of what he wanted; a lovesick girl feeling used and lied to after her man left her for someone younger and more exciting. Besides Mor's general mindfuckery, I'd somehow ignored all the sexism baked into our relationship too.

I didn't know if the guys around me meant what they said, or whether they were secretly like those jerks who yelled at Marilyn Webb at the rally. I wondered if any of those rally guys had been the boyfriends of feminists, who themselves may have been stymied by their love or lust for someone who unconsciously—yet fundamentally—saw them as second-class citizens.

After the success of her 1976 report on female sexuality, researcher Shere Hite decided to conduct a similar study on men. She published it in 1981, long after feminist ideas had spread past radical circles into the mainstream. Some male respondents praised women's liberation as a long time coming, while others called it "ridiculous," "the worst thing that ever happened to women," "a farcical gyration of dykes." When discussing whether the women's movement had affected their relationships, most men said it hadn't at all—at least not in a way they were conscious of. Some said it had a positive effect, like the man who wrote that because of "women's lib," his wife had become "more independent and more aggressive—more fun to be with." Others resented the havoc it wreaked on the status quo: "Women's liberation has fucked up a number of relationships with women for me," one guy wrote. "We have to communicate a hell of a lot more than we did before. . . . The result is that it's gotten a lot easier to offend people." Overall, there was a lot of yearning for the good old days: "Women are too liberated. I want romance back, and more love." Still other respondents expressed a lot of equivocation. Like this guy: "Many feminists, especially radical and militant ones, make me nervous and uncomfortable (even though I consider myself to be a feminist), because I feel that they dislike me or see me as a man, and not a unique human being. (I hate being stereotyped by anyone.)"

I emailed some of the early members of the women's movement to ask how men around them adapted to such fast-moving changes. When it came to their intimate male partners, they told me, hostility toward feminism wasn't so blatant; as it had with Mor, it took the form of a jumbled ambivalence that had the power to make reasonable women feel utterly disoriented.

Some men thought women's liberation was hot. "I was lucky to have boyfriends who were interested in my pleasure, liked my brain, and overcame their fears," Erica Jong, longtime sexual liberationist and *Fear of Flying* author, told me in an email. Other men didn't adapt quite as well. Men would seem supportive, then act threatened. Many relationships formed pre-feminism, like feminist writer Vivian Gornick's marriage, did not survive. Gornick's husband "really got behind feminism" at first, she told me, but once her consciousness had been raised, "there was no going back." This well-meaning man was completely at sea. She remembers him saying, "It took me forty years to learn the ropes, to learn the rules of how to act with a woman, and now you're pulling the rug out from under me."

If my mom had been alive for me to ask her, she might have steered me toward those letters Bob wrote her in the emotional wreckage of their breakup. In them, he expressed complicated feelings about a movement whose power he clearly recognized. "It ought to please you to learn that ultimately I blame my dilemma"— the seeming impossibility of modern heterosexual love—"on the oppression of women by men," he wrote. Perhaps he was "looking for a scab—that is, a woman who can love a man."

Love. A depressingly effective force against political ideology. Second Wave feminists were well aware that heterosexual romance presented a major roadblock to political clarity. If Bob's "scabs" were women who chose to love their oppressors, men were the bosses themselves—who, as any union organizer will tell you, are in an inherently adversarial position, no matter how benevolent. Newly radicalized women struggled to figure out whether there was any such thing as a true feminist man, or whether love would always cloud their judgment. "When we are fighting against the feelings of love which seem capable of debilitating us," British feminist Daphne Davies wrote in a 1978 article in *Red Rag*, a Marxist women's liberation magazine, "we should be constantly vigilant about the way we feel, attempting to understand why we behave as we do, and not accepting love as unfathomable and unchangeable."

My mother struggled with this dynamic, first when she initially joined the movement and then when she fell deeply in love with my dad at the start of the eighties. Members of the Sex Fools, the women's group my mother met with for fifteen years, remember the early days of my mother's intense connection with this commitment-phobic man. Though he'd evidently learned a lot since the days when he was married to Jane, my father was well-known for being a "womanizer," itself a politically ambiguous term: Was a man automatically a sexist because he was less than honorable in his romantic relationships? How much of it was patriarchy, and how much was just his personality?

Alix Kates Shulman recalls feeling "delighted and excited for Ellen" but that the group felt protective and worried for her too. Another group member, Bonnie Bellow, acknowledged that if you were in a relationship with a man in the midst of Second Wave feminism, there was always the fear that you'd be seen as "consorting with the enemy." If something negative happened, like an affair, it was an embarrassment. But Bonnie remembers their group discussions being less about any one particular man's misogyny and more about offering "support to each other to stick up for ourselves, create our own space within these powerful relationships. . . . It was support to be more independent."

Of course, when obsessive love is involved, living up to those ideals becomes much easier said than done. In retrospect it seems ludicrous that I was in love with Mor, but at the time it felt like the only conceivable diagnosis. And, more to the point, why I couldn't see how retrograde our gender dynamics were. In the same article, Davies acknowledged how difficult it is to stick to our guns in a romantic situation: there comes a time when we are "forced to fight against feelings in ourselves which we know (in theory) to be unacceptable, but which we find almost impossible to combat in practice."

* * *

It's not just the blinders of romantic love that stand in the way of seeing our relationships with men clearly. The feminists who responded to my questions about those early days cited familiarity, the conviction that they *knew* these men. It's always easier to reject an outsider on account of sexism—somebody else's ex-boyfriend or a megalomaniacal boss, but not your friend, your brother, the man with whom you're currently spending so many hours in bed. Decades later, now that such blatantly misogynist behaviors like rape, domestic violence, and harassment are in theory no longer tolerated, we've convinced ourselves that the specific men in our lives would never engage in them. The dudes you know and love must be well-intentioned, or else why would you love them?

In those early months of 2017, when the election was fresh but before the #MeToo accusations had come, some of us were still clinging to the pipe-dream exceptionalism embodied by that little phrase, brilliant for its simplicity: *not all men*. The meme dates back to when Joanna Russ, in her 1980 feminist novel *On Strike Against God*, wryly repeated the bad-faith motto. It was the echo of every man wishing to exempt himself from misogyny by pointing out that not all men—and especially not him—manspread, mansplain, manterrupt, catcall, harass, intimidate, hit, rape. But it was also every woman hoping he was right, hoping that her inner circle didn't include those kinds of creeps.

We're all gripped by a constant cycle of negotiation and for-giveness with the people in our intimate lives. A gay friend of mine tells me he waves off an occasional whiff of homophobia from his sister because he knows "she's not like that." A woman of color I know tries not to call out every racially off-kilter comment from her white friends because she knows where their hearts are. But as Second Wave feminists were fond of pointing out, other kinds of oppression are much more compatible with pursuing separatism. Patriarchy is unique in that heterosexual women are oppressed by the very people they want to love, live with, and have sex with. This mucks up the justifiable anger women feel toward men who are violent, hateful, or even just sleazy. "Man-hating is everywhere, but everywhere it is twisted and transformed, disguised, tranquilized, and qualified," Judith Levine wrote in *My Enemy, My Love* in 1992. "It coexists, never peacefully, with the love, desire, respect, and need women also feel for men. Always man-hating is shadowed by its milder, more diplomatic and doubtful twin, ambivalence."

It's icky to think about the anger we're burying, but the alternative is equally uncomfortable. Wouldn't that mean seeing every human as an insignificant speck of a larger problem rather than individual balls of contradiction and messiness? Wouldn't we also have to confront the roles we might play in the pain of others, and in our own pain too? Not to mention the problem of trust: If you can't count on the men you know to not be dicks, how can you count on the randoms?

● ● ●

By February, just six weeks out from my low point on the couch mourning both Aaron and Mor, dating seemed more daunting than ever. Between my emotional tenderness and my political rage, my standards were sky-high. I only wanted to deal with guys who had a highly developed sense of gender consciousness, *and* who would not fuck with my fragile heart, *and* who wouldn't disappoint me in bed, *and–and–and–and*. In the name of politics, my impulse to self-protect swelled up again, while my benefit-of-the-doubt tolerance hit rock bottom. I prematurely ended a promising thing with a sexy, attentive writer I'd known for years, because of one awkward condom incident and because he'd interrupted me a few times. I said "thanks but no thanks" after one date to a guy with a sweet, crinkly smile and a flawless Obama impression because I thought our end-of-the-night kiss had been bad. Most men didn't even get to the meet-up stage, because I began stretching dating-app chats over days or even weeks, circling a guy to make sure he met all the criteria. Virtually none of them did.

Normally I would have gravitated to the many men who were now identifying themselves as allies or writing "Fuck that pussy-grabber" on their dating-app profiles, but I was even—no, especially—wary of them. There was a reason why I was having trouble trusting self-proclaimed male feminists: they all reminded me of a date I'd gone on the previous summer, when my hackles were not yet up.

On a July weekend when Aaron was out of town, I agreed to meet a guy named Max the day after we matched on Tinder. He was in an open relationship, just like me. He talked frankly and respectfully about sex. He said he was a "giver." He had twinkly eyes and a brawny physique that was less ice sculpture than tree climber. He agreed on "no sexpectations" when we made plans for a last-minute date. I can't say for sure because he would later un-match me, but I think his profile boasted that he was a feminist.

Once at the bar, I couldn't tell if I was attracted, but we had a pleasant time anyway. Max seemed adventurous, smart, fun, and horny. He told me he worked with survivors of sexual trauma. He touched my leg almost immediately, then said, "Let me know if this is too much." After an hour or two, I decided we would have a light hookup to see if there was any physical spark. I went back to his place, around the corner from the bar, after announcing my boundaries. "Just a make-out," I insisted. He said that was fine.

After a few minutes in his bedroom, it was clear it was not fine.

We had started kissing and I felt mildly turned on. Then I didn't. I told Max I had to go, but he pressed. Coquettishly, quietly, I said, "Stop." He pressed more. I said, "No, really, *stop*." When I faced away from him to jiggle my bra back in place, he came up behind me and tried yet again. At one point, he pushed me onto his bed and said, "Wait a minute, I still haven't made you come."

Eventually, I was firm—"I REALLY have to go!"—and made my way to the door, although I kissed him good night rather than leaving in a huff. As soon as I was on the street, I sniffed back confused tears, disappointed in myself for letting my guard down so quickly and then not even acting angry. Did that scenario really just happen between two Brooklyn feminists?

● ● ●

I had intended to write about this incident immediately, but I kept putting it off. That summer's election coverage and violent upheaval kept me plenty busy at my editing job. Then the end of 2016 came, and the media was having an existential crisis about the election results. The self-flagellating think pieces piled up about What the Media Got Wrong. I decided to redirect my political and personal restlessness into something useful. I pitched a series of road trips to recruit local writers that would take me far, far away from my bubble of New York City. To my delight, my editor in chief went for it. At the start of March 2017, I left to go on a monthlong road trip across Texas.

The first stretch was a long, sunny, nondescript drive on the 10 going east from Central Texas. I had a lot of time to feel the emotions pinballing around my body for the last few months. Contemplation careened into anger, which simmered down to melancholy, followed by bouts of numbness, and back again. The nature of those emotions went from macro to micro, from "How do we start a revolution?" to "Will I die alone?" Somewhere between a pit stop in Flatonia and the maze of highways in Houston, I started thinking about every piece I'd ever wanted to write, and this long-lost date with Max again crossed my mind, as it had many times over the past few months. I had a name I used for guys like him, a type who seemed to proliferate postelection: the woke misogynist.

A woke misogynist is a guy who talks a big game about gender equality and consent, uses vocabulary like "triggering" without rolling his eyes, prefers to date feminists and may freely call himself one too—then turns around and harasses you, assaults you, or belittles you. As with the word *woke* itself, he's comfortable with both performance and appropriation. (This was 2017, when *woke* had recently been stolen from Black people by white leftists and was not yet used as an epithet by conservatives.) Perhaps his behavior throws you off because, unlike the whimpster or emosogynist of the aughts, he's confident in himself and his pro-woman bona fides. Or because he apologizes nicely and engages you in a thoughtful conversation after the offending incident. Or, most likely, because his misogyny is far more ambiguous and subtle than that of serial abusers like Harvey Weinstein or R. Kelly.

The woke misogynist is harder to pin down than the garden-variety progressive men who yelled at Marilyn Webb onstage. That appalling disconnect was hypocritical in a grander sense, in that someone purporting to be for human rights shouldn't go around harassing or putting down women. But unlike the woke misogynist, the bigotry of the men at that rally was unflinching, their hostility blatant. They certainly never claimed to be feminists.

Some of these modern male feminists are genuine, even if they're not perfect. Many men now want to be equal partners and parents. They believe a woman should be president. They follow the Squad on Twitter. They will try and sometimes fail on their way to enlightenment. We care about the men in our lives, so we are often willing to discuss mistakes they make. We will explain to our partners that waiting for us to delegate housework tasks does not lighten our cognitive load. We will chide our guy friends for being avoidant with their female lovers. We will point out how our brothers' favorite films don't pass the Bechdel test. The problem is, there's no definitive way to be sure how much they really care, or how much of their deeply embedded sexism is here to stay. The line between sincere allyship and simmering misogyny can be paper-thin. And some of them reveal themselves to be wolves in pink pussy hats.

Shortly after the date with Max, I initiated the digital equivalent of a consciousness-raising session to compare notes. I emailed a couple dozen friends, who then passed along my email to others: *Had they taken note of these woke misogynists too?* Emails flooded in about behavior all across the spectrum: The college guy who bought his girlfriend feminist zines and also hit her—then taunted her about not living up to her ideals by staying with him. The boss who was an enemy of the patriarchy on the internet but regularly intimidated and talked down to his female employees. The outspoken women's rights advocate who went out of his way to call Kellyanne Conway ugly. Women recalled chronic patronizing, compulsive interrupting, and classic sexism excused with self-awareness ("I know this is super-scummy of me, but . . ."). Riot grrrl icon Kathleen Hanna, who flayed her woke misogynist fans in her song "Mr. So and So," told me she was raped in college by a guy who'd read more feminist books than she had.

I heard countless versions of my awful Tinder date: a supposedly feminist guy who tramples on one's boundaries in some uncanny, unexpected way. The worst thing about this phenomenon, one woman remarked, is that it's often "a general feeling, not necessarily a momentous incident. And that makes it feel less real." Since woke misogyny comes with a hefty dose of gaslighting, it's difficult to tell whether it's calculated or not. These guys usually seem nice. Reasonable. The kind of man you'd feel comfortable confronting about the very behavior he claims to denounce. And when those confrontations actually happen with a woke misogynist, it can be the biggest mindfuck of all.

• • •

When I got home from the date with Max, I noticed he had texted me: Home safe? Haunted by my conciliatory good-night kiss, I decided to recap what had just transpired. If anyone could have a rational conversation about consent, it was us two, right?

Yeah I got home safe, I wrote. But I do have to say, I feel a little funny about what just happened.

I called him out for ignoring my boundaries, for not stopping when I put my foot down. To my immense relief, he responded with all the right things: I feel like an animal and not good, he texted back. Are you ok? :(I am really not happy with myself and I am sorry.

The conversation went on for an hour. I admitted that my initial arousal had thrown me off. He admitted he really wasn't listening. I asked him what exactly he was thinking. At the moment, I have no excuse, he replied. But what was in my head was a playful vibe and perhaps a struggle to present myself as more masculine. I don't know . . . I've heard the other side. Your side. From so many lovers, partners, clients, and empathize but have never been on the end that I am now.

I went to bed feeling shaken, but also validated and encouraged that a genuine dialogue had taken place. But I wasn't sure: Did he really mean what he said? Was this a sincere exchange or a manipulation? If it was the latter, was this his MO?

The thing about being a woke misogynist who attracts confident feminists is that he's more likely to get challenged. These men, in turn, are unusually willing to Talk It Out, often leading to maddening head games. After Clara, one woman who emailed me, was assaulted by a male feminist, she launched into a "long, ill-advised, fruitless campaign to get him to admit what he did." Her rapist initially explained his behavior by offering that his last girlfriend liked rough sex and he thought she would too. Five years later, he sent her a Facebook message saying that "he regretted something 'weird' going down between us because he thinks I'm really cool."

The morning after the Tinder date, I woke up to another text from Max. I'm available if you have more thoughts to share, he wrote. Sorry, again, that I blew it. Then, a moment later, the most tone-deaf text in the history of tone-deaf texts:

> Date redo. I can set my table up and gift you a mock massage! With def clear boundaries. ;) or i make you dinner or a yummy smoothie.

It was the moment I knew that either he was totally clueless or he was playing a long con. Sure, I'd been willing to talk about what went wrong, but apparently I hadn't made it clear that I never wanted his hands anywhere near my body again. He unmatched me on Tinder shortly after I politely declined. Later I found out from a mutual Facebook friend that a few months back, she had booked Max on a panel she organized. The topic was good sex, a discussion about consent and pleasure.

The mutual friend had no idea whether he did this a lot, but she assured me this was an age-old pattern, that people often go out of their way to condemn the very things they're most ashamed of, like an evangelical, homophobic male senator who secretly sleeps with men. It was heartbreaking to see the language of feminism co-opted by someone who clearly didn't get it. And yet no one who heard this story was surprised. During eras in which feminism becomes fashionable, it's always been harder to tell who our true allies are.

• • •

By the late 1970s, men started using the language of liberation to their advantage. An article in *Esquire* in 1978, "New Rules in the Mating Game," quoted a thirty-one-year-old woman describing a date with the type of guy who claimed to love "strong women": "You invite [your date] to a work-session dinner. He asks how you can advance his career. Then he asks you to sleep with him. No commitment. Then he washes the dishes." Many men interviewed in *The Hite Report on Male Sexuality* linked women's liberation and sexual availability. As one guy put it: "I like the part of women's lib that says yes to sex more frequently."

Meanwhile, men who identify with the women's movement have existed almost as long as the movement itself. A couple of years after my date with Max, while researching something completely different, I would stumble upon a minor but prescient men's liberation movement that formed when the women's movement had just burst on the national scene on the cusp of the seventies. A young leftist psychologist named Jack Sawyer published a 1970 article called "On Male Liberation" in *Liberation*, a New Left magazine founded by David Dellinger, of all people. "Male liberation calls for men to free themselves of the sex-role stereotypes that limit their ability to be human," Sawyer wrote. A year later, *Life* magazine published a feature on men's liberation—written, of course, by a dude, and nested between hilariously sexist ads (a wife preparing a picnic of Pepsi and crudités while the men relax by a badminton court; an ad for Puerto Rico featuring a woman in a white bikini).

"So many guys have it in the back of their minds that they have to be a jock, some kind of supermale, just to exist," said Mike from Berkeley, who got into men's liberation when being laid off gave him intense feelings of inadequacy. He'd placed an ad in the *Berkeley Barb* for an all-male consciousness-raising session. The men's group he subsequently formed would eventually stage a protest at the Playboy Club in San Francisco (sample sign: SMASH COMPULSIVE MASCULINISM) and publish two issues of a men's liberation newspaper called *Brother*. "Our enemy isn't women, it's the role we're forced to play," Mike told *Life*.

The reporter travels across the country, talking to men in these newly formed discussion groups. One group in Flint, Michigan— nine men, mostly autoworkers, who met weekly in church after Sunday services—weren't as immersed in countercultural language as their West Coast hippie counterparts. But they were making headway too: "Give women economic equality and there will be more freedom for human beings to get what they want from each other," a man was quoted as saying. Once, the group showed their solidarity with a women's picket line by bringing them sandwiches and drinks.

The nascent movement was driven by a basic principle, one

that's now an accepted (though sometimes neglected) part of mainstream feminism: that men are hurt by gender roles too. That men may have more institutional power but are still imprisoned by their aggression or emotional constipation or both. In a 1972 article in *The New York Times* headlined "Men's Lib—Almost Underground, but a Growing Movement," an industrial designer explained that his discussion group was "not just rapping about politics or baseball scores; we're talking about feelings." The countercultural search for authenticity turned out to be a boon for feminist ideas; the women's movement "raised questions for me about the phony parts of masculinity that I had bought—and that had always existed," another man said in the same article.

The piece also quoted Warren Farrell, then a PhD student at New York University writing his doctorate on the political power of the women's movement. He'd recently joined the board of the New York City chapter of the National Organization for Women, the members of whom tapped Farrell to help organize men's consciousness-raising groups. Eventually there were several hundred groups across the country, usually made up of less than a dozen men, mostly meeting in one another's houses.

I emailed Farrell, curious to hear more about his early male feminist days. On the phone, he was avuncular and even-keeled. He described having a "fire in [his] belly" to explore the women's movement and remembered the halcyon days of consciousness-raising to be extremely gratifying. As a facilitator of these groups, he'd pose questions like "What is the biggest hole in your heart?" The point of these discussions, Farrell told me, was "to confront everything men are told to be." Men would offer their peers support, but they'd also encourage one another to change.

By the mid-1970s, a handful of high-profile books had been

published—against the backdrop of recession and the Nixon scandal—that grappled with masculinity, including Farrell's own *The Liberated Man*, Deborah S. David and Robert Brannon's *The Forty-Nine Percent Majority*, and Marc Feigen Fasteau's *The Male Machine*. These books brought men's liberation beyond discussion groups to theory. Farrell wrote of the deep psychic costs of restrictive masculinity, arguing that men's "denial of dependency" on their loved ones "and emotions leads to silence and the creation of a male mystique." While women were sex objects, men were "success objects"—valued only by their ability to gain status and make money. Feigen Fasteau's book imagined "a view of personality which will not assign fixed ways of behaving to individuals on the basis of sex." The December 1974 issue of *People* magazine profiled Marc's egalitarian marriage with his wife, Brenda Feigen Fasteau, a feminist lawyer he'd met at Harvard who later cofounded the Women's Action Alliance with Gloria Steinem. In the article, Marc vows to help raise his children in a way "work-obsessed fathers" can't. He and his wife founded a law firm together. They each added the other's last name to their own.

Many feminists supported this new movement; everyone from NOW founder Betty Friedan to Toni Morrison appears in *The Liberated Man*'s acknowledgments. Liberal feminists began to warm up to the idea of framing the women's movement as a more inclusive, less threatening "sex role debate," which took the focus off misogyny in favor of the psychological liberation of both sexes. Steinem wrote the introduction to Marc Feigen Fasteau's book, calling him "a spy in the ranks" of the white male elite.

I felt mostly heartened and even excited when I found these books and articles. This movement seemed at times sweet, earnest, and open-minded. The dudes involved with it seemed as evolved as the male friends of mine who did housework and proudly wore their babies around Brooklyn, perhaps even more so, since their political activism included actually talking to each other. But certain sentences set off my Spidey sense, in the same way allegedly feminist men on dating apps did. "If a woman has her own life and destiny to control she will not be as likely to feel the need to control her husband," Farrell declared in 1971. "Men may be even *more* restricted in their identity as *human* beings," he wrote later in *The Liberated Man.* "Support your wife's assertiveness during marriage, her educational and occupational development, and anything else that will make her an autonomous, independent person," wrote psychologist Herb Goldberg in his 1976 book, *The Hazards of Being Male: Surviving the Myth of Masculine Privilege.* Why? Because "during divorce it will make you less vulnerable to guilt."

These moments felt conspiratorial with a men-going-their-own-way tinge, as if feminism was a great way for men to get women off their backs. In 1983's *The Hearts of Men,* Barbara Ehrenreich argued that men's resistance to traditional roles long preceded the women's movement. Before feminism was in fashion, Ehrenreich writes, this rebellion came in the form of what she calls the Gray Flannel Dissidents. This was the type of suburban white man immortalized in *Mad Men* who "lived by the rules. He accomplished his major 'developmental tasks' by his late twenties, found a wife and made the appropriate adjustments to marriage, established himself in a white-collar job. . . . But (maybe because he was just a little smarter than other men) he knew that something was wrong." It was angst over "conformity," a rough equivalent to Betty Friedan's "problem that has no name" and what Richard Yates called "the great sentimental lie of the suburbs" in his 1961 novel, *Revolutionary Road.*

Men who decided to avoid conformity (and its perceived cause: status-obsessed wives) became playboys and beats. Ehrenreich suspected a certain strain of the seventies men's liberation movement was simply this same "old male revolt in a new disguise." Though the movement was "in part a sincere attempt to respond to feminism," she concedes, it also opened up a way for men to "articulate all the old grievances and resentments, but in a way that no longer sounded spiteful or misogynist." In 1970, my mom observed this same veiled hostility, writing in a letter that she had "great hope for men's groups, eventually, but so far most of the trials of that idea that I know of have failed. The men end up criticizing women and the women's movement, or giving each other support in their oppressiveness, complaining about how their wives have been pushing them."

I began to look into what other feminists to the left of Steinem and the more mainstream NOW thought about this new "male revolt" and found that, like my mom, they weren't feeling it. Radical feminists were suspicious of recasting women's liberation as the "sex-role debate"; not only did it depoliticize sexism but it ignored the power imbalance between men and women. Socialist feminists like Carol Hanisch pointed out that many of the ideas coming out of men's liberation were just unacknowledged critiques of capitalism. All this "whining about being a . . . 'success object'" simply means "men don't like their jobs," Hanisch wrote in the 1975 anthology *Feminist Revolution*. It's time for men to name and fight "their real exploiters": capitalists.

But men's libbers didn't align themselves with broader political movements like socialism. Instead, the movement remained mostly limited to straight, white, middle-class men who felt stuffed into the breadwinner role—which in turn led to class and race blindness. Farrell estimates that out of the three hundred college men's groups he helped start, only 1 percent of the members were Black and Latino. Why? The participants tended to be "those who have the luxury to be educated and not be worried about survival needs," he told me. Also, Black and Latino men "were more traditional in their masculinity norms."

It's true that breadwinner pressure was less of a concern for men of color; in most Black and Latino families, both men and women worked. But those men's masculinity required negotiating all kinds of other expectations and oppressions. And yes, there was plenty of "traditional" misogyny in these communities, too, but for different historical reasons than white ones. From slavery on up, a white-supremacist culture sought to simultaneously emasculate and hypersexualize Black men. So their racial liberation often included "a self-conscious quest for manhood," as historian Paula Giddings put it, which could mean doubling down on "their male prerogatives" and dominating Black women. In a similar way, some scholars believe machismo to be a response to colonizers' subjugation of Indigenous men; others posit that it was a way to mirror the conquistadors themselves and better assimilate into colonial society. In short, much like their white female counterparts, white male liberationists failed to engage with any of these layers of competing loyalties (let alone scratch the surface).

The theories behind the men's liberation movement were also straight-up classist. Psychologists critiquing male gender roles in the seventies developed a model of a man's life cycle: boyish aggression, adult masculine coldness, and then (if you're lucky) liberation. "The official ideology of liberal sociology and men's liberation was egalitarian," Ehrenreich wrote in *The Hearts of Men*. But metaphorically, the underlying idea was that working-class men were "culturally retrograde." Not only did men's libbers ignore the nuances of the lives of poor men and men of color, but pitting stoic types against belligerent types didn't account for polite society's wife-beaters, fratty rapists, or men who would grow up to be aggro, entitled toddlers in upper echelons of government like, say, Brett Kavanaugh.

But it seems the main reason why the movement didn't get very far is because men themselves just weren't that into it. The articles written by male authors about men's liberation in mainstream publications had obvious strains of contempt; in the *Life* feature, for instance, the author called these groups an "embarrassing vanguard" and used paternity leave as an example of the world becoming "too sensitive." A 1975 *New York Times* review of several books on masculinity wrote off all of them as making their arguments "piously," "turgidly," and in a "self-indulgent" way.

Even Warren Farrell admitted to me that men weren't exactly joining in droves. At the movement's peak, only a few thousand men across the country had been involved in the discussion groups. "On some level every man is resistant to being in a men's group," Farrell recalled. "The essence of what you learn to be [as a] man is to not feel, not express your feelings." In *The Liberated Man*, Farrell recounts endless roadblocks and conflicts in men's groups he facilitated. At one point, he quotes a letter from Norman Mailer, snidely declining Farrell's invite to a men's lib group: "Obviously I would rather write a good book than go around raising my consciousness."

In the end, Farrell became a sort of genteel, sympathetic fairy godfather of the modern men's rights movement. In 1993, he wrote *The Myth of Male Power*, known as the "bible" that inspired professional misogynist Paul Elam, who would go on to found the flagship men's rights activist website A Voice for Men. During our phone call, Farrell repeated a refrain he's told other reporters and Redditors before about how every movement has both their MLKs and their Eldridge Cleavers, how politicized incels who spout violent rhetoric are akin to Valerie Solanas, whose *SCUM Manifesto* called for eliminating the male sex and who later shot Andy Warhol. He told me the radical wings of any movement usually exaggerate and "have an anger in their heart," but their anger reveals a germ of truth. You have to ask, he said, what's the pain they're expressing, and is it worth listening to?

Before we hung up, Farrell posed an analogy: since the first years of Second Wave feminism, he explained, "there's been a war in which only one sex has shown up, and men have put their heads in the sand and hoped the bullets would miss [them]." It's a vivid metaphor, and yet its meaning is malleable. You can interpret this the way many MRAs do, that women won that war, made men an oppressed class, and now should be prepared for a well-deserved comeuppance. You can interpret this the way I believe Warren Farrell does, that men have just as many legitimate grievances as women (such as being told to shut up while feminists fought for basic civil rights), and they finally need to stand up for themselves. Or you can interpret this the way I have chosen to, in my most charitable moments toward men like Farrell and Max: The war is between patriarchy and every human under its spell. And no one—not even men who spout platitudes and wield feminist jargon—is safe from the flying bullets.

* * *

On a quiet afternoon in Houston, I finally finished my article about Max and woke misogynists. It was strange to be writing about this very specific type of progressive guy after having swiped through

Texas Tinder for the last week, seeing none of the same tropes I'd written about. A few of the men used American flag emojis or wore MAGA hats, but most profiles avoided the current political climate entirely. Instead, they listed heights and hobbies, shared pictures of bar nights and cute babies. ("My sister's, don't worry!") They were not bragging that they were feminists.

That night, I matched with a guy who was brawny and fresh-faced in that *Friday Night Lights* kind of way. At first blush, Kyle was not the best candidate for an enlightened fuck sesh. His messages didn't contain anything objectionable, but it was clear he didn't know from feminism, or politics at all, really. Raised Christian in a Houston suburb called Sugar Land, he bashfully revealed to me during our first chat that he'd never before had casual sex, and he wanted to try it. If we were to sleep together, Kyle admitted, I'd be his second sex partner ever.

Over old-fashioneds (seriously) at a tiny hidden jazz club around the corner from my Airbnb, this non-woke non-misogynist and I discussed our fantasies and boundaries and anxieties and mutual desire to feel valued, if only for one night. Later, at a bar named Poison Girl, he asked if he could kiss me. Then we boned and cuddled for many hours. We didn't talk about who we voted for or what movements we identified with, a nice change from most of my dates in Brooklyn. We didn't have to. Most of the time, a hot one-night stand simply requires being a decent human.

My woke misogynist piece published the next day, just as I was driving down the Gulf coast to South Texas. The internet reacted with a burst of recognition and righteous anger, but all I could think about was my sweet night with Kyle. The withering rage I'd channeled into the piece was already intertwining with another feeling. Hope, maybe? Optimism?

Eventually I realized that in the absence of buzzwords, I'd instead relied on good old intuition during my date with Kyle. I tried to tune in to who he was, not who he *said* he was. Trendy language can be superficially employed, but kindness, patience, and perceptiveness cannot—though that doesn't mean these qualities are impossible to learn. The whole premise of restorative justice, developed by Indigenous communities and championed by prison abolitionists, is that harm can be repaired, that no one is irredeemable. I still remembered a story I'd heard years ago from Black feminist and reproductive justice advocate Loretta Ross. A sexual assault survivor herself, Ross was working at the DC Rape Crisis Center in the seventies when she received a letter from William Fuller, a Black man serving time for rape and murder at Lorton Reformatory. She remembers the letter saying: "While I was on the outside, I raped women. Now on the inside, I rape men. I want to stop raping. Can you help me?"

Her immediate reaction was "We don't even have the money to help rape victims. How dare a rapist ask us for help?" But after some ruminating, she and other staff members agreed to work with Fuller and a group of other self-confessed rapists at the prison. The men formed the country's first male-led anti-sexual-assault group, Prisoners against Rape. Ross met with them regularly. She shared her own experiences with sexual assault. She brought them copies of bell hooks's *Ain't I a Woman*. A decade later, Ross ran into William Fuller on the street. She considered running the other way, but she stayed around long enough for him to thank her for changing his life. He'd gotten out and was working in construction. "He was a transformed man," she reflected in the mid-aughts. "But he did that himself . . . he was his own mentor."

If Ross could grant a man like William Fuller such grace, I

could do the same for the dudes in my life. Acknowledging that patriarchy seeps into all our relationships didn't mean I had to think of all men as lost causes, nor subject them to my arbitrary, ultimately useless litmus tests. I still needed to honor my own boundaries, of course. I still needed some standards. But I also needed to stretch the limits of my own empathy and sense of what was possible, or else I'd never be able to stop second-guessing every guy I met.

There's a moment in one of my mom's essays when she recalls her time in 1970 in Colorado working with antiwar GIs. Fresh off her feminist radicalization, she allowed herself to be angry at the men around her. "So often they simply *didn't get it*," she wrote, "a solid, dumb lump of resistance masquerading as incomprehension of the simplest, clearest demands for reciprocity." At the same time, a working-class feminist began confronting my mother and other middle-class leftists about the various ways they were oppressing her and the mostly working-class soldiers:

> And I began to see it all from the other side: my good intentions; my struggle to see myself as my friend saw me, to change; my continual falling short; my friend's anger and hurt when I just *didn't get it*; my own dumb lump that, to me, often felt indistinguishable from the core of my identity. Male guilt made me furious ("Don't sit there feeling guilty, just get your fucking foot off my neck"), but now I was mired in guilt, resentful about having to feel guilty, guilty about being resentful, and so on.

This train of thought made my mother feel even more despair, more hopelessness. But a similar realization provoked the opposite reaction in me. We've all hurt others, all violated other people's boundaries to certain degrees—I definitely have as a white, privileged person. I still remember my thoughtless racist comment my junior year of Wesleyan when I declared that "all" students of color there were middle-class, and a Black friend reminded me that he grew up in the projects and hadn't I heard of the Boys and Girls Clubs? I wince each time I recall when I flippantly misgendered a writer I was editing. In each case, they cared about me enough to say something, and I, in turn, was grateful for their patience.

It was a reminder I would desperately need when the #MeToo movement exploded later that year. During those months, when the stream of allegations was fresh and shocking, I tried to truly grapple with the effects of this harmful behavior. I didn't push away my anger toward these men and the people enabling them. But I also told myself that if I was redeemable and lovable and capable of growth, "bad" men could be too. Even the woke misogynists. Even the MRAs. Even the sexual harassers and the men in prison for rape.

● ● ●

After a necessary visit to the Selena Museum in Corpus Christi, I headed to McAllen, a border town in the Rio Grande Valley. The plan was to meet with people from Neta, a media platform run by a group of young Latinx journalists, activists, and artists. I clicked right away with a writer and newly minted drag queen named Gabriel, who, upon learning that I loved Stevie Nicks, promised to perform a Fleetwood Mac medley at his drag performance the next evening. I showed up at midnight the following night at the oldest gay bar in South Texas.

I observed the bar's mostly male patrons: one guy ruffling

another guy's hair, a straight dude cuddling with his girlfriend, men in motorcycle jackets, men in cowboy hats and jeans, men in full drag, all with their own unique and complicated relationships to masculinity. I felt my phone buzz in my hand just as Gabriel took the stage in a green Stevie shawl. It was the guy with the crinkly smile and the Obama impression, texting almost three months after our first and only date:

> Hey Nona, remember me? Gotta say this or I'll regret it. Still think about you sometimes, and I'd love to see you again.

If I'd gotten this text a few weeks earlier, I would have assumed the worst: that he wasn't respecting my initial rejection, that his unassuming tone was just an act so he'd have another chance to fuck me. I knew that same reflexive mistrust would probably rear its head again, but in that moment, in that South Texas bar, I listened to my gut. Even though I doubted I'd say yes to another date, I took this guy's motivations at face value. I saw his text for the brave, sincere gesture it seemed to be. I sipped my beer and cheered loudly for my new friend.

7. In It for the Dick

God didn't make me gay, I fucking earned it.

—ANDREA LONG CHU

I noticed Leila immediately, her hazel eyes glowing against her teal jumpsuit, her wavy black hair getting in her face. It was during the summer of 2015, an intimate affair at an outside bar. I tried to cultivate some conspiratorial, close-talking banter. She seemed interested in me too. Before she left, she grabbed my phone and stored her number in it.

This wasn't the first time I'd been attracted to a woman, and it wouldn't be the last. I'd had a handful of same-sex hookups, mostly in spontaneous circumstances where I was being pursued. But this time, my infatuation with Leila was fueled and sustained by me. I was intrigued by her in a way I hadn't been by other women. I spent an inordinate amount of time on her social media. I felt fluttery when I texted her. I noticed a sinking feeling when her Instagram indicated that she was seeing someone. My fantasies weren't necessarily sexual, but this was an honest-to-goodness crush.

We proceeded to play text tag for nearly two years—making plans, then breaking them; exchanging flirty innuendos but never escalating. We rarely hung out in person, and when we did, neither of us really acknowledged our text rapport, to the point where I wondered if it was all in my head. Either way, my lack of initiative was out of character. If things were stalling out with a man I wanted to fuck, I usually blurted out something explicit like, "Hey, do you want to kiss me?" I wasn't the type to flake out on people whom I genuinely desired.

So what was my problem? I considered the possibility of my own internalized homophobia but assumed I wouldn't face negative social consequences among my progressive circle; if anything, being queer seemed far more modern than clinging to heterosexuality. I was still with Aaron when I met Leila, and he, like many straight men who feel threatened only when there's another dick involved, had given me the green light to pursue her. Maybe my crush was more intellectual and aesthetic than romantic or sexual? Maybe I lacked the confidence to move forward without the typical sexual cues I received from men? Or maybe I was trying to turn this friend crush into a sex thing because I wanted to think of myself as gayer than I actually was. Because then I could be something other than just an unhappy, trapped straight woman married to a man.

Whatever the reason, I did notice that after a disappointing experience with a dude, my interest in Leila would spike. She had unapologetic misandrist and anti-hetero energy that she dished out generously. Throughout the years, I gave Leila bits and pieces of my romantic life—just enough for her to know I was ambiently dissatisfied, searching for . . . *something*. A scroll through our texts revealed that I hit her up right before my breakup with Aaron, then again during the Mor turmoil. Now I was engaging her again, right after I published my woke misogynist piece on the Texas road trip, and just as I was struggling to fully trust men. She often reinforced my own skepticism. At one point, Leila texted me a link to a piece by a hetero woman describing in detail just how bad men were at giving oral sex. God I would hate to be straight, she wrote. This is really tragic.

Leila's pity for the straights wasn't just about sex. It was an indictment of the participants in a system where women just expect that men will fail to have full emotional capacity, care about women's orgasms, text back in a timely manner, do dishes, or take on their share of childcare—and where men often meet these lowered expectations. Most hetero people simply accept a certain amount of Mars versus Venus discord, or worse, romanticize it. Leila was expressing relief that she'd sidestepped that endless cycle of loving men, getting hurt, then emerging bruised but ever wry and ever optimistic.

But also, it *was* about sex. In later conversations she'd make it clear that she had never had great sex with a dude, and believe her, she'd tried: it was just so dull, so uninspired, so one-note. She listed reasons for why she preferred women, both specific (they know their way around a clitoris; they have softer skin) and broad (male privilege isn't built into the relationship; they're more in tune; they just *know*). In the bedroom, she assured me, women were light-years ahead of their male counterparts.

She wasn't the first person in my life who'd made it clear just how unevolved she thought heterosexuality was. Most of my queer friends who didn't fuck cis men poked similar fun, and hetero people themselves had gotten into the self-deprecating habit of denouncing their own orientation as hopeless and depressing. I was known to occasionally mourn my stubborn heterosexuality to friends when a man was causing me angst. But Leila's offhand text stuck in my mind. It made me feel shamed. Exposed and uncool. *I can't help who I want to fuck*, I thought. Though several of my hook-ups with girls had been enjoyable, to me they had confirmed that when it came to sex, I preferred the bodies and energy of cis men.

Still, my lingering attraction to Leila herself, to her wholesale dismissal of men, and to her affirmative reasons for preferring women made me wonder more deeply if my sexual orientation was as much of an immovable given as I'd assumed it was. Did I "hate to be straight"? Did I think of my love life as "tragic"?

My initial answer was no, though perhaps I hadn't been thinking hard enough. It *was* a little weird that I considered it a rite of passage to be treated like shit by dudes, that I demanded so little emotional capacity from the men who'd shaped my sexuality in my teens and twenties. I *did* feel, for all those years, that following the rules of heterosexuality meant I had to remain on Team Chill. I'd also had a lot of bad sex with men, due to behaviors ranging from clueless to sinister: consent breaching, selfishness, jackrabbit sex, stubble during cunnilingus, untrimmed fingernails, sloppy kisses, and belligerent drunken rants, to name a few. The last year or so of my personal life had contained transcendent, transformative, and just plain hot moments with men whose bodies and personalities I truly enjoyed. But yes, those moments had also been wrapped up in that familiar, distinctly gendered pain and ambivalence that I'd felt ever since I started having crushes on boys.

Leila's contempt for heterosexuality—not just for men, but for women like me who resigned themselves to this doomed cycle— punctured my own narrative of sexual awakening. I'd turned my whole heart inside out since the day I moved out of Aaron's and my apartment, trying to reach for liberation from fear, from repression, from dusty scripts I'd followed for too long. But I'd been doing it by fucking guys, obsessing over how to love them, trust them, forgive them, relate to them. In one sense I'd remained loyal to the most basic script there was. It wasn't hard to imagine a lesbian listening to my long, winding story of the last year and thinking, *When will straight women ever learn?*

"Born this way" has long been a rallying cry of many queer people, particularly gay men, meant to strike back at conservative bigotry that's justified by the idea that gayness is a "choice." Because of pervasive homophobia, many queer people throughout history have hoped and wished they could "choose" to be straight, and they hold up their inability to do so as proof that sexual orientation is innate. Why select oppression if there was a world without it? My presumption that queer was "cooler" in progressive crowds ignored the persistent trauma, depression, and shame many queer people still had, even in the best-case scenarios; they, too, grew up in an overwhelmingly hetero-dominated society, after all. Not to mention the fact that supposedly progressive people could still have moments of homophobia too. The ease of having straight privilege is something many gay people would be happy to feel.

Yet even before the impressive acceleration of social acceptance and legal rights for LGBTQ people in the last decade, there was a tradition of radical lesbians who framed their orientation as not only a choice but a joyful choice, one that frees you from the fuckery of men and heterosupremacy. To Leila, continuing to have sex with men and hoping it would result in long-term happiness looked like voluntarily staying in a prison of my own making. It looked like I was turning my back on happiness and pleasure. It looked like giving up.

• • •

In Rita Mae Brown's 1973 autobiographical novel, *Rubyfruit Jungle*, a spunky lesbian named Molly Bolt has a heated exchange with Polina, a beautiful, Italian, married professor. Tipsy on wine, the older woman ponders why Molly would reject heterosexuality.

"It bores me, Polina," Molly says. "I mean men bore me. If one of them behaves like an adult it's cause for celebration, and even when they do act human, they still aren't as good in bed as women."

"Maybe you haven't met the right man?" Polina says.

"Maybe you haven't met the right woman," Molly replies.

Continuing to drink, Polina pushes her: *What exactly is so different about having sex with women?*

"For one thing, it's more intense," Molly tells her. "It's the difference between a pair of roller skates and a Ferrari." Next to lesbianism, she says, the heterosexual world looks "destructive, diseased, and corroded." Without warning, Molly goes ahead and kisses Polina, who is shocked and appalled.

"Why don't you climb off your sanctified prick," Molly taunts. "You dig it. Anyone with half a vagina left would dig it. Women kissing women is beautiful. And women making love together is dynamite. So why don't you just let yourself go and get into it." Polina, predictably, lets herself go and gets into it, kicking off an affair propelled by Polina's growing lust for Molly.

This kind of scene, a sapphic inversion of the classic "you know you want this" coercion, unfolds more than once in *Rubyfruit Jungle*. From the time she's in sixth grade, irresistible, rough-and-tumble Molly turns out one pretty girl after another, most of whom swear they're not lesbians. To Molly, being gay is a no-brainer, and any woman who actively chooses straightness is a fool.

In this case, art imitated life. By the time the novel came out, Rita Mae Brown had helped ignite a full-on lesbian political movement. Born to an unwed teenage mother and adopted by distant relatives, she had a white, working-class Southern up-bringing. In the mid-sixties, she was effectively blackmailed with the loss of her scholarship to the University of Florida, for some opaque combination of being a lesbian and instigating civil rights actions on campus. Shortly afterward she hitchhiked to New York and started writing for underground newspapers like *Rat*. She also joined the local chapter of NOW in late 1968, though she never felt like she fit in. Rita Mae was twenty-four and still fresh out of Gainesville; these fancy ladies were at least ten years her senior and wore "pretty Emilio Pucci dresses," she recalled in her 1997 memoir. Still, "the act of women gathering in one room to discuss being women in a political context was exciting," even if they complained about men too much. Eventually, Rita Mae worked on NOW–New York's newsletter and was a fixture at meetings.

During one meeting in 1969, she spoke up and came out: "I'm tired of hearing everyone moan about men," she said. "Say something good about women. I'll say something good. I love them. I'm a lesbian."

These days this speech would be unremarkable in a feminist group. But back then, many liberal feminists were openly homophobic. Betty Friedan and other hetero feminists from NOW worried that lesbians were too "butch," too unpalatable to the mainstream, and would hobble the movement's power. Pretty soon, Friedan was declaring NOW's lesbian faction a "lavender menace" and cutting the Daughters of Bilitis, a lesbian civil rights organization, from the list of sponsors of the First Congress to

Unite Women in November 1969. As for Rita Mae, she was pushed out of NOW shortly after her declaration.

She decided to try the radicals downtown instead. She showed up at a few Redstockings meetings but found she had little in common with them either. Though they were "polite" and "took it in stride" when Rita Mae raised the issue of lesbianism as a site of oppression, "they had no intention of considering the reality of a gay woman's life." The presumption that women were heterosexual, and therefore motivated to transform personal relationships with men, was key to the Redstockings' strategy. For Rita Mae, that felt like a lot of wasted energy. She felt she had no choice but to go out and organize other lesbians.

She persuaded a group of lesbians in the Gay Liberation Front to start raising the issue of heterosexism not only in the outside world, but among other feminists. On May 1, 1970, the opening night of the Second Congress to Unite Women, the ragtag group staged their first big action. Before the proceedings started, about forty lesbians stormed the auditorium, many of them wearing light purple T-shirts with LAVENDER MENACE stenciled on the front. The women held the floor for two hours while they explained the realities of being a lesbian in a straight world. The group, who would later call themselves the Radicalesbians, also handed out what would become a formative text of lesbian feminism: "The Woman-Identified Woman."

The paper spent a lot of time dispelling feminists' assumptions about lesbians—that they all want to mimic men, or that experimenting with women was just part of the groovy counterculture, or that being a lesbian is solely about whom you fuck. It reframed lesbianism as not just a private bedroom activity but a political choice, one that allows women to "withdraw emotional and sexual energies from men, and work out various alternatives for those

energies in their own lives." Even more than that, lesbianism offered psychic freedom from the "male-defined response patterns"
ingrained in women. The paper was the first major document of
the women's movement that deemed lesbianism as inseparable from
female liberation. It blended lesbian sexual politics with a broader
sense of community, solidarity, and bonding among women. The
bedrock of this argument was that lesbianism was a holistic, pro-
woman ethos that one could opt into.

In some circles, declaring oneself a lesbian became a prerequisite to feminism, while heterosexuality was a weaker reformist
position. Male supremacy was the fault of not just men but also
women who reaped the privileges of heterosexuality. "Lesbianism
is the key to liberation," Charlotte Bunch, a member of the lesbian
separatist group the Furies, wrote in 1972, "and only women who
cut their ties to male privilege can be trusted to remain serious in
the struggle against male dominance." Radical lesbian Jill Johnston, who reclaimed the term "lesbian chauvinist" from skeptical
straight feminists, wrote in her 1973 polemic *Lesbian Nation* that
male privilege would be eradicated only "through instant revolutionary withdrawal of women from the man or the system," which
she saw to be inextricable.

This separatist hard line didn't resonate with many lesbians of
color, who found it unfair—and besides that, racist—to be made
to ignore their shared oppressions, and therefore solidarity, with
Black and brown men. "We reject the stance of Lesbian separatism
because it is not a viable political analysis or strategy for us," read
the 1977 statement of the Combahee River Collective, a Black
feminist group that included lesbians like Barbara Smith and Audre
Lorde. "As Black women we find any kind of biological determin-
ism a particularly dangerous and reactionary basis upon which to

build a politic." Or, as Chicana lesbian feminist Cherríe Moraga put it in the introduction to the landmark 1981 anthology she edited with Chicana feminist Gloria Anzaldúa, *This Bridge Called My Back*: "The lesbian separatist utopia? No thank you, sisters. I can't prepare myself a revolutionary packet that makes no sense when I leave the white suburbs of Watertown, Massachusetts and take the T-line to Black Roxbury."

Still, many women of color also saw their lesbianism as a full-throated choice, as bigger than just who they slept with, and as a welcome relief from a culture poisoned by deep-seated misogyny. "Being lesbian and raised Catholic, indoctrinated as straight, *I made the choice to be queer* (for some it is genetically inherent)," Anzaldúa wrote. Black poet and activist Cheryl Clarke, who called lesbianism "an act of resistance," framed that identity as an affirmative choice in 1983: "I name myself 'lesbian' because I do not subscribe to predatory/institutionalized heterosexuality. . . . I name myself 'lesbian' because it is part of my vision. I name myself lesbian because being woman-identified has kept me sane." It wasn't an affinity based just on sex, and not even based just on politics, but on self-protection and survival.

Of course, there was a thin line between making space for a positive choice and setting up yet more mandates for moral and political purity. The equation of lesbianism with feminism itself ended up alienating many women who slept with men, sometimes outright banning them from meetings (the Feminists, for example, had quotas of how many married women could be in the group). Bisexual women felt rejected by both sides, not only marginalized in the straight world but also labeled as traitors by lesbians—a double bind that persists to this day. Lesbian activist Sharon Dale Stone, looking back on her separatist days in the seventies, regretted how she dismissed bi women as "unsavory characters who fed on lesbian energy," their orientation "proof of their male identification." Bisexual activists like Lisa Orlando, June Jordan, and Lani Ka'ahumanu pointed out how harmful and discouraging this could be for women who were seeking sexual freedom. "The desire to identify with a community often forces bisexuals to repress a part of themselves," Ka'ahumanu wrote in 1987. "If I kept myself quiet for another's sense of pride and liberation, it was at the cost of my own."

Much of lesbian-feminist theory also rejected butchness and BDSM as "too male," playing into social stereotypes of women's kinder, gentler sexuality. Some lesbians even defined the connection between women as something distinct from sex. Sue Katz, in her influential 1971 essay "Smash Phallic Imperialism," wrote that her "coming out meant an end to sex," which to her meant sex acts with penises. Lesbians, she averred, practice "sensuality" instead. Sex was transactional, exploitative, and "localized in the pants," while sensuality was diffuse, up for interpretation, and not driven by orgasmic goals.

This dubious distinction mirrored the debate around "pornography" versus "erotica" in the anti-porn movement, a faction of radical feminism that focused on the sexual victimization of women and overlapped with lesbianism. The dichotomies of pornography/erotica and male sexuality/female sensuality were invoked by feminist writers all over the map, from Andrea Dworkin to Gloria Steinem to Audre Lorde. The contrast was often framed as so innate, so obvious, that anyone who disagreed was lying to herself: "Every woman here knows in her gut," wrote Robin Morgan in 1978, "that the emphasis on genital sexuality, objectification, promiscuity, emotional noninvolvement, and coarse invulnerability, was the *male style*, and that we, as women, placed greater trust in love, sensuality, humor, tenderness, commitment."

Other women's guts begged to differ. Plenty of lesbians and non-lesbians enjoyed aggressiveness, found traditional gender roles erotic, and loved to play with power dynamics during sex. Many lesbians cared very much about orgasms, not just sensuality. "I am a lesbian," proclaimed feminist writer Dorothy Allison at the 1982 Barnard Conference on Sexuality. "I occasionally do S&M sex; I like anal sex; I like dildoes; I have two silk dresses and very high heels; I do public sex, fuck at night in bars, and come very loudly." In a phone conversation, Cherríe Moraga told me that the distinction between sensual lesbian sex and aggressive hetero sex was "embedded in class privilege" and "made people who wanted to have different kinds of sex feel really, really guilty." Obviously, Moraga said, the women endorsing that dichotomy hadn't spent much time in lesbian bars with women who were there because they "wanted to fuck."

Plus, the idealization of lesbian relationships as "pure as snow, ego-free, and non-profit," as Susan Helenius described them in 1971, raised the eyebrows of lesbians who didn't wish to be placed on a pedestal. To many, the idea of lesbianism as the primary way to fight against misogyny was facile and moralistic, but more to the point, ineffective. Dajenya, a biracial and bisexual writer, reminded all the separatists in her life that not only would this strategy harm the possibility of solidarity, but "both black people *and* lesbians are capable of being quite as oppressive within a relationship as anyone else."

In the age of gender fluidity, strap-ons, and queer Dommes, much of political lesbian writing now comes off as an easy target for anybody who bristles at sanctimony or blanket statements. Designations like "lesbian" and "gay" have since expanded to a whole spectrum of more specific, creative labels we can all choose from that don't necessarily align with particular ideologies. (After reading this chapter, one gay friend of mine remarked, "Well, you're not a lesbian, but you might be heteroflexible!") Yet for all their flaws in hindsight, I couldn't deny how courageous and powerful it was that the radical lesbians pushed beyond grievance toward an actual solution. Many modern queer people who don't sleep with men remain frustrated with women who won't leave men behind. I could only imagine how much worse it was to date men in the pre-feminist sixties, how much more urgent it felt to create a joyful alternative to the dismal sex and dysfunctional relationships about which women constantly, idly complained.

Which is why I kept coming back to *Rubyfruit Jungle*. Despite kicking off what would eventually become political lesbianism—an attempt to distinguish the identity of "lesbian" from simply the act of two women having sex—Rita Mae Brown stands out to me as being one of the earliest Second Wave writers to eroticize the lesbian experience, to portray it not just as a vehicle for solidarity with women and an escape from heterosexuality, but also as an exciting, satisfying way to have sex.

I suspect my mom appreciated *Rubyfruit Jungle*'s horniness, because while she was vehemently opposed to both separatism and prescriptive feminism, it was she who handed me the novel in the first place, when I was fourteen and bored during a weekend upstate with my family. (My mother often preferred to gift me books instead of talk directly to me about thorny topics; she'd done the same thing with Joan Morgan's *When Chickenheads Come Home to Roost*.) The book was the opposite of boring. In fact, it was downright thrilling, laden with lush descriptions of playful, voracious romps and the book's titular term for the vulva: Women are "thick and rich and full of hidden treasures and besides that, they taste good." I didn't quite comprehend everything I read, but it was obvious that Molly Bolt was not running to lesbianism because it was a safe, genital-free haven from men's (or anyone's) advances.

At the same time, the novel upends the fantasy of lesbian relationships as idyllic and conflict-free. Molly's trysts certainly didn't align with Robin Morgan's stereotype of perfect love and perfect trust between women. (Yes that's a quote from *The Craft*; yes I think Nancy was supposed to be bi!) Molly, after all, basically forces Polina to fuck her because she thinks she knows best:

> I was a good five inches shorter than Polina, but that didn't stop me from going over and bodily putting her on my mattress. Before she could double up her soft hands to belt me, I gave her another kiss. And I touched her breast, pressed her thighs, and Polina decided that she didn't know the other side of the story and forty-one years is a long time in the dark. So here she was and how convenient it was too because I had half forced her into it. This way she could avoid responsibility for making love with another woman; the wine helped a lot on that account, too.

This passage makes me cringe every time. It's a reminder that anyone assuming they know more about your desires than you do is ultimately not going to help along your liberation, a fact well-known to the women being pressured by hippie dudes to "put out" at the height of the sexual revolution. And because this seduction scene is designed not only to make a political point but to titillate its presumably female readers, it obliterates the theory of women's "true" fantasies as devoid of aggression.

In other words, *Rubyfruit Jungle* is an illustration of lesbian pleasure rooted not in an idealized fantasy of harmony but in a flawed, messy, lusty, uniquely human reality—one that's at times adversarial and contradictory. When I dug further into lesbian texts of the era as I wrote this book, I found more and more examples of lesbianism that were unapologetically sexual and pleasure-centered and multilayered, not born out of grudging necessity or the moral purity of sacrifice.

These women made compelling cases for lesbianism as a way not just to escape misogyny but to more fully appreciate women's humanity in a way that men have been systematically taught not to. They didn't shy away from the reality of homophobia yet made it clear that lesbianism was worth the trouble. They described relationships that were expansive, full of possibilities, with uncertainty built in. Sometimes, the pleasure these writers described came from the thrill of a scriptless future, a chance to shape a life that doesn't get reduced to the drudgery of the nuclear family. Other times, sex itself—not sensuality—took center stage. In an erotic poem by Cheryl Clarke, she describes "a lesbian adventure one splendid night / of furtive, fixed stars and fully intend- / ing to have you suck my breasts and fuck me / til dawn." The way Cherríe Moraga describes an older lover in her prose poem "The Slow Dance" is striking for both its sexual tension based in power dynamics and its eroticizing of older women: "I want age, knowledge. / Your body that still, after years, withholds and surrenders—keeps me / there, waiting wishing . . . / Willing. Willing to feel *this time* what disrupts in me." In another poem, she craves the "animal hunger" of her lover, watches her "leave and enter me / my eyes, liquid / prey before her hunter."

What they all had in common was the sense of sexual agency, that lesbianism wasn't a purely political default setting but something one explores largely because, well, it feels good. Anybody who declares themselves anything but straight has by definition gone out of their way to think about, accept, and affirm their own desires—and to stop bullying themselves into a life that feels wrong for them. I started thinking of this as an expansion of the "yes means yes" theory of enthusiastic consent; much like a yes should be the bare minimum for having good sex, an emphatic yes should be required for declaring *any* sexuality, whether queer or heterosexual.

In Adrienne Rich's essay on compulsory heterosexuality, she wishes straight people would acknowledge that for women, "heterosexuality may not be a 'preference' at all but something that has had to be imposed, managed, organized, propagandized, and maintained by force." Women, both straight and closeted, who fail to examine their true desires with clear eyes "share the pain of blocked options, broken connections, lost access to self-definition freely and powerfully assumed," Rich writes. Given how much of our sexual preferences are socialized and expected, the only way to know how authentic our sexualities are is to be an active participant. Against the impassioned endorsements of lesbianism, settling into the privilege of automatic, explanation-free heterosexuality seemed passive, even cowardly.

Even my mom, who clearly admired the sexual boldness of *Rubyfruit Jungle* and mined the other layers of her identity until she hit the molten center, had never bothered to delve into her orientation on the page. The only mention I could find is a sentence she wrote in 1969, as she observed the first inklings of lesbian separatism: "My commitment to heterosexual sex is very basic and I want, need love and companionship." What did she mean by "basic"? And how did she know? If she did ever explore sex with women, it received nary a footnote.

It would take me years after Leila's comment to truly contem-

plate what it would mean for me to select my sexual orientation—
to thoughtfully weigh different kinds of happiness and pleasure and
satisfaction. Despite my self-image as a down-for-whatever chick,
despite the considerable amount of hookups I'd had with women,
I hadn't truly ever questioned my heterosexuality. So what would
it look like to affirmatively choose to leave men behind like the
radical lesbians had?

• • •

While radical lesbianism was thriving, there existed a parallel universe of "experimentation" among hippies and swingers that involved sex between two women, often in the context of orgies,
often suggested by men in the spirit of leaving one's "hang-ups" at
the door. At the time, bisexuality wasn't taken seriously as an identity and was instead thought of as a trend, or "bisexual chic," as
some media outlets obnoxiously labeled it. By the nineties, queerness was gaining acceptance and, much like pro-sex feminism, this
period sprouted a palatable uncanny valley of mostly straight
women getting with other mostly straight women in the name of
sexual freedom.

There was a fratty, spring break version of this. While straight
men had very little room to experiment with other men, women
were often encouraged to make out with their friends on dance floors
to appear more carefree and adventurous to the dudes they would
fuck at the after-party. There was also an urbane version. Like white
people searching for "authenticity" by taking pilgrimages to Mississippi's blues towns, dabbling in queer culture promised a kind of ca-
chet, a fleeting intervention into hetero people's normie existence.
Each time a "straight" woman "experiments," it's nearly impossible
to discern her exact reasons, or how genuine they are. She could be

any combination of earnest explorer, performer, and appropriator. Regardless, none of it seems to threaten her heterosexuality.

During my teenhood, the idea of "experimentation" was alive and well. I got the message that any forward-thinking woman hooks up with her female friends, just to try it, and maybe to turn on a guy in the process. My inaugural same-sex kiss was inseparable from the reward of male approval. It was in ninth grade with my best friend, Sarah, who was tagging along on a family vacation. When my parents were asleep, we stole my dad's bottle of vodka from the freezer and got blind drunk. Right before everything fades to black in my memory, there's that kiss: sloppy, giggly, fun but not exactly sexy. The moment wasn't private for long—the instant we returned from the vacation we told Sarah's boyfriend all about it. His arousal was palpable, and we liked it.

Later, in my early twenties, I had a handful of experiences that were not filtered through the fantasies of men, though they weren't exactly my own fantasies either. They were all with self-assured, Molly Bolt–like women who knew what they wanted: me.

Valentina, a lithe Puerto Rican bartender I worked with at a dive bar, was one of these women. One day upon my arrival for my shift, I was greeted with a matter-of-fact advisory from a fellow cocktail waitress: "Val says she's going to fuck you tonight." Um, whoa. I hadn't even realized she slept with women, but I was flattered by her attraction. It was sexy to be pursued like this outside the context of male aggression. The hookup itself was hardly the mid-seventies lesbian stereotype. It was an exciting mélange of ass eating, spanking, and Spanish dirty talk, and also kind of mortifying in an AC-less, late-summer, early-morning way: chests splotchy, bodies awkwardly splayed, my confidence ratcheted down to the newbie energy I had when I was a teen. This encounter with Val was straight-up hot, but an abstract sort of hot. An overall feeling of spontaneity and submissiveness, not *her* or her body, is what most turns me on about the memory.

The rest of my hookups with girls, usually women I knew through friends who would hit on me at a bar or a house party, were . . . fine. None were actively bad or gross or alienating. None were initiated by me. I never felt violated, but I can't say I was a wholly active player in pursuing pleasure. I usually felt a certain level of dissociation during them, as if I were watching myself being devoured from ten feet away. Most of it felt "dimly good," as Molly describes her first sexual encounter with a boy in *Rubyfruit Jungle*, because it's fun to admire and pleasure a pretty body. I didn't have orgasms with any of them, though, and at times I actually struggled to get wet. I suspected that the chief reason I participated in these encounters was ultimately to beef up my own self-image as an intrepid woman whose sexual repertoire was vast.

I didn't doubt my heterosexuality at the time, but later I would wonder: Is it possible that I simply didn't have enough experience? I'd slept with dozens of men; in total, I'd hooked up with just five cis women, half of whom were under twenty-five at the time, and zero people who were trans, nonbinary, or any other gender. In most cases my partners hadn't had much sexual experience with other women either, partly because we were all so young and partly because many lesbians roll their eyes at the idea of hooking up with a mostly straight girl looking to rebel. I'd certainly let myself explore cis men thoroughly and openly in a way that I hadn't explored any other gender. Cringeworthy sexual encounters with them had also not caused me to rethink my sexual orientation.

The next phase of my exploration didn't come until a couple of years after my flirtation with Leila had slow-faded into nonexistence. (She started seriously dating someone and then moved to the Pacific Northwest, both of which put a damper on our standard-issue what u doin tonight? texts to each other.) By this time, around 2018, the era of heteropessimism was in full bloom. In *The New Inquiry*, Asa Seresin defined the phenomenon as "performative disidentification . . . regret, embarrassment, or hopelessness about the straight experience . . . rarely accompanied by the actual abandonment of heterosexuality."

At the same time that powerful men were getting called out for rape, domestic violence, and power abuses, study after study came out showing that queer women were having more orgasms, had more flexible views on monogamy, and were better communicators. I continued to doubt that someone with my values and interest in sexual exploration would fail to tap into their queer side, especially because things between men and women were so plainly bad. So I tried to stretch myself. I watched a bunch of porn featuring all genders; I sexted and flirted with all kinds of people; I had a couple of threesomes with another woman present. None of it made me any queerer. (I did, however, discover my penchant for gay male porn. Unlike most straight porn, it was actually designed for people who love men's bodies.)

Ironically, what made me feel most hetero was the best and most mature hookup with a woman I've ever had. Raye was absolutely gorgeous, tall with pale skin, freckles, and wild curly dark hair. She was smart, breezy, a great communicator, an utter mensch about both sex and non-sex. We were equal partners in pursuit. We went on actual dates. We had sex sober. There was no one to impress but myself. It was lovely, comfortable, and invigorating in the way that making a new friend can be. But even this brief time with Raye, during which I experienced my favorite same-sex hookups, did not produce the same level of desire and arousal I feel for a male body with a biological dick. It wasn't the difference between "roller skates and a Ferrari," as Molly Bolt explained—more like being gifted a Ferrari when you don't have a driver's license, and anyway, you live a block away from the subway.

I had also never felt strong romantic feelings for a woman, which later led me to think hard about what, exactly, romantic feelings *were*. There's that deep and sustained longing I've felt for at least a dozen men throughout my life, all of which included physical attraction. I thought back to my crushes before my pubescent hormones kicked in, crushes that did not entail sexual fantasies, but rather a generalized, slightly painful obsession. This included overthinking everything they did; constantly wondering what they were up to; a heightened awareness of when they were around; a literal butterfly sensation in my stomach; wanting to be physically close to them (though not necessarily touching); marveling at how brilliant or hilarious they were; having a dynamic aesthetic appreciation of physical qualities one cannot see in a photograph, like the way their lips curl when they smile or the exact way strands of hair fall against their face. Even well after puberty, I experienced this kind of not-quite-sexual but nevertheless strong desire for women. I've had crushes on female camp counselors a few years older than me, feeling a mix of envy of and desire for their glossy hair and perky breasts. I've basked in the honeymoon rush of new friendships with women that really feel like mind melds—and far less of an emotional battlefield than playing a male romance exactly right.

As intense as these female crushes could be, they all felt rather separate from the highly recognizable sensation of sexual desire. This all may very well be ingrained, unconscious behavior, so internalized that my vulva and my brain's neurochemicals have learned not to respond to female bodies the same way they respond to cis male bodies. Still, it felt nevertheless deeply, indisputably true. Short of a long-term, concerted effort to get me to love sex with women, I don't know how it couldn't be. I concluded that if I were to stop fucking men, the sexual and romantic element of any relationship would likely have to be secondary at best, absent at worst.

Could I live with that, given all the other benefits of trading in the poison of heterosexual culture for a more imaginative, flexible community that wasn't so bogged down by centuries of misogyny and conflict? I tried to picture it. I could sincerely attempt to re-frame romantic love as an entity separate from sex. I could still fuck cis men sometimes, but partner with someone of a different gender. The idea of one's partner fulfilling every romantic and sexual need is unrealistic anyway, right? I thought about my eight-year relationship with Aaron, and how virtually the entire reason for its demise was that I couldn't stand its lack of both sexual passion and a true romantic bond, even though there were lots of things about it that worked. But through the lens of a lesbian defec-tor, maybe an Aaron-like relationship with a woman wouldn't be doomed if it came with transparent honesty, and without the crushing pressure that we'd fill every little void in each other's emotional and sexual worlds.

It seemed that becoming a lesbian despite having a clear sexual attraction to men would require admitting that heterosexuality is beyond repair, or at least not worth the energy to transform. It's not a ridiculous assertion. Maybe I'd never feel "at home" fucking women. Maybe I'd always wish I could have sex and build a life with men in a way that would be holistically satisfying. But even if you have an ideal stuck in your head, it's not unreasonable to throw up your hands and choose another life, sick of waiting for a political revolution that may never come. Considering the conditions of male-female relations in the seventies and eighties, I can't blame some women for leaving their straight life behind. I wouldn't blame them now, given how much repression, trauma, and even death heterosexuality causes. Even my parents' relationship—my lifelong model of a functional, loving partnership—was marred with inescapable heterosexual traps that had become so much clearer to me as an adult.

Besides, as the radical lesbians pointed out, I wouldn't be just running away from something bad but embracing something good. Perhaps I'd feel respected, supported, and safe in a world that presented straight women with unending obstacles to happiness. I'd have access to the intuitive comfort and openness I've often felt when surrounded by women, a bond based on mutual understanding rather than mystery. I could form relationships devoid of the exhausting negotiation and rejection and remixing of hetero norms. Talking about my feelings has always been so much easier with women; seldom have I gotten the vibe I sometimes get with men I date that I've revealed "too much."

But now I could feel myself slipping on the same unhelpful rose-colored glasses that many lesbians had warned against. Because again, no queer community was free from the consequences of homophobia, both internalized and from the outside world. And seeing the full humanity of queer people meant recognizing their bad qualities too. As Carmen Maria Machado writes in *In the Dream House*, her terrifying memoir of an abusive lesbian relationship: "Some of us are unkind, and some of us are confused and some of us sleep with the wrong people and some of us make bad decisions and some of us are murderers. . . . *Queer* does not equal good or pure or right. It is simply a state of being—one subject to politics, to its own social forces, to larger narratives, to moral complexities of every kind." The fantasy of the "lesbian paradise" is dangerous; the space between it and reality creates extra pain when it's punctured by something like abuse. "All of this fantasy is an act of supreme optimism," Machado writes, "or, if you're feeling less charitable, arrogance." Sure, I could romanticize women's spaces, but that didn't mean I was guaranteed an emotionally safe queer relationship.

Ultimately, it was the denial of my desires that would stand in the way of me giving up on heterosexuality. The compromises I'd have to make sounded not like the joy that Cherríe Moraga and Cheryl Clarke and Rita Mae Brown described, but like a desperate last resort. They sounded no better than a secretly gay person who marries someone of the opposite sex for social acceptance, or a straight woman who marries a rich man she doesn't love because he's rich. Sexual attractions can't be created, but they can be discovered. That, more than "gay is best," appears to be the most useful thing a hetero woman like me could learn from the radical lesbians. Every one of these women had thought affirmatively and deliberately about their desires, deeming them essential to living a satisfying life.

And perhaps I had even more to learn from bisexual women, who commit to their desires despite the risk of both homophobia and the toxicity of hetero relationships, despite the pressure from both queer and straight people to "choose." They *would* genuinely be happy with women, but they still don't subdue their attraction to men. Carol Queen, a bisexual writer and sex educator, writes about how she hung out with a lesbian crowd in the seventies, but also got pleasure from sleeping with and fantasizing about men. "I knew I had lesbian blood," she wrote in the 1991 anthology *Bi Any Other Name*. "So why did I continue to fuck men? For fun, for one thing—for the near effortless heat of it." She worried about "rebelling against the lesbian and gay community's rules," but then she slowly began to own her bisexuality, rejecting the stereotype of indecisiveness: "I make a decision each time I have sex," she wrote. "I choose to honor the purr in my cunt that says, 'Gimme.' I choose the thrill of attraction and the promise of pleasure, the clit, the cock, the fire in the eyes." Her desire, ultimately, won out.

• • •

Throughout the years, I've engaged in tons of identity pessimism. I've pointed out that I'm a New Yorker, not an embarrassing American, or I'm Jewish, so my family never enslaved anybody. I've said similar things to distance myself from my middle-class intellectual roots, my marital status, and, of course, my heterosexuality: *Sure, I like to fuck men, but I get with women here and there. I'm not monogamous. I like to dominate my male partners from time to time.*

These qualifiers, while tempting, wash one's hands of any duty or accountability. They mute the rallying cries of revolution. "To be permanently, preemptively disappointed in heterosexuality is to refuse the possibility of changing straight culture for the better," Seresin wrote. If I really was committed to loving and fucking men, I would have to stop feeling sheepish and inert. That meant taking a little bit of ownership, acknowledging a tiny stake in something larger, a responsibility for making it better.

I didn't fully understand what this commitment could look like until one fall weekend in October 2020, when I started reading Jane Ward's book *The Tragedy of Heterosexuality*. It turns the typical narrative of queer suffering on its head, calling for "renewed investigation" into the assumption that heterosexuality is easier than being queer. The sole focus on the trauma of queerness, she writes, "masks the gendered suffering produced by straight culture, as well as queer sensations of freedom that result from having escaped not homophobia but heterosexual misery."

The book came out in the midst of the pandemic, at the tail end of the supremely stressful 2020 election, and during another moment when I was very turned off by most men. "Am I straight? Do I ever want to have sex with another dude (another person?) again?" I wrote to my journal in melodramatic frustration. "Right now I feel scared, pearl-clutchy, like no guy can strike the balance of sexy but not aggressive, tender but not crushingly boring. I want something but I have absolutely no idea what. How can I know that something is missing but not have the imagination to fill that space with my desire?" And then, the classic complaint: "I'm not queer, but not asexual, but I also profoundly distrust men right now."

Amid all this, a press copy of Jane Ward's book arrived. I eyed it nervously. I was already in a deep shame spiral about how I could never fully access the part of me who might be queer, that my heterosexuality was so indoctrinated that even my vagina's arousal mechanisms had learned it. Did I really have to read a book that would worsen my mood?

At first, yes, the book made me felt like hetero garbage. Chapter after chapter outlined in harrowing detail how broken and bleak straight culture is, how much pain it's caused and yet how little it's challenged by its participants. There's a chapter full of quotes from queer interviewees that are essentially different versions of Leila's God I would hate to be straight text. But then I got to the last chapter, where Ward describes the concept of "deep heterosexuality":

> Deep heterosexuality proclaims: if straight women and men
> are actually attracted to each other, that is excellent. Now let's

expand the notion of heterosexual attraction to include such a powerful longing for the full humanity of women, and for the sexual vulnerability of men, that anything less becomes suspect as authentic heterosexual desire.

Ward says the solution isn't to accept the "tragedy" nor to defect to queerness. Echoing Carmen Maria Machado and other queer theorists, she warns that idealizing queer relationships is counterproductive. Ward also doubts the proposed strategy of queering straight relationships with things like pegging, BDSM, or polyamory. Honestly, I was relieved; I didn't think I could accept anyone telling me what kind of sex act would liberate me, especially if the goal was political purity. As the writer and activist Yasmin Nair put it, "The revolution will not come on the tidal wave of your next multiple orgasm had with your seven partners on the floor of your communal living space."

The solution, Ward writes, is actually to become *more* straight—owning that identity and resolving to enact the best version of it. If heterosexuality weren't considered the default, Ward asks, "how might straight women and men articulate what propels them toward each other, despite all the difficulty?" For men who date and have sex with women, that would mean taking a cue from lesbians (who share their sexual attraction to women) by actually liking and identifying with their female partners. This necessitates being a partner who knows how to recognize and reject the misogyny built into so many hetero relationships. Ward notes that many lesbians observe some men's contempt for women and find it suspicious: *If you're supposedly so straight, why do you seem to care more about impressing other men than the women you purport to desire?*

But, she says, straight women also have work to do. Once

they've affirmed their commitment to being straight, Ward advises them to "not just blindly follow a script, but to find their own unique heterosexual desire." That means being able to articulate the specific reasons they love men and/or are attracted to them.

I arranged a phone date with Ward, nervous she would pity my listless complaints about straightness like Leila had. But she didn't, at least not to my face. Instead, she told me it was refreshing for hetero women to say they were emphatically "in it for the dick." If women love sex with men, "great," Ward said. "You're working from a place of desire." Seresin describes a similar feeling after hearing the writer Larissa Pham on Harron Walker's podcast *Why Do I Like Men?* "Pham does cite reasons why she finds men desirable, such as 'big arms,' 'penis,' and 'the way men smell . . . most men.' . . . For all their obviousness, these observations are quite rarely voiced. Hearing them spoken so plainly exposes how heteropessimism has worked to silence articulations of women's desire."

Harron Walker, a trans woman who used to identify as a gay man, initially had a different question than her podcast's title. It was the same question the radical lesbians asked, and the same question I'd been asking myself: How can I stop liking men? "No matter how many times a man ghosted me, disposed of me, casually crossed my boundaries, or treated me however he wanted, I would still come back for more," she wrote in *W* magazine. "It confused me, how I could change something as seemingly fixed as my gender if for no other reason than the fact that it caused me pain, yet there I was, powerless to change my desire no matter how painful I found its consequences." She decided that asking *why* she desired men was perhaps a more productive line of inquiry.

I similarly realized that I'd spent a huge amount of time figuring out why I wasn't a lesbian, but not all that much time thinking about Walker's titular question, why I loved and lusted after men in particular. So I made my own list, which included rather specific items like "narrow, smaller bodies with dicks," "cum: looking at it, tasting it, watching it spurt out," "spooning a cute, muscular, hairy butt," "the aching desire an erection exposes." Once I saw it all written down, it occurred to me that my "deep heterosexuality" had already been in process for a long time.

Until a few years ago, I had almost exclusively been attracted to tall men. They made me feel small and protected, exactly how our culture tells us a male partner is "supposed" to make us feel. Men who were my height or below seemed desexualized or effeminate to me. The first thing that had drawn me to Aaron all those years ago was his towering height.

Then, gradually, I started sleeping with shorter men I found hot not despite but because of their stature. There was Mor and his pint-size, tanned torso. There was Rob's authoritative energy despite his modest height and delicate bone structure. There was a one-night stand I had in DC a few years back with a petite guy named Josh. The beauty of his tiny waist and broad shoulders eluded me at the time but had made some surprise appearances in my fantasies lately. My limited standards of the past had faded so much that I now *preferred* a man of a similar height who could easily switch roles, who could cuddle me or be cuddled, who could make me feel small or big depending on the mood, who welcomed the chance to submit and be nurtured.

The romantic and emotional aspects of my attraction with men were harder to explain, but they weren't any less profound. At first I thought I might be hetero in the traditional sense: attracted to difference and unknowability. But Ward challenges this idea, explaining that for some radical queers, identification fosters eroticism. It has for me too. My love for a man has at times grown out of similarity: a movie that made us both cry, an inside joke we both find hilarious, the loss of a parent breeding deep mutual empathy. My bond with Mor wasn't just physical; it also involved the act of overthinking, a distinctly Jewish quality we shared.

Finally, after turning it over and over in my mind, I sort of understood what my mother meant by her "basic" love for men. I decided that perhaps the answer to why I loved the men I loved was too intrinsic, too elemental, to break down. And that, ultimately, I didn't owe anyone an explanation—another lesson I've gleaned from queer friends who refuse to back up the authenticity of their sexual identity with data points. Once a desire has been consciously determined, the reasons start to seem less important. As Walker concluded, after all her interrogation: "Who cares? I like men, and that's that."

Still, it was a treat to slow down and recall these sweet moments of my heterosexual life, hard-earned yet primordial, outside the context of rubbing one out or regaling a friend with a sex story. For the time being, the practice of loving men didn't seem like surrender. It wasn't embarrassing or doomed, inherently "tragic" or toxic. I had an urge to go back to the day I received Leila's text, to reply that she didn't have to feel sorry for me, because I'd learned the same thing about myself as she did the day she abandoned dick, as bisexual women do when they refuse to "repress a part of themselves," as anybody does when they affirmatively express what they want. The tragedy isn't heterosexuality, I wanted to tell her, but giving up on one's desires—or never uncovering them at all.

8. The Fallow Period

Sex is the refuge of the mindless.

—VALERIE SOLANAS, *SCUM MANIFESTO*

It was the sort of excuse I'd used before, when I wasn't brave enough to straight-up reject someone I wasn't into. When I'd heard it from others, I knew to take it as a tactful letdown. In April 2017, I texted it to Dom, the crinkly-smile guy who'd sent the sweet Hail Mary message while I was watching the drag show in the Rio Grande Valley bar. This time, though, it wasn't an excuse. It was actually true.

I'm taking stock and not really dating, I wrote. Like at all. I feel like I need to "do me," as they say.

Not long after I got back from Texas, my ability to fuck simply shorted out. I couldn't do it. I canceled on sex dates. I ignored u up? texts. I used masturbation more as a sleep aid than a sexual release. Even so much as peeking at the apps made me sick. Not only did I not seek out sex, but I also just didn't feel horny. I didn't develop new crushes; I didn't stalk people's social media feeds; I didn't fantasize about anyone who passed me on the street. I'd gone cold turkey and was not even fighting against the pull of withdrawal.

The first thing I noticed was how much time I had on my hands—and how much better I managed that time. The political moment was demanding a lot from me. We were just a few months into a presidential administration that hoovered up all my energy and poured it into my job editing features for a leftist website. Suddenly I was writing more and became a fountain of assignment ideas. Instead of late-night booty calls, I was actually showing up to protests and organizing meetings. I was more clearheaded during tax season, when I was tasked with tallying up my dad's sprawling web of medical deductions. Also, I finally remembered that my friends needed me to listen to *their* problems, not just hear mine.

My mood was also so much more even-keeled: no nervousness before a date, no flood of chemicals during a date, no sleep deprivation and overthinking after a date. No getting distracted and flustered by midday sexts, no heart sink from being left on read, no need to fend off random attempts at boundary crossing. After the extended tizzy of the last few months, my personal life was muted, less exciting.

It was a relief, and it also freaked me the fuck out. The memory of my sexual frustration during my marriage was still fresh. The scarcity of those years put me in a state of years-long permahorniness, and I couldn't have imagined forgoing sex (or at least good sex) voluntarily. I'd also had a sex-free few months during my freshman year in college, which felt very much against my will. "This is the time when everyone gets the most ass of their life," I pouted to my journal. "Not me. I haven't had a dry spell like this since, well, never. I feel completely undesirable, bored, ugly, and like I have no game. Not to mention COMPLETELY and

TOTALLY sexually frustrated. Seriously, that area has not been stimulated in quite some time. I could cry. What the hell is wrong with me??"

This more recent sexless period felt different, like a part of my identity was slipping away. I had just learned so much about myself through fucking, by thinking and talking and writing about it. I'd turned my whole life upside down largely because I'd determined that sexual pleasure was a gigantic priority of mine. Now that portal of self-discovery appeared to be closed. I knew— well, hoped—it wasn't permanent, but how could something that seemed so crucial to me just a few months ago feel not only useless but even . . . silly? If I wasn't the woman who had lots of sex, who even was I?

. . .

In the summer of 1968, Dana Densmore, a systems programmer at MIT working on the *Apollo* missions who was eager to join the feminist revolution, decided to attend a free workshop in Boston. The topic was Valerie Solanas's *SCUM Manifesto*, run by an anti-war activist named Roxanne Dunbar. Solanas had just shot Andy Warhol, and her polemic had spread through the radical feminist underground like wildfire. Solanas's ferocious, witty, nasty misandry struck Dana as "perfectly exhilarating." The other women who came to the workshop seemed perturbed by what they saw as "paranoid rantings"; to Dana, "anything less would have seemed an underestimation of the problem." Among many other declarations, Solanas had denounced sex: if a woman could "condition away her sex drive," she'd be left "completely cool and cerebral and free to pursue truly worthy relationships and activities." By the time the workshop was over, Dana and Roxanne were on their way to plotting a revolution and shortly afterward formed their own militant group called Cell 16.

The next month, the two of them met eighteen other feminists from around the country for several days in Sandy Spring, Maryland. In historian Alice Echols's recounting of the conference, much is made of Roxanne's insistence that the *SCUM Manifesto* was "the essence of feminism," but Dana remembers another dynamic that got under her skin. She kept hearing women describe awful, toxic, sometimes abusive relationships with men. The women's reasons for not leaving? "We need sex." If they didn't get it, they'd "dry up inside." Dana's suggestion—"rather mild, so it seemed to us"—was that autonomy was more important than sex. That suggestion was met with shock and anger.

When Roxanne and Dana returned to Boston, they got to work on Cell 16's first issue of their journal, appropriately titled *No More Fun and Games*. The issue included Dana Densmore's now classic piece on celibacy, where she refuted this supposed "need" for sex: "Some people go through their whole lives without engaging in it at all, including fine, warm, happy people. It is a myth that this makes one bitter, shriveled up, twisted. The big stigma of life-long virginity is on women anyway, created by men because woman's purpose in life is biological and if she doesn't fulfill that she's warped and unnatural and 'must be all cobwebs inside.'"

Not only was sex "a minor need" that was "inconvenient, time-consuming, energy-draining and irrelevant"; it was also anathema to effective political energy. "The guerrillas"—the real revolutionaries—"don't screw," she declared. "They have important things to do, things that require all their energy. . . . Erotic energy is just life energy and is quickly worked off if you are doing interesting, absorbing things."

The piece is a cousin of radical lesbianism, in that it was a stark rejection of women's dependency on men. But in another essay in the same journal, Dana comes for gay sex too: "Homosexuals are usually at least as obsessed with sex as the rest of society," she wrote. "So much wasted energy! So much emotional turmoil, anxiety, jealousy, plotting and dreaming to distract and cloud the rational faculties!" For any gender, of any orientation, sexual desire often just masks other desires, like the "need for attention, affection, ego gratification, security, self-expression, to win a man or conquer a woman, to prove something to somebody." In a sentence that could be confused with a Buddhist monk's (or perhaps a wellness enthusiast's Instagram caption), she wrote, "Happy, free, self-confident people exist more in their minds and imagination, often forgetting about their bodies, feeling at one with them, but not dictated to by them."

In the same issue of *No More Fun and Games*, in a piece called "Asexuality," Roxanne Dunbar similarly praised the mind-clearing, monastic properties of rejecting sex completely: "The person who has been through the whole sex-scene, and then becomes, by choice and revulsion, a celibate, is the most lucid person." The lucidity isn't in service of religious enlightenment or even moral superiority, but rather a "women's revolution." Nowadays, the identity of "asexuality" is understood as an innate lack of sexual attraction, not a defiant reaction to toxicity. Back then, though, "asexuality" was Dunbar's term for conscientious objection.

Some feminists even flirted with the use of sex strikes for achieving political goals—distinct from touting the benefits of celibacy in that sex, in this case, was not merely an inconvenience but a weapon. Sex strikes had been employed globally as protest for centuries, but seldom had the punishment so perfectly fit the crime. Journalist and activist Judith Levine, recalling a Lysistratan policy her women's liberation group adapted circa 1971, wrote that if any man they knew "committed a crime of piggishness against women, he would lose his privileges. Until he reformed, his wife, girlfriend, or any member of Women's Liberation would refuse to have sex with him."

Sex itself wasn't the only thing standing in the way of said revolution. Around the same time, radical feminists attacked the disruptive nature of love and infatuation too—a characterization that was hundreds of years old. By the late sixties, it wasn't even new to feminism: Twenty years earlier, Simone de Beauvoir posed the possibility that one day "it will be possible for woman to love not in her weakness but in her strength, not to escape herself but to find herself." But until that day comes, love will take the form of a "curse that lies heavily upon woman confined in the feminine universe, woman mutilated, insufficient unto herself."

Despite these precedents, it was a particular sect of American radical feminists who declared that love was actually a roadblock to a successful revolution. Ti-Grace Atkinson positioned romance as the enemy of independence and fortitude. "What is love but the payoff for the consent to oppression?" she declared in 1968. "What is love but need? What is love but fear? In a just society would we need love?" Others reasoned that until conditions improved, heterosexual love was too tied to marriage and societal expectations of what it meant to be feminine. Shulamith Firestone characterized romance as "a cultural tool of male power to keep women from knowing their conditions" in the *Dialectic of Sex*. "Love is being psychically wide-open to another. It is a situation of total emotional vulnerability"—which isn't "inherently destructive" among two equals, but dangerous under the circumstances of patriarchy. After all, she writes, "whoever heard of logic in the bedroom?"

Even women who weren't militant feminists admitted that sex could be an unwelcome irritant that clouded their ability to feel stable and successful. "I think sex is a damned nuisance," said one respondent in Shere Hite's 1976 national study of female sexuality. "For a few weeks of 'rapture' a lot of us suffer and often go weeks of agony with someone we don't get on with, all because of some kind of passion we felt."

In the same study, some women mentioned that celibacy could feel actively good, because "I'm not dependent on anyone for anything," because it "gave me time to turn my life around—a beautiful and peaceful time," because it "leaves you remarkably clear about what you really want, and from whom," because "I feel I am in total control of my body and my life." Celibacy, one woman said, could be "the fallow period before new things can grow."

• • •

When I first read the work of the political celibates during my own fallow period, it filled me with the same kind of shivery jolt that Dana Densmore might have felt in Valerie Solanas's *SCUM Manifesto* workshop in Boston. Their work was way, *way* out there. They couldn't give less of a fuck about seeming sexy. Political celibacy flew in the face of everything I'd been taught. It called into question my deeply held beliefs about the centrality of pleasure and connection.

I didn't trust this horniness ebb at first, and I also didn't like it. But as I got used to it, I could see that though pleasure seeking had been a way to steer my own life, that didn't mean a sex pause erased that pleasure or made me a traitor to the cause. My indifference to sex started to feel like nothing less than rebellion, not only from the relentlessly sexual you-go-girl nineties but from my mother too.

Though my mom often expressed admiration for overtly

sexual celebrities, like Madonna and Courtney Love, I didn't get the message from her growing up that a constant high sex drive was required. The whole twenty-two years I knew her, I never heard her praise or criticize another person's sex life, including mine. But in 2015, I learned she subjected herself to mandates she would never dream of putting on others. That year, my mom's ex-boyfriend, Bob, wrote a memoir about his early life as a downtown bohemian wherein my mother is prominently featured. The book revealed that after her first marriage to Henry, a relationship that left her feeling unloved and bottled up, my mom decided upon compulsory sex as the solution. "She proposed a rule we stuck by for three and a half years—that neither of us could ever deny sex to the other," he wrote.

Bob put in that detail, I guess, to illustrate her voraciousness and/or her commitment to a transcendent sexual politics? But when I reread that sentence during my period of no sex, I winced. It sounded simplistic and immature, with more than a tinge of gym teacher voice. I thought, *Wow, Mom, way to bury yourself under pressure!*

Granted, my mother *was* in her mid-twenties and in the middle of a radical transformation coming out of an enormously repressive era. I'd be surprised if she stuck with this sex-no-matter-what rule after the flush of revolution wore off. In fact, in a letter she wrote while she and Bob were breaking up, she criticized his tendency toward "compulsive lovemaking when things are going wrong," remarking, "There are times when what's needed is a rest from sex." Still, even the existence of such a policy seemed like an incredibly risky move in a relationship. I doubt it would have produced anything but resentment in me during a libido-less period like the one I was experiencing.

My mom wrote in 1979 that "sexual love in its most passionate sense is as basic to happiness as food is to life," and that the independence lost by love—"surrendering detachment and control, giving our lovers the power to hurt us by withdrawing their love, leaving, or wanting someone else"—is worth what we gain. She, like most pro-sex feminists, considered political celibacy cutting off your nose to spite your face, grouping the celibates in with the "Neo-Victorian" lesbian separatists. To her, it was way too soon to be reclaiming something like celibacy, which was tightly tied to oppressive misogynist religions.

At the same time, it put the movement at risk of ceding the transformative gains of the sexual revolution for the sake of political purity. My mother didn't call for sex strikes, but she did see "men's need for sexual love from women" as "our biggest weapon in both individual and collective struggle—and that our own need for *satisfying* sexual love from men was our greatest incentive for maintaining the kind of personal confrontation feminism required." Like defecting to lesbianism, she thought a hetero woman declaring celibacy was giving up not only on personal happiness, but on the movement itself.

To me, with the benefit of hindsight, the biggest obstacle to political celibacy wasn't the theory behind it—some of it made a lot of sense—but rather the logistics. I had a hunch there was no way anybody stuck to that lifestyle. My assumption was confirmed years later when I started writing this book and delved into the personal lives of the radicals who denounced, or at the very least de-emphasized, the importance of sex and love. I dredged up an email conversation I had with Rosalyn Baxandall in 2012 while I was fact-checking a eulogy I'd written for Shulamith Firestone. When I asked if Firestone was actually celibate, Baxandall replied that, on the contrary, she remembered her as "boy crazy." Judith Levine admitted that, faced with a sex strike, "our troops couldn't quite muster the discipline." And in a phone call with Dana Densmore, she rather crankily informed me I'd taken her piece too literally: "There wasn't anyone in Cell 16 that was celibate," she said. "All of us were, at times, between relationships, and we could see that relationships are positive." At the height of her involvement in Cell 16, Dana was dating "a lovely man who I think is wonderful."

That's not to say these women were hypocrites; I can understand the difference between theoretical polemic and autobiography. But the fact that so few people could commit to celibacy on principle, even the ones touting its merits, shows that, in the words of early radical feminist Amy Kesselman, "you have to promise people a better life, not a narrower life." Celibacy, like lesbianism, could be presented as an alternative but not a decree on its own. That 2017 spring, I was authentically feeling a sense of clarity and freedom from avoiding the maelstrom of sex, but I would never have tried celibacy in the name of feminism, or the #resistance, or anything else if my sexual urges hadn't naturally fallen off a cliff after Texas.

Half a century after "On Celibacy," the more useful way to view it is not as a prescription, but as an antidote to a society where sexuality is deemed essential to a fulfilling life. Part of the reason Dana was annoyed with me, in fact, was because I'd missed what she considered the most important sentence of her essay: "This is a call not for celibacy," it reads, "but for an acceptance of celibacy as an honorable alternative, one preferable to the degradation of most male-female sexual relationships." Sex "should be something you have if it's bringing joy into your life," Dana clarified on the phone.

But conditions were "really bad in 1968. It felt like life and death. The sexual revolution had happened, but feminism hadn't, so it felt really desperate for some women. There was a lot of pain. That's why it felt important to tell women they could walk away from bad relationships."

Perhaps I missed her "honorable alternative" sentence because I'm conditioned to be skeptical of women who insist feminism is simply about "choice." It could also be because it's the *one* nuanced sentence in an essay that's overflowing with barn-burner sentences. Or maybe I missed it because, by the time of our 2020 phone call, it already felt familiar. The extreme poles of the repressive fifties and the porny aughts—frustrating for people who didn't fit into mainstream norms, and doubly frustrating for feminists who didn't fit into feminist norms—had started to loosen.

Both the sexual revolution and Girls Gone Wild feminism had the side effect of alienating not only people who preferred emotion with their sex, but also people who weren't interested in sex at all, temporarily or ever. *The Hite Report* quoted lots of women who felt that they "should" be sexual to keep up with the times, even though they had different things on their mind. "I feel a heavy social pressure to have lots of sex, but sex is something I do not have time for now, as building my career takes all of my energy," wrote one. "I guess I'm not as interested in sex as I should be." Some people were simply sick of its exaggerated importance. One woman quoted in the report complained, "We are taught that every little twinge is a big sex urge and we must attend to it or we'll be an old maid. I'm getting sick to death of sexuality—everywhere sex sex sex! So what? Sex is not the end all and be all of life. It's very nice but it's not everything!"

In the last few years, journalists have expressed concern that young people are having too *little* sex. In 2018, Kate Julian wrote of the "sex recession" in *The Atlantic*, citing stats on how teens are having sex later, and young adults are on track to have fewer sex partners than previous generations. The experts and young adults she spoke with pointed to lots of reasons for this downturn: skyrocketing anxiety, the alienation of modern life, internet porn, increased screen time. But she glosses over the one reason I felt in my bones those celibate months, a reason my mother might have felt less equipped to take advantage of: people, especially women, may now feel more empowered to shrug at sex they won't enjoy, or turn down romantic partners they don't feel strongly about.

Even when you'd rather not be celibate, refusing to accept what men are offering can be a way for women who have sex with men to harness agency in a world that insists you *must* have sex to maintain dignity. There are online communities of women who identify as *femcels*, describing themselves as unable to have sexual or romantic relationships as a result of a toxic blend of misogyny and impossible beauty standards. The label itself is a female take on the male *incel* (a portmanteau of "involuntary celibate"). Incels often claim on forum threads that femcels don't exist. All women, they say, have a choice about whether or not to be sexually active; if they aren't, they're just being too picky.

Most femcels acknowledge that they probably *could* find a man to have sex with, but that sleeping with men who disrespect them, abuse them, or are ashamed of them makes this "choice" akin to choosing between starving and eating poisoned food. As someone with the username Feelinveryblue put it on a femcel site called ThePinkPill: "A woman can get sex if she has next to no standards, doesn't care about whether or not she has an orgasm, and doesn't mind being used as a human fleshlight."

Most women would probably not identify as femcels, but they might relate to the frustrating expectation that they should prefer awful sex to no sex at all. Most women are quite aware that men often express their aggression, power, or contempt for women—especially those deemed "undesirable"—through sex. Black feminist writer Brittney Cooper has written about the rawness of feeling invisible, seemingly punished for having standards while at the same time being the subject of others' narrow views of sexuality. "Recognition is a human need, and there is something fundamentally violent about a world that denies Black women recognition on a regular basis," she writes in her book *Eloquent Rage*.

I think also of my friend Samhita, who told me recently that women like her—fat women of color in their forties—"stand outside the gaze of heterosexuality." After a string of degrading experiences with dudes, she told me that she "looked around and was like, *What the fuck am I doing?*" She was killing it professionally, which made her unfulfilling dating life appear even more unacceptable in comparison. She could no longer bear to sleep with people who refused to see her full humanity.

So Samhita got off the apps. She cut off her existing entanglements. Her period of celibacy has lasted more than two years. There are moments when she wonders whether she's preempting rejection—"I make assumptions about people, so I take myself out of the running," she told me. But for the time being, declining to participate feels better than accepting less than she feels she deserves. "I refuse to subject myself to it," she said, "because I know I'm devalued inherently."

The cultural conversation around abstaining has noticeably ripened since my fallow period of 2017, but that doesn't mean my spikes of self-doubt disappeared. When my libido plummeted again during the height of the pandemic, I went through an echo of the same identity crisis—this time while writing this very chapter. "I'm a fucking fraud and should not be writing a book about sexuality," I declared in my journal, in a moment of "way harsh, Tai" self-censure. "It doesn't mean anything to me anymore. . . . Maybe there are real limits to what sex can accomplish and how it figures into happiness. Maybe its power is illusory, cruel, built to be self-defeating. Like, tricked ya! I feel so foolish."

Angela Chen's book about asexuality, *Ace*, came out just as I was on this emotional roller coaster. She tells of the pressure she felt to have loveless sex in her twenties, even though she'd never felt sexual attraction. She wanted "to be modern instead of old-fashioned, a good feminist who lived out my beliefs, and to not be repressed." The sexually repressed woman, she writes, "is embarrassing."

Ultimately, Chen's realization that she had the neutral identity of "asexual" was an act of self-kindness. When she embraces the identity of asexuality (a community that has just started to gain visibility in the last few years), she understands that "not having a super-exciting sex life does not make one a political failure. . . . Stop assuming that sexual behavior must be linked to political belief or that horniness is an interesting personality trait. That's closer to what I mean by real choice." It was what I needed to hear at that moment. I knew I'd be pursuing sex only so I could somehow cling to a static identity of "sexpot." My sexual freedom, let alone my individual appeal as a person, didn't always mean having as much sex as possible. In fact, it was *more* liberating to accept these natural dips and embrace how the contours of our desires, or lack thereof, can still surprise us.

• • •

Throughout my sex pause, most of the guys I'd been seeing fell off the map. But for some reason, I kept texting Dom, even after I told him sex was not an option.

He was six years younger than me, a New Jersey native who was in business school and went to church every Sunday. Not exactly the guy I'd go for on paper. Still, I liked texting back and forth with him. He was friendly, thoughtful, and a great conversationalist. We weren't dating or fucking, but the vibe was not platonic. It wasn't even devoid of sex; we delved into the topic in a studied way. We told hookup war stories, asked each other for tips on our dating profiles, and traded links of good Tumblr porn. Gradually, imperceptibly, a crush developed.

On one of the last nights in May, my interest in sex came rushing back. Our texting seamlessly evolved into sexting. As I looked at flashes of this man's slender body and listened to audios of his muffled moans, I felt sexual desire for the first time in months. Along with that familiar squirmy warmth, relief coursed through my body. I was grateful that neither he nor I had pushed it; no one was tapping their feet waiting for my libido to hurry up and come back. It had returned on its own, just as vivid as ever. One thing now seemed certain: at some point, some way, Dom and I were going to have sex.

9. Fire Needs Air

Yes, love is free; it can dwell in no other atmosphere.

—EMMA GOLDMAN ON THE STUMP

Your promiscuity tears my very vitals, fills me with gall and horror and twists my whole being into something foreign to myself.

—EMMA GOLDMAN IN A LETTER TO HER LOVER BEN REITMAN

In June 2017, I left to go on another weeks-long road trip to recruit writers, this time through the Rust Belt. Dom and I texted every couple of days, bouncing between media-heavy sexts and riffs on topics like religion, the fallacy of "Real America," the temptation of molly, and Youngstown's cringey dating scene. He seemed too dorky and normie for me with his Christianity, his apparent sympathy for capitalism, and his conventional clean-cut good looks. Still, I was intrigued. I also loved his naked body, or at least what I saw in pictures and videos. By the end of the trip, we agreed that an in-person meet-up was in order. I didn't want a Mor redo, so I asked him: *Think we can keep a happy medium between staying too chill and getting carried away?*

He gave me the only answer a question like that deserves: I think I could, but I don't 100% know.

It was suddenly summer, atmospheric and sticky, perfect for

outdoor movies and barbecues and bike rides through the park. We did all that. But what I remember most about that time is spending hours and hours in Dom's air-conditioned bedroom in Ridgewood, Queens, fucking, laughing, and pillow-talking—sexually, it *was* kind of a Mor redo, but without the drama or dishonesty. I gushed about it all to my friends: about his great dick, his endless energy in bed, how he "drowns me in oxytocin." We probably won't get serious, I told them, but I sure do like to have sex with him.

As I got to know him I realized he was not a normie at all, but actually one of the most unusual people I'd ever met. Yes, he was getting his MBA but also was . . . a democratic socialist? He was proudly half-Jewish and raised secular, but had recently started going to a hipster church in Williamsburg, but also thought the Bible was bullshit, but also truly felt *Christian* and not just "spiritual." He was totally straight passing but talked openly about his hookups with dudes and, unlike many cis men, was equally open about his experiences with trans women. The pieces of his life that had given me pause started to seem like not only nonfactors, but ripe topics for debate—which was fun, because he was less dogmatic than me and asked lots of questions. I even started to look past his square jaw and notice his wackier physical features like his rubbery, expressive cheeks; his mischievous brown eyes; his duck-like walk. Much to my relief, the guy was a fucking weirdo.

Dom and I began to acknowledge our mutual crush. I think you legit have ruined hummus for me, I texted him shortly after he declared the spread nothing more than "salty mud."

Well you ruined other women for me so we're even I guess? he replied.

One August morning, when he left early for his internship after two rounds of wakeup sex, I took my time getting ready, my eyes lingering on the toiletries atop his dresser. I saw a stack of yellow Post-its and suddenly felt compelled to put my surging affection into note form. "Fuck the happy medium. I can't get enough of you," I wrote. My cheeks burned as I wedged the Post-it under his pillow. I'd written tons of love notes, but they mostly lived in my personal records. I'd seldom actually *given* them to people. I'm with you, he texted me a few hours later. I can't be moderate either.

The day after that note, a white supremacist killed Heather Heyer in Charlottesville, Virginia. The news site I worked for happened to have sent a reporter to cover the rally, so I spent that Saturday afternoon frantically communicating with the writer and photographer while we pieced together the breaking news. In between, Dom and I engaged in an electric text exchange about everything that was going down. Our connection was so immediate, so raw. During a date later that night, we couldn't stop swooning and making out in public. Afterward, we had baroque, drunken role-play sex, then rolled around cuddling for hours.

It was the opposite of the lonely night after the Dallas police shooting the summer before, when I craved connection with Aaron but instead received the clarity I needed to end things. This time, I felt like I'd found someone who could provide equal parts comfort, insight, and exquisite escape amid the chaos of the world. When he said "I love you" that night, I barely let him finish before I said the same.

I couldn't believe this was happening. *How was I falling in love less than a year after my marriage ended?* Breaking up with Aaron had required making peace with the possibility that I might be single forever. I needed to see that state as more appealing than staying in a relationship that made me unhappy. Of course I wished for love, but it seemed like a far-off possibility, certainly not something I could count on. "I still have the hope that I'll find what my mom did," I wrote a month after I moved out, "even if it's later in life like she did. Even if it's after I'm able to have children."

Yet here I was, nine months later, one half of this daunting, bottomless, unexpected love story. I had episodes of self-doubt, unsure whether my feelings were real, because how could they be? This relationship was fitting together, and things never fit together! There would soon be hard parts, but falling in love was not one of them.

We started saying outlandish things to each other, wildly committal things that I'm mortified to write down. Things like, "It's all you," "This is it," "You're my person," "I never want this to end." From the hummus comment on down, they were all couched in the classic only-have-eyes-for-you mold—partly because that's how we genuinely felt, and partly because that's the vocabulary we all have for the extremely strong limerence phase of love. My mind swelled with so many thoughts of him, both romantic and sexual, that I couldn't imagine fitting in anyone else. We'd discussed my history with open relationships in a levelheaded way during our courtship, but then delighted in how our mutual obsession seemed to overtake those questions. **Love doesn't care what we believe about monogamy, it's asserting itself,** he texted me. **But also it's not necessarily true that our love will be any less the moment one of us does want to fuck someone else,** I texted back.

I hoped I believed that but was also pleased with this spontaneous devotion. We were free to fuck others, yet didn't want to. It felt sweet, organic, and romantic, yet dangerous too. Why was I taking comfort in this traditional barometer of whether someone loved me? Even after all the mistakes I made with Aaron's and my nonmonogamy, I still believed that it was immoral—and besides that, ineffective—to try to control someone else's desires. So why did I feel like I'd won something?

Dom had never been in an open relationship himself, but the last few people he'd casually dated seemed a lot less attached to the idea of monogamy. And he'd seen firsthand with ex-girlfriends how possessiveness and jealousy could erode a relationship. At twenty-seven, he knew he wasn't done with his sexual or romantic exploration. I'd been single for less than a year between him and Aaron. That September, I'd moved into my own apartment for the first time, an ultradreamy prewar studio in Clinton Hill, Brooklyn. So even in the fog of all-consuming love, we promised each other that, despite our current feelings, we'd never feel obligated to be monogamous out of principle. I meant it, but I also knew the true test hadn't come yet.

● ● ●

I hadn't always been so suspicious of monogamy. For the first decade of my romantic life, I hung on to the idea that a pledge of exclusivity was the ultimate grand gesture. I didn't accept any of my relationships as "real" unless I got that pledge. In a kiss-off email to a guy I was seeing unexclusively right after college, I wrote: "If this will EVER work out, it has to be without you fucking other people and me not wondering when you're doing it and why I'm not enough for you." Then, in the second half of my twenties, I absorbed more complex messages in bits and pieces. I learned about the term "monogamish" from reading Dan Savage's column in *The Stranger*, and I read Laura Kipnis's polemic *Against Love*, which framed fidelity as something naive, fruitless, and self-defeating. I also observed that most of my gay friends had much more flexible policies with the people they were seeing.

Even though I was convinced that having sex with one person forever was probably unrealistic, the allure of "exclusivity" endured. It was a combination of osmosis from the prevailing culture and a result of inconsiderate college-age men, none of whom actually knew the basics of ethical nonmonogamy. My desire for it wasn't related to the far-reaching devotion of marriage. To me, in the context of serial dating, it seemed like the easiest way to affirm, *Yes, I like you the best.* That's what was on my mind that night in 2008 with Aaron at the techno club and the lychee martinis, when I blubbered that it was either me and only me or we had to end it. His acquiescence only served to reinforce the idea that this type of commitment was the ultimate heterosexual prize, the most powerful booster of self-worth.

Two years later, however, I was the one suggesting that Aaron and I open things up. Since I didn't really have nonmonogamous friends at the time, I went on a polyamory reading spree instead. I started with books about the sixties counterculture, which had repurposed the term "free love" from the sex radicals of the nineteenth century. People experimented with all forms of nonmonogamy, from the more conservative and emotionally detached swingers to the love-focused, all-in group marriages like the one portrayed by writer Robert Rimmer in his bestselling 1966 novel, *The Harrad Experiment.* Open relationships became a fascination among scholars and psychologists, spawning a cottage industry of manuals seemingly all written by straight couples—books like *Open Marriage* by Nena and George O'Neill, *Group Marriage* by Larry and Joan Constantine, and *Beyond Monogamy* by James and Lynn Smith.

I wasn't surprised to learn that much of the hetero free love movement was—like the sexual revolution in general—practiced through a distinctly male lens, and there were double standards for men and women. Feminists often criticized this 1960s male iteration of free love. In 1971, radical feminist Barbara Leon called the "male supremacist attack on monogamy" nothing more than "emotional abandonment by men," echoing some of the complaints about modern dating. "'Smashing monogamy' is nothing new for men," she wrote. "They have been doing it for centuries. . . . What is new however, is its elevation to the level of an ideology." Even my mother revealed herself to be skeptical of the project in a 1972 opinion piece about marriage, because sexism was still rampant in relationships. "Until there is genuine equality between the sexes," she wrote, "'open marriage' can be nothing but a cotton candy slogan."

But my mom also took issue with the premise that women were more innately drawn to monogamy. Most women in consciousness-raising sessions seemed to prefer it over open relationships, but feminists were divided about what it all meant: Did it reflect "these women's true desires, their objective interest given a sexist culture, or the psychology of the oppressed"? What about the minority who *didn't* prefer monogamy—was it "the difference in their situation or their emotional makeup, did they have false consciousness, or what"? It was clear that my mother believed you couldn't judge things like fidelity or jealousy outside societal context, especially among heterosexual couples.

Meanwhile, the gay liberation movement always had more laissez-faire ideas when it came to monogamy. Since queer relationships weren't subject to entrenched norms, the people in them made up their own rules. The famed pre-AIDS gay bathhouses weren't the cold, anonymous places that some people assumed they were. "Places devoted to sex are usually depicted as harsh, alienated, scary environments, where people have only the most utilitarian and exploitative relationships," wrote Gayle Rubin about the S and M leather fisting club the Catacombs in San Francisco. "It was a sexually organized environment where people treated each other with mutual respect, and where they were lovingly sexual without being in holy wedlock." Open relationships were also often the norm in all-female communes and lesbian communities of the 1970s. A popular lesbian button at the time sported the slogan "Smash Monogamy" along with a triple woman's symbol: ♀ ♀ ♀

As I moved forward in time to polyamory's New Agey period, I read Dossie Easton and Janet W. Hardy's sanguine nineties manual *The Ethical Slut*, where I learned that feeling jealousy is totally okay, but behaving badly because of it is not. (I also learned that full immersion into a poly lifestyle was probably not for me; sex was great and all, but I wasn't ready to cede even more time thinking about it than I already did, much less build a whole community around it.) Deborah Anapol's *Love without Limits* introduced me to the concept of "responsible nonmonogamy," which seemed to boil down to being accountable and not being a sketchy asshole. I read Tristan Taormino's *Opening Up*, which led me to eighties and nineties queer sex writers like Susie Bright, Patrick Califia, and Celeste West. I read Christopher Ryan and Cacilda Jethá's *Sex at Dawn*, which argued that prehistoric humans were polyamorous as hell. (It was entertaining, though everybody told me to take it with a grain of salt.)

And then there were the perennial polyamory-safari trend pieces, like when *New York* magazine spent time with a cozy gay throuple upstate, or when rumors flew about celebrities like Tilda

Swinton and Carla Sarkozy exploring open relationships. Poly-amory and group sex also seemed to be major pastimes of Burning Man enthusiasts. It was unclear to me whether the polyamory of this community, which was ickily cozy with Silicon Valley by the time I was aware of it, was propelled by philosophy or if it was just another element of the Burners' "radical self-expression," like face paint or psychedelics.

Armed with all my new knowledge, I became one of those insufferable, self-assured nonmonogamous people. The more hostile or weirded out people acted, the more I evangelized. Which was rich, because despite the sincerity of my spiel at parties, I had an inkling early on that Aaron and I were not the ideal test case for an open relationship. Our nonmonogamy was not "responsible," at least on my end. To the extent that sleeping with other people had anything to do with our breakup, it mostly served the purpose of holding up a mirror to our problems. Because of that, I did not regret the whole enterprise, even if I always suspected our bond wasn't strong enough to withstand an open arrangement.

By the time Dom and I started dating in 2017, nonmonogamy had become more mainstream, and therefore less politically charged. Open relationships were *so* relegated to the personal realm, in fact, that people who talked up the radical dimensions of nonmonogamy often received a sneer. "If you want your sex life to heavily rely on google cal i frankly do not care," writer Brandy Jensen tweeted in 2019, in response to an article about polyamory and socialism, "but please don't pretend you are Being Leftist."

Though I, too, was skeptical of ideology driving sexual identity, it seemed obvious to me that monogamy as default *was* political. Just as with Adrienne Rich's critique of compulsory heterosexuality, the culture's encouragement and expectation of romantic exclusivity meant that it could never simply be seen as a value-neutral choice—and therefore neither could nonmonogamy. I thought it was fair to lambaste woke misogynists and overly smug lifestylers for presenting polyamory as a political imperative or for wielding it to apply peer pressure—but they were not wrong about our mass indoctrination either. If nonmonogamy wasn't necessarily the answer, there was also no inherent reason monogamy deserved to be our baseline.

Of course, there was the matter of jealousy, possibly the most unpleasant and wrenching of all human emotions. Most people I knew who declined to pry open their exclusive partnerships did so not for moral reasons but because they didn't trust their own threshold for pain and complication. They hated feeling jealous, and they believed that giving their partner more freedom would stoke it. "Intellectually, I totally get it," a friend emailed me in 2011. "People need lots of things, and no one other person can possibly be expected to provide all those needs." But she didn't seriously consider nonmonogamy because "I'm way too needy and kind of raw to tangle myself up in multiple people's relationship whatever."

On its face, minimizing jealousy would appear to be a personal endeavor, not a political one. But because of the societal slant toward monogamy, it's impossible to know whether jealousy is intrinsic or socially learned. Regardless of whether there's a biological element to it, it's fair to say that social dynamics inevitably stoke its intensity. The way it plays out is often gendered. Male jealousy toward women has been historically tied to men's need to control and defend their property—not to mention their egos. Female jealousy toward men has its own age-old patterns: women worrying about economic abandonment, men searching for relief from over-whelming obligations; women being encouraged to concern them-selves with sentimental matters, men being encouraged to disengage from their feelings. We often present wounded pride as natural or a given when a partner sleeps with somebody else, but pride itself is a social construction, based on cultural standards of romance and respect.

I sympathized with the impulse to self-protect in this way. Just because the source of feelings and reactions may be cultural, that doesn't mean we experience them less viscerally in our stomachs, behind our eyes, and in our windpipes. Yet it was precisely jeal-ousy's outsize intensity that made it seem politically relevant to me. "For the philosophically polyamorous, jealousy presents an oppor-tunity to examine the insecurities that opening a [relationship] lays bare," journalist Susan Dominus wrote in a thoughtful piece on open marriage. "Jealousy is not a primal impulse to be trusted be-cause it feels so powerful." For those same reasons, "it is an emotion worth investigating."

By the time Dom and I were dating, I thought I had read ev-erything under the sun about nonmonogamy. But only when I looked back even further in history could I begin a serious inquiry into jealousy, and the political and personal truths it reveals.

• • •

It was the beginning of the twentieth century, decades since Mary Gove Nichols wrote her anti-marriage screeds, even longer than that since Christian perfectionist John Humphrey Noyes founded the Oneida Community and created complex marriages, wherein each man was a husband to all women and each woman a wife to all men. ("The new commandment is, that we love one another," read the community's *First Annual Report*.) While the nineteenth-century free love movement had always focused less on pleasure than on marriage abolition, now a diffuse, more sexually charged rebellion flourished among the bohemians in Greenwich Village and Harlem in the form of Ethel Williams's dancing, Mina Loy's erotic poetry, A'Lelia Walker's sex parties, and Mabel Dodge's salons. For most of these partygoers, this sexual fluidity was not necessarily born out of political ideology; it was part and parcel of more ambient transgression and, for middle-class white people, a way to craft an avant-garde, freewheeling persona. But for at least one attendee of Dodge's "Evenings," the radical potential behind free love could not have been more central to her anarchist politics. Her name was Emma Goldman.

Emma wasn't cool or glamorous or conventionally sexy. She wore tiny glasses and schoolmarmish clothes and had a severe (yet motherly) energy. When she first met Mabel Dodge through a mutual friend, she made them both a humble homemade dinner of beefsteak and potatoes. She was a hard-core activist, not a lifestyle type; unlike most dandies and intellectuals in these circles, Goldman was regularly hunted by the police. For her, a thing like sex wasn't simply a matter of taste—it was the basis for revolution. This urgency came through in the fiery lectures she gave across the country, on things like birth control, workers' rights, and sexual freedom. On Emma's first official "Evening" at Mabel Dodge's, she wowed the genteel bohemians with a passionate speech about equal sex rights for women, daring any man in the room who hadn't experienced premarital sex to come forward. Not one man did.

Emma had fought long and hard to escape a provincial life of sentimentality and make her mark on the political life of the big city. Born in Lithuania to observant Jewish parents in 1869 and raised in Saint Petersburg, Russia, she was from the age of twelve an autodidact and teenage Nihilist who swore she'd only wed for love. She emigrated to Rochester, New York, with her sister when she was sixteen after her dad threatened to marry her off. A year later, though, nothing much had changed in the New World: she was still a factory seamstress, and the relatives who'd taken her in still wanted her to get married. But then she met twenty-one-year-old Jacob Kershner, another recent Russian immigrant who, like her, loved to read and dance and yearned to travel the globe. Eager to leave factory work, Emma got engaged and quit her job to start her life as a proper wife.

It was her wedding night in February 1887 when Emma discovered Jacob was impotent. She felt lonely, disappointed, and confused. Her sexual frustration mixed uneasily with the trauma of violation: a rape when she was fifteen had left her with a profound fear of being touched by men, even as "their lure remained strong." It was a contradiction she described as existing "between two fires." The sexual rejection also dredged up unpleasant childhood memories, like when her mom threatened to whip her for masturbating and slapped her when she got her first period. She and Jacob grew further and further apart. Emma's dream of exploring the world with her husband began to fade.

At the same time, recent headlines lit another match in her brain. A group of eight anarchist revolutionaries were being tried for conspiracy to murder in the aftermath of a Chicago labor protest, known as the Haymarket Affair, that had ended in bloodshed. She was deeply shaken when the activists were executed. Around the same time she began reading the anarchist newspaper *Die Freiheit* and learning as much as she could about the movement. She wrote in her autobiography that her newfound political passion saved her from "utter despair." After less than two years wed and a brief, ill-advised reunion with Jacob, Emma did what pretty much no one in her traditional community had: she left him for good and moved to New York City on a sweltering day in August 1889. She was twenty years old.

Over the next few years, Emma became a full-time rabble-rouser. She quickly met the Lower East Side radicals at their famous meeting place, Sach's Cafe on Suffolk Street, and by the next year, Emma had given her first public lectures on the eight-hour day in Rochester, Buffalo, and Cleveland. She kept lecturing and traveling and marching and organizing on behalf of workers' and women's rights—regularly getting arrested in the process, and serving ten months in prison in 1893. By 1906, she was devoting nearly her full attention to editing and promoting *Mother Earth*, the anarchist magazine she founded.

Amid all this, she established herself as one of the preeminent opponents of the repressive institution of marriage. Like the European anarchists and the free lovers of decades past, she opposed the legal and religious institution of marriage but went even further by challenging monogamy and insisting that eroticism was central to one's well-being. She assessed sex as natural and healthy, "as necessary . . . as the functions of the stomach, the brain, the muscles, etc." She believed that liberation of women included *sexual* liberation too—a woman's "right to support herself; to live for herself; to love whomever she pleases, or as many as she pleases."

She was drawn to the sex theory of Sigmund Freud, social reformer and doctor Havelock Ellis, and utopian socialist Edward Carpenter. Perhaps her most famous free love document is her stump speech "Marriage and Love," first published in 1911, which insisted that love, inherently wild and uncontainable, and "that poor little State and Church-begotten weed, marriage" were diametrically opposed. She railed against the expectation that a woman should have to remain a virgin until a suitor snapped her up. "Can there be anything more outrageous than the idea that a healthy, grown woman, full of life and passion, must deny nature's demand, must subdue her most intense craving, undermine her health and break her spirit, must stunt her vision, abstain from the depth and glory of sex experience until a 'good' man comes along to take her unto himself as a wife?"

She also condemned "the green-eyed monster" in a speech titled "Jealousy: Causes and a Possible Cure." She challenged the assumption that jealousy, which she called "the most prevalent evil of our mutilated love-life," was human nature and therefore an emotion we should coddle. The entitlement to control our partners' sexual activity was "the artificial result of an artificial cause . . . handed down from generation to generation as a sacred right and the basis of purity of the family and the home." Jealousy was a contemptible emotion, wielded as a weapon by the establishment to preserve marriage supremacy and protection of property. A claustrophobic union, "dependent upon each other for every thought and feeling, without an outside interest or desire," is a breeding ground for hate, suspicion, and distrust. This type of coercive love isn't love at all, and should be an embarrassment, Goldman insisted. If your relationship is truly solid and harmonious, you should be able to dispense with jealousy altogether.

Goldman often defended a person's right to be a "varietist," but like the earlier free lovers, she wasn't advocating for meaningless, casual sex. Rather, she pushed for a view of organic, nonbinding love that's ruled by the principle of free will. "Each [person] is a small cosmos in himself, engrossed in his own thoughts and ideas," she says in her speech on jealousy. "It is glorious and poetic if these two worlds meet in freedom and equality. Even if this lasts but a short time it is already worthwhile. But, the moment the two worlds are forced together all the beauty and fragrance ceases and nothing but dead leaves remain."

How dreamy, how positively intoxicating! I can't imagine a more appealing vision for authentic love. It's easy to see why Goldman inspired the people who came in droves to watch her speak, why she became a major influence on Second Wave feminists and, because of that movement's excavation of her work, an enduring leftist giantess. But the Emma Goldman who spoke at Mabel Dodge's salons had not yet had to seriously grapple with self-paradox. She did not yet know that the political conviction that so inspired her audiences would end up being, when put into practice, a source of her unbearable pain. She did not yet know just how hard it was to live up to the glorious, poetic, jealousy-free love she so espoused.

• • •

When Emma Goldman arrived in Chicago in 1908, she was already enveloped in controversy. Two days before her arrival, a Russian immigrant had attempted to assassinate the police chief, as a response to police violence against demonstrators during a huge march of the unemployed several weeks earlier. The crime inflamed the local right-wing press, who called the man "a disciple of Emma Goldman, 'Queen of the Reds.'" The police threatened to raid any lecture hall that allowed her to speak. Worn down from exhaustion, Goldman was convalescing at fellow anarchist Dr. Becky Yampolsky's house when Ben "Hobo King" Reitman, a rakish radical gynecologist who treated prostitutes and other outcasts for STIs, stopped by to offer her the use of his Hobo Hall.

Ben showed up with silk ties around his neck and a cane in his hand. A black cowboy hat hid "a mass of black curly hair," she recalled in her autobiography, "which evidently had not been washed for some time." Emma was intrigued by this rough-and-tumble "brute" who'd once hopped boxcars—so different from the refined intellectuals she hung around with in New York. "From the moment he had first entered Yampolsky's office, I had been profoundly stirred by him," she wrote. "In the quiet of the night, alone with my thoughts, I became aware of a growing passion for the wild-looking handsome creature, whose hands exerted such fascination." Ben quickly became her lover and tour manager, her partner in revolution and lust for three blissful months on the road.

At first it was all rapture and fantasy. Ben, who was a decade younger than the thirty-eight-year-old Emma and also unduly obsessed with his mother, called Emma his "blue-eyed Mommy." When he returned to Chicago in mid-tour, they wrote love letters to each other, in which she professed how he "opened up the prison gates" of her "womanhood," releasing all her pent-up passion and desire. "You fill me, fill every nerve and atom, you intoxicate me, you are the great passion of my life," she rhapsodized. They exchanged eroticisms in a code that eluded notorious moral hysteric Anthony Comstock's obscenity laws but would make the most avid erotica reader blush. She longed for his face between her "joy mountains." Her treasure box craved his Willie. "I press you to my body close with my hot burning legs," she wrote, in a passage about oral sex. "I embrace your precious head." They flustered each other so much with these letters that they sometimes had to cool off in the tub to dampen their passion.

Meanwhile, Emma's anarchist crowd tsk-tsked her affair with Ben. Alexander "Sasha" Berkman—Emma's longtime friend, one-time lover, and intellectual soul mate—didn't approve of the man he deemed as having "no rebel spirit" and who "didn't belong in our movement." Anarchist photographer Senya Fleshine thought Emma was just dickmatized by this opportunistic newcomer; ACLU cofounder Roger Baldwin called him "overbearing, arrogant, possessive, and dismally disagreeable." Emma thought they were all being pretentious and hypocritical, turning up their noses at a man less sophisticated than them. She and Ben fantasized about hightailing it to Australia, where they might escape the demands of work and the judgments of others.

Pretty soon, and in spite of her dearly held principles, Emma was crushed by jealousy. After months apart, Ben began sleeping around, in line with their free love beliefs. Sometimes he'd divulge a new relationship right away, and other times Emma found out long after the fact, but each revelation drove Emma absolutely nuts. The fallout of one of these affairs torpedoed the Australia plan. She cherished Ben's high libido, but she also bemoaned it. In letters they exchanged while she was traveling—and after an especially wrenching confession that Ben had been seeing other women and lying to her about it—she told him, "your promiscuity tears my very vitals, fills me with gall and horror and twists my whole being into something foreign to myself."

To be sure, Ben wasn't playing fair. Much like the dirty-haired fuckboys that would follow him, he couldn't help but be evasive about his other lovers—hardly what Deborah Anapol would call "responsible nonmonogamy." He often flouted basic human decency, like when Emma would be giving a lecture on the misconceptions of free love and he would stand in a corner checking out other women, eventually leaving to consummate his conquest before Emma had even finished speaking. She began giving a new lecture called "False Fundamentals of Free Love," which made a distinction between hidden, illicit promiscuity and real, honest spiritual union. "Your love is all sex," she wrote Ben around the same time she first gave the lecture, "with nothing but indifference left when that is gratified. . . . My love is sex, but it is devotion, care, anxiety, patience, friendship, it is all. How are the two to harmonize?" One wonders how their affair would have shaken out had Ben erred on the side of honesty and tenderness. (Then again, she might not have been as attracted to him.)

Even when Ben's trysts were on the up-and-up, Emma was still wracked with insecurity and a sense of loss. Though she knew she couldn't condemn his behavior on political grounds, she certainly didn't play it cool. "I don't think you love me," she wrote in another letter. "Maybe while I suffer, you are with someone else." Ben, an otherworldly lover, had ruined her ability to enjoy an affair with a mere mortal: "Do you think that one who has heard the roar of the ocean, seen the maddening struggle of the waves, who has been carried up to snow-peaked mountains; in short, do you believe that one who has known all the madness of a wild, barbarian primitive love, can reconcile one's self to any relationship under civilization? I believe you have unfitted me for that, hobo mine."

There was Schtick Emma: uncompromising, independent, against possessing any lover. And there was Human Emma: someone who believed in free love but found it excruciating to practice with a man she felt blew every other out of the water. Their affair, which lasted nine years, shook Goldman's political beliefs to the core. "I have no right to speak of Freedom when I myself have become an abject slave in my love," she wrote to Ben. She even condemned her own "Marriage and Love" lecture because it was "hateful to me. . . . I used to think it could perform miracles, poor fool that I was." Emma knew she had to hide her anguish and pessimism from the public. Her ideas were already so radical, she worried, that any inkling of personal failing would discredit her. "If ever our correspondence should be published," she wrote him in 1911, "the world would stand aghast that I, Emma Goldman, the strong revolutionist, the daredevil, the one who has defied laws and convention, should have been as helpless as a shipwrecked crew on a foaming ocean."

The love affair is also highly downplayed in Emma Goldman's autobiography; she never lets on that her relationship with Ben led to her questioning her life's work. Jealousy is an emotion she scornfully attributes to others in her autobiography, but not to herself. She'd written hundreds of letters to Ben, and she requested he return them during the time she was writing her life story. But once she reread the letters, she couldn't bear to even get them transcribed: "It is like tearing off my clothes to let them see the mad outpouring of my tortured spirit, the frantic struggle for my love, the all absorbing devotion each letter breathes, I can't do it!"

It wasn't until the 1970s that feminist scholar Candace Falk stumbled upon these letters quite by accident in the back of a Chicago guitar shop where a friend worked. By then, Emma's autobiography was "required reading" within the women's movement, Falk recalled. These letters became the basis for Falk's 1984 biography, *Love, Anarchy, and Emma Goldman*, a book I devoured in a single sitting at the New York Public Library, just a few months into my relationship with Dom. Through their letters, it tells the story of "a woman who could not envision these two powerful forces—love and anarchism—coexisting peacefully in her life." At the time of publication, a *Kirkus* reviewer dismissed Falk's book as "monotonous, trite," and "mired in trivia"; the idea that one's personal life could undercut and pose doubt to their ideology was "ridiculous."

The same review also pronounced Falk's book as "inferior" to *Emma Goldman: An Intimate Life* by Alice Wexler, another biography published the same year. Wexler, of course, knew of the Reitman-Goldman affair and had seen some of the letters, but she deemed them "unimportant" for her book. "Reducing her story to a saga of relationships . . . suggests the tendency of even contemporary feminists to collapse the political into the personal, losing sight of the anarchism that was surely Emma Goldman's most enduring passion," Wexler wrote in a letter to *The New York Times* in 1985.

Times have obviously changed, because I for one appreciated the portrayal of Emma Goldman as an emotionally complex being. (Falk confirmed I wasn't the only one: her biography is now regarded as a classic, as "people changed in their understanding of what a full person was and what love was," she told me.) It was humbling to see this pillar of the Left be so hard on herself. She suffered from needing to be what Alix Kates Shulman calls "the model of the superwoman," having unattainable standards of political purity that spurred inner chiding when she herself fell short of them. That same scorn and whiff of victim blaming, Shulman writes in an anthology of Goldman's writings, that same demand for perfect willpower at all times, would trickle down to other women who might watch Goldman on the stump and think, *Why can't I be that strong?* Even Kate Millett, author of the feminist classic *Sexual Politics*, felt inadequate after reading Goldman's autobiography. "A lifetime given to the anarchist cause without a moment's doubt," she marveled. "I am all waver, I doubt everything. . . . Better not to try anything."

• • •

By the time Ellen Willis was writing about love and sex in the seventies and eighties, emotional nuance in radical politics was far more welcome. Her writing about nonmonogamy echoes Emma Goldman's utopic ideal—unsurprising, given that she was an avowed fan. Ellen wrote in 1979, in an essay about the once and future meaning of family: "I suspect that in a truly free society sexual love would be at once more satisfying and less terrifying, that lovers would be more spontaneously monogamous but less jealous, more willing to commit themselves deeply yet less devastated if a relationship had to end."

At that point, she'd had only limited experience with nonmonogamy herself. During the most experimental years of the sixties, she was in two mostly exclusive relationships: with Bob and then, after that fateful acid trip in Colorado, with Steve. She left the former for the latter because she saw the potential for a freer kind of love with more trust, less ownership. In a letter she wrote to Bob shortly after they split, she confidently explained that she and Steve "really believe that possessiveness doesn't work, that it's destructive." Open relationships were the answer because infatuation (or, in polyamory lingo, "new relationship energy") was both something she craved and something that couldn't last in a long-term relationship: "I think there is a sick part to infatuation that has to do with uncertainty and insecurity. . . . But that there is also a healthy part, and it has to do with a kind of innocent wash of emotion . . . a sort of throwback to the time when things weren't so complicated, when you just felt intensely, with no reservations, and the reality principle hadn't quite taken hold."

In order to achieve a more enlightened partnership, though, she felt that both she and Steve would have had to be "born again, into a different world." Raised instead by a society that elevated the sacred couple form, they ended up virtually monogamous by default. The one time she and Steve ventured outside their twosome, with another couple named Larry and Marge who lived upstairs in their two-family house in upstate New York, it resulted in searing pain. "It hurt, it was disruptive, it made me for a time feel like killing two people," she wrote in 1989, with the benefit of twenty years of hindsight. Yet she didn't regret it, and she remained faithful to the concept of free love. "The power of that urge to stretch the limits could not cancel out jealousy and possessiveness," she wrote, "but it could compete. And, in a sense, win."

She wrestled with herself in that essay, and included shades of regret and pain within a piece that ultimately endorsed sexual freedom. But as I would discover after she died, a performance of emotional complexity is not the same as being truly honest. It turns out she'd felt a deep heartbreak and yearning for monogamy that she never expressed in public. It involved a very Ben Reitman–like figure, who entered her life at the start of the eighties: my dad, Stanley Aronowitz.

When I was younger, my parents mentioned that there had been some drama before I was born, followed by couples therapy. But, as with puberty and sex, I never got too many details because my mom maintained clear boundaries around the mother-daughter relationship, and I almost never had personal conversations with my dad. I was curious, though. My parents rarely argued in front of me; what was so bad that it had put them at odds? I got some answers shortly after her death, when I was organizing my mom's papers for her archive, in the form of pieces of loose-leaf covered in her tight, crowded scrawl.

• • •

CIRCA 1982, WHEN THERE'S A BAD VIBE:

Paradox: Compulsive monogamy is joyless. Monogamy that one asks for, demands, intimidates the other person into— monogamy inspired by duty, moralism, guilt, habit, lack of imagination, timidity, desire for peace at any point, of fear that the other person will do it if you do—isn't worth having. But spontaneous, voluntary monogamy—monogamy based on an intensely focused passion such that sleeping with anyone else seems superfluous, an unneeded and unwanted distraction—is entirely different. Times when I've felt that way . . . have been times of great happiness for me—and great emotional freedom. Yet I never dared to consciously want someone to feel that way about me; I think I felt a deep superstitiousness about it: to actively want it is in a sense to ask for or demand it and therefore negate it.

When Stanley said, "When I'm in love I'm monogamous" and many other things to the same effect, it liberated that unconscious or half-conscious desire. I allowed myself to believe he was giving me this gift of spontaneous exclusivity, precious because unasked for. Part of the pleasure I felt had to do with who he was, as a sexual person: a man who was very attractive to women and had many sexual opportunities, a man who believed in his right to sexual freedom and would

*exercise it if he wanted to—and yet he didn't want to, <u>chose</u>
not to.*

• • •

CIRCA 1983, WHEN ALL IS REVEALED:

living in a miasma of falseness . . .

*I still cling to the fantasy that we can make a new
start—that moving is symbolic of that—that I can heal the
wounds I've inflicted, that S. will respond in kind—even
that joy in the baby will bring us closer (sound of cynical
laughter by hordes of parents . . .)*

*But how [to] make a new start without truth? How [to]
talk about what's happened when what I know has happened
is being denied? How to say "I feel horribly hurt but I've
learned something"? How to admit to anguish when I know
it will only be dismissed as irrational + baseless (i.e., crazy)?
What do I do when the alternative is roiling silence or a
conversation that will immediately descend to the level of
cops-and-crooks, "you did," "I didn't"? How do I tell where
the lies end + truth begins? (I can't help wondering what he's
told <u>her</u>—that he's staying with me out of a sense of responsibility, because of the baby? That he doesn't want to spring
anything traumatic on me while I'm pregnant?)*

*I feel as if S's insistence on denial in the face of the most
blatant evidence has the force of a compulsion—certainly it
makes no sense in terms of rational self interest—instead of
avoiding trouble it creates trouble—destroying trust—
magnifying what might be a minor incident into a crisis . . .
It seems to me that denial, on many levels, is Stanley's life*

strategy—he feels he needs it for self-protection—is desper-
ately committed to it—I feel despairingly that he'd rather lose
me than change it, or try to—that if I can't stand it any more
he will stoically + "understandingly" accept my leaving—
assuming that my pushing this issue doesn't drive him to
leave me first . . .

So in grimly lucid moments I feel the awful sinking con-
viction that something is dead or dying—namely the terrible
hope that we can have a kind of love the world tells us is
impossible, have it now, not after the revolution. That this
is a turning point, + what lies beyond is the descent into
resignation and spiritual exhaustion—whether we stay to-
gether + have one of those nice, agreeable lives (the hope +
grief pushed aside as useless baggage, not real life), or wheth-
er we split.

At the same time I feel this incredible tenderness toward
S.—tenderness and desire—as if in defiance of impending
loss—as if to say "Yes I do love you, love you deeply, what-
ever my failures I've really tried. . . ."

• • •

CIRCA 2004, WHEN MY MOM WROTE A NEVER-PUBLISHED,
THINLY VEILED FICTIONALIZED ACCOUNT OF MY DAD'S AFFAIR:

"What was all that, then, about not believing in compulsive
monogamy?" [he said.] "Was it all just bullshit? If you want
a regular traditional deal—say so. Don't expect me to read
your mind."

"You are missing the point, Aaron. We are not even
married, and you are treating me exactly like a traditional

wife. I get to be the stable boring partner who takes second place to TV and gets lied to and patronized, someone else gets to have the passion and to know more about what's going on in my life than I do. What shit, Aaron! What fucking sexist shit!"

He was quiet for a minute, looked down at his large hands, frowned.

"Suppose . . ." he began. "Suppose that you—I—just wanted something . . . separate. Not in competition with our relationship. Just . . . separate."

Louise understood that desire now. Maybe she had even understood it then. At least she had experienced an instant of confusion, though it had not shaken her conviction that honesty was the core of love. What was the point, if not to get naked with each other emotionally and spiritually as well as physically? Of course, you could never totally achieve that, but that had to be the project. . . .

Louise could not decide what to do, and then her period was late.

• • •

This shattered and demoralized woman, this alienated couple—they were utter strangers to me. Ellen's despair, on paper, would seem to signal the precipice of this relationship's collapse. Stanley's remoteness and inept dodging had derailed her "terrible hope" for a love emptied of guile, an effortless devotion, a thing "the world tells us is impossible." It was a moment when she told *herself*, on a piece of loose-leaf, that it was impossible.

Of course, their relationship didn't collapse. My parents would go on to have a twenty-five-year-long union that, by all accounts, was real and bighearted and fulfilling. The first time I read these diary entries, at the age of twenty-four, I tried to remind myself that the laughs and excitable mealtime debates I'd heard them have were results of genuine affection. I felt fairly secure in my assessment that their love had been special. That security was mixed with feelings of protectiveness for my mom, withering anger and a little pity for my dad, then gratefulness to both of them for somehow working it out. Barely through my first year with Aaron, I knew little about the way long-term relationships are often a series of episodes of drifting apart, then coming back together. I couldn't fathom how they'd saved their union from the brink.

The next time I read these entries, years later when I was writing this book, I started thinking about my parents as just two out of so many poor souls who try to square their personal lives with their politics. Like Ben Reitman, Stanley was sexually indulgent and didn't have much respect for others' emotions. Like Reitman, he still hewed to the old-fashioned way of nonmonogamy, which is to say he lied. And like Goldman omitting those letters from her autobiography, like me in France writing and scribbling over the pros and cons list, it seemed to "tear my mother's very vitals" to look herself in the face and admit that what she wanted clashed with a politically perfect idea of herself. Perhaps that was why she felt the need to fictionalize her life, even in the context of a piece of writing meant only for her.

I was particularly fascinated by this idea of "spontaneous monogamy," which was clearly a persistent desire of my mother's, though she felt self-conscious about it. Deep down, she wanted to be completely fulfilled by one single person, and she wanted to uncover everything about him. She saw space—the separateness Stanley wanted but didn't know how to directly ask for—as threatening the "project" of true love, even as it might have also been fueling her desire.

* * *

For the first few months of our relationship, Dom and I enjoyed the spontaneous monogamy my mother had hoped for. It was okay to recognize the positive things that came with it, even if it might be temporary: The relief to not face your vulnerabilities while dating. The time and energy to focus on someone you're legitimately obsessed with. The thrill of knowing for sure that you're on the same page with someone. The trust buildup, the simplicity, the "emotional freedom," as my mom called it.

But we kept the channels of communication open, and eventually the conversation inched toward the possibility of nonmonogamy again. I was nervous, but I was hopeful it could work. We were living in a time when we didn't have just stump speeches and abstract free love philosophy books, but actual manuals and millions of advice columns about how to conduct an open relationship. There were coping strategies, methods for befriending your jealousy and learning more about yourself from it. There was a whole vocabulary, entire emotional scripts associated with it.

Less than a year into our relationship, we set some ground rules and dipped our toes in. It was perfect timing to try it out, we figured, because I was about to go on a trip to Los Angeles and the high desert, and at the same time, he was going to be in Buenos Aires for a business school–related trip. What's less threatening than vacation sex? The very first night he was there, he had a whirlwind hookup with a young blond French girl who was staying at his hostel. In accordance with our rules, he checked in with me before he proceeded and told me the details the next morning.

I was taken aback by my instantaneous feelings of jealousy while lying on my friend's air mattress on the east side of LA. I felt my heart thud through my whole body. My face radiated heat. Fresh air suddenly seemed like a dwindling resource. Jealousy, as the polyamory manuals point out, is actually more of a composite feeling. In my case it was a mix of competitiveness (*He hooked up with someone else before I did!*) and feelings of inadequacy (*His night sounded so fun, he's such a natural flirt, I am a loser in comparison*). That night we spoke on the phone, and I decided to just say out loud the same thought Aaron had once conveyed to me: his hookup made me feel like everyone in the world wanted to fuck him, and no one in the world wanted to fuck me.

I also had a strong urge to tell him, *Please never touch anyone else as long as you live*. Yet that scenario scared me too—boxing him in and cutting myself off from other experiences until the erotic charge in our relationship was thoroughly burnt out, inviting resentment and boredom and a feeling of constraint. I intellectually understood that we should allow each other sexual space and privacy, to give each other a mechanism to feel distance and mystery, to see each other as sovereign beings. You simply cannot possess another person. I felt strongly that to try to do so would be tantamount to emotional abuse, or at the very least aiding and abetting self-delusion and the stunting of personal growth.

Still, I was desperate to rebalance our power dynamic, so I made a loose plan with a guy named Cole whom I'd fucked a few times shortly after Aaron and I broke up, and who now lived in LA. I didn't *really* want to see him, but I felt I had something to prove: my desirability, and also my independence from Dom. I couldn't fully submerge myself in this love affair, as wonderful as it was. I needed to hold on to a vestige of my pre-Dom self. I hated the idea of my entire sexuality being subsumed by a guy I met nine months ago. Wasn't I still capable of layers and richness, of surprising myself?

At that point Dom's and my relationship had already formed a dynamic that was unfamiliar to me: although he was sure of how in love with me he was, he wanted more space than I did. I could talk and fuck forever, while he had a lower tolerance for intimacy binges. He also had a stronger need for privacy than I did, which sometimes made him feel so far away, so unreachable. Sex therapist Esther Perel employs an analogy for maintaining the erotic charge in relationships: Fire needs air in order to burn. "The grand illusion of committed love is that we think our partners are ours," she writes in her book *Mating in Captivity*. "In truth, their separateness is unassailable, and their mystery is forever ungraspable." It was disconcerting to realize that Dom's unassailable separateness was the very thing that both hurt me and kept me loving and desiring him. In most ways he was not Stanley, but he related to my dad's wish for something "not in competition with our relationship. Just . . . separate."

Our dynamic could be partly explained by our individual circumstances. The intense intimacy of his nuclear family could be overwhelming, stoking his need for space, whereas I feared abandonment and desired security because of how my own familial bonds had loosened. Personal histories and attachment styles will always muddy one's ability to live out political ideology. Emma Goldman, for instance, grappled with feeling unloved, unwanted, and deprived as a child.

But politics were powering my jealousy too. Some of my reactions had been internalized through culture, though I'd stuffed them down so deeply that I hadn't even known they existed. Many of my intrusive thoughts, I knew, were coming from corrosive conservatism: *Don't make a fool out of me*, even though there wasn't hiding involved; *What does she have that I don't have?* while scrutinizing this French woman's body on social media. Others had to do with keeping my libertine reputation intact, wanting to feel "empowered" and not vulnerable, especially with friends who doubted that open relationships could work. Still more thoughts came from a third realm, from a misguided interpretation of polyamory (and from Emma Goldman's speeches) that cast the very presence of jealousy as shameful and pathetic and relied on personal willpower as a solution.

It didn't help that most of my friends were either in monogamous relationships or wanted them. When I expressed my tangle of feelings after Dom's Buenos Aires hookup to a few of my friends, they affirmed my first set of reactions, the ones that had made me feel so entrapped by the dominant culture. They offered up petty comments about the French girl out of solidarity, not realizing that they were reinforcing how toxic monogamy and sexual competitiveness could be. They gently suggested that maybe an open relationship wasn't what I really wanted. I didn't blame them; it wasn't easy to stare down the source of one's jealousy, and nobody wants to see a friend in pain. Normally my friends were ports in the storm of various relationship snags, but this time I felt incredibly lonely. They didn't understand my desire to see my way through the bad feelings and learn from them, rather than immediately surrender to them. It was the first time I wished I was part of the poly community, corny Burner aesthetic be damned.

They were right about one thing, though: I was putting pressure on myself in order to even the score. I canceled my date with Cole. It had been set up for the wrong reasons. I spent the whole night thinking that perhaps my friends were right, that I secretly wanted monogamy, that I was just like every other woman who wanted to tie her man down.

And then, just a few days later, during a weekend trip to the high desert, I saw a cute guy at the Joshua Tree Saloon.

His name was Adrian, a park-ranger-in-training who was in town visiting his sister. I remembered how great it could all be: the rush of meeting someone new, of flirting, of having eye sex across the room, and then the bonus of knowing I had Dom's blessing. We ended up having a semi-naked, semipublic hookup in the parking lot next to a sky-blue school bus. I still remember the feeling of his warm, tanned stomach, his hands urgently spreading my bare ass, his fingers gripped around my curls. It was a perfect encounter, and it had come at the perfect time. I knew symmetry was a crutch, that I couldn't always rely on it saving me. But at that moment, I'd needed the reminder of my own desires, and Adrian had given me that. Dom reacted graciously the next day. "Get it, girl," he told me, seeming far more impressed than threatened. My floaty feeling of expansiveness lasted for days.

● ● ●

After our mutual forays into vacation sex, we went on for two years without much conflict. We both hooked up with people—he slightly more often than I—and there were small flare-ups of jealousy and discomfort. But each time he'd reassure me, and equilibrium would be restored. We experimented with sex parties; we explored getting with other genders. It was fun and exciting to visit these pockets of freedom, then come back to the bubble of our love. But we talked openly about a frustrating paradox, how the encounters felt less than fulfilling *because* they were finite and sex-based in accordance with our monogamish-ness and not true polyamory, because the potential was sucked out of them. In some ways, it felt like backsliding into Team Chill, an overly controlled way to experience intimacy. Destiny was less of a factor; unless something went way off the rails, the outcome (an eventual end) seemed predetermined, and therefore both less meaningful and less exciting. One day sometime far away, we said, we might want to forge real connections with other people, connections that would necessitate more than one- or two-night stands.

During the pandemic, those thoughts came home to roost. The air between us was nonexistent in quarantine, and our natural inclinations amplified. I became extra-reliant on our bond, while he needed more space than ever. I couldn't imagine hooking up with others, instead craving nothing but monogamy and the chemical rush of cuddling, while he was feeling isolated and in need of a more consistent connection than a onetime encounter could provide. Like the rest of the world, my anxiety reached unimaginable heights; there were days when my worry and despair about Dom's and my relationship mimicked my mother's resignation after the discovery of my father's affair. I eventually understood that what I was feeling was envy—that Dom was stretching and I wanted to be able to also. "I can't deny that my relationship with Dom is strong and full of love and sexual attraction," I wrote in my diary. "But I also want something else. Something that doesn't resemble my 2017 self in the slightest. Something that can be a respite from this intensive dyad of fully relying on him, pouring every bit of myself into him. I need something on my own, in multiple ways, but one of them is physical and emotional. And romantic even."

Again, symmetry saved me: My own desire for exploration came inching back. As the months pressed on, I began to pursue new sex buddies, both IRL and digital. The much-needed space created by those encounters paved the way for a horny streak with Dom too. I'd been nervous to have anything but an ultracasual hookup, but once I started seeing one person consistently, I could more clearly see how to appreciate people on parallel, not competing, tracks. I admired Dom's ability to tell me what he wanted, and I strived to feel the security he felt, to have as much faith in our partnership as he seemed to.

It wasn't the emotional freedom of spontaneous monogamy. It wasn't the dull comfort of security and routine. The uptick in "serious talks" was exhausting and kept both of us on edge. I had to keep reminding myself not to accuse but instead to ask for reassurance; he had to fight against his urge to conceal in order to protect his own privacy. I constantly fretted that our intermittent separateness would come at the expense of eventually losing each other—too much air, after all, blows out a fire. And sometimes, I just wanted a break from having to think about my own insecurities.

Still, this new, harder back-and-forth was the most active commitment I'd ever experienced. I thought back to that Susan Dominus piece, when she describes the type of person who pursues nonmonogamy. "Open marriages . . . are not just for people who were more interested in sex, but also for people who were more interested in people," she writes, "more willing to tolerate the inevitable unpacking conversations, the gentle making of amends, the late-night breakdowns and emotional work of recommitting to and delighting each other."

As I write this chapter, I struggle with deciding how much to reveal about the contours of Dom's and my particular tensions. The first version tied up everything in a bow. (Because I didn't want to make polyamory look bad? Because I didn't want to be seen as one of *those* couples who fought all the time?) The second version had the tenor of a rambly therapy session—too many mundane details, too little useful insight. The best truth I can offer is that while nonmonogamy is not at all relaxing, it also feels worthwhile to try to excavate the deepest wells of my own generosity and trust. It's nerve-racking but ultimately thrilling to invite someone I'm in love with to search for things that don't include me, and for me to do the same. And as long as monogamy remains the standard, breaking with that standard will always mean extra emotional effort. It means being confronted, even more than normal, with the politics that inject paradox into romance—no matter how tempting it is to think of your private life as private.

10. The Real Experts

People always talk about the moment of shock they feel when they see those two lines on a pregnancy test they hadn't planned on taking. *How could this have happened?* they think with their head in their hands. Well, I knew exactly how it happened. Dom and I had unprotected sex right before I ovulated.

After years of procrastination, I had finally resolved to learn fertility awareness method. Dom and I went to a class together in the fall of 2017, where the instructor invited us to stick our fingers in bowls of lotion and egg whites so we could familiarize ourselves with the nuances of cervical fluid. After charting for a few months, I was delighted to find out that I did ovulate, that my hormones were strong and functional. By the beginning of 2019, I'd been charting for more than a year, recording my temperature every morning and examining my cervical fluid when I went to the bathroom. I knew what ovulation looked like on that little chart, and I knew I'd ovulated early that month. I knew, too, that the length of my luteal phase—the two weeks or so after ovulation—is identical from month to month. So when it was one day longer than normal, I knew I should find a pregnancy test that would measure minuscule levels of HCG hormone in my urine.

But somehow, despite what felt like an encyclopedic knowledge of the female reproductive system, I still didn't *really* think I'd get pregnant by having sloppy, cummy, caution-to-the-wind sex at the exact wrong time.

Though I worried about accidental pregnancy in my twenties, I was now in my thirties and part of a privileged, urban, blue-state demographic that seemed to fret far more about impending infertility. Maybe it was because I couldn't fathom all the steps of pregnancy falling perfectly into place, or because, as much as I'd talked about sex and pregnancy with my friends, I couldn't recall many details about their actual abortions. The reality of being pregnant, and the medical intricacies of deciding not to be, felt abstract.

This is not to say I never thought about abortion. At that point I'd written and assigned countless articles about reproductive rights, pregnancy, and birth control. I closely followed reporting on abortion, which usually focused on the legal obstacles, cultural judgment, and complex emotions about the desire to be a parent, rather than the nuts and bolts of actually having one. I'd had discussions with my partners about what we would do in the event of an unplanned pregnancy.

I'd also thought about having kids and was very sure I wanted at least one. Dom and I talked about it a lot, but in a sentimental, one-day-far-away tone. On the day I got a positive pregnancy test, I was barely two years broken up from Aaron. I was loving my little solo routines in my own apartment; Dom had started a punishing consulting job and lived with two roommates; we still regularly stayed up boning and chatting until late into the night. Domesticity seemed a million miles away. I wanted to live in this sweet phase—independent yet immersed in romance—for as long as I could. After allowing ourselves a brief moment to picture the alternative, we agreed the same day of the test: *Let's just enjoy each other for a while.*

Since 2011, I had been aware of the spate of "heartbeat bills," the medically inaccurate name for a law banning abortions after the detection of a fetus's electrical cardiac activity, which would make the cutoff for an abortion as early as six weeks. I had been angry about them in a generic way, knowing that many people don't even know they're pregnant at that early stage. Still, I didn't quite understand the depths of these bills' cruelty until I learned there's such a thing as showing up too early for an abortion.

When I went to my ob-gyn's office a few days after the pregnancy test, the ultrasound technician informed me she couldn't yet see anything in my uterus. It's rare, she explained, but sometimes an embryo implants in the fallopian tubes or elsewhere to form an ectopic pregnancy, so it could be ineffective or dangerous to initiate an abortion without visual confirmation of an intrauterine pregnancy. "Come back next Friday," she told me. I obliged. That second ultrasound deemed me eligible for an abortion, and my appointment was scheduled for five days later.

I Googled around furiously: *Is this normal?* I learned that this protocol is common in the US but not necessarily required. I trusted my doctor, but I also recognized the irony that, in this case, being ultra-tuned-in to my reproductive health had done me zero favors: all I could do was wait—and obsess.

In those few pregnant weeks, tits swollen and stomach queasy, my first impulse was to tell everyone what had been taking over my brain. "How are you?" a friend would ask, and I'd often say, "Well, I'm counting down the days till my abortion, but otherwise I'm fine!" I quickly realized that wasn't the norm even in my progressive circles. My friends were supportive and sweet, never questioning my decision not to continue the pregnancy. But some, even the ones who'd had abortions themselves, betrayed a moment of surprise or discomfort that I was talking about my impending procedure without a reverent tone or that I was complaining about first-trimester symptoms over martinis. A few times, I got the distinct feeling it was gauche or TMI, like divulging an obscure sexual fetish. I related to feminist writer Maya Dusenbery, who encountered "so many hushed voices . . . utterances of 'I don't know what to say'" among her own crowd. She remembered thinking at the time that "women who have abortions are more closeted than gay people."

At the same time, a few close friends who'd gone through the experience did volunteer personal abortion details, some of which were brand-new to me: they hadn't told me back when it happened, and I also hadn't known to ask. One friend recalled that she'd had to wait seventy-two hours—the mandatory "waiting period" in Missouri, where she lived. Another said she'd had an "incomplete abortion," so she needed to get a vacuum aspiration two weeks after she'd taken the pills. And more than one person revealed that they, too, were told to wait for a visual confirmation of their pregnancy.

Other life experiences had worked this way too. I hadn't truly comprehended the pain of, say, death or divorce until it affected my life. In the aftermath of both, other people who'd experienced the same thing came out of the woodwork, like Dane the breakup doula, or the many people who reached out to me after my mom died with their own stories of a parent's death. Still, the secrecy around abortion—which I hadn't even really noticed until I had to get one—weirded me out. One in four women will get this procedure at some point, and most won't go through it completely alone. They'll seek comfort and help from partners, healthcare workers, counselors, parents, friends. "Everyone loves someone who had an abortion," the modern feminist adage reminds us. So why was it still so hard to talk about?

• • •

In April 1968, after she was divorced but before she joined the women's movement, Ellen offered her couch to a teenage girl who was in New York City to get an abortion. The doctor's price was seven hundred dollars—more than five thousand in today's dollars—but at least he was a well-known, respected abortionist. Still, Ellen worried when he didn't prescribe antibiotics, and worried more when the girl was in pain the next day. Panicked but afraid to confront police at the hospital, they wasted hours calling private doctors and hoping the pain would somehow subside. Finally, after her friend's fever skyrocketed, Ellen called 911.

The hospital was a nightmare. Amid the chaotic tangle of tubes and shots, the doctor harangued the terrified girl: *You went to a quack, right? That was a stupid thing to do, wasn't it? How much did it cost you?* When the girl asked him if she was going to die, he refused to say no. Mercifully, the nurse was kinder than the doctor: *She's full of penicillin*, she reassured Ellen. *It's going to be all right.*

The girl had gotten an illegal abortion, but at the time, New York was one of the few states where the procedure was legal under certain narrow circumstances. Since 1828, it had been permitted for "therapeutic" exceptions, when a person's life was at risk by continuing her pregnancy. (Women in the know often employed the trick of threatening to kill themselves in order to be eligible.) The New York State legislature started flirting with abortion reform in the sixties and, in the winter of 1969, the state announced that they would hold legislative hearings on abortion reform. Fourteen men and a nun had been selected as expert witnesses.

Only ten months had passed since Ellen had taken the girl to Bellevue Hospital, but the political climate had changed considerably. The women's movement was well underway in New York City by then, and abortion rights had emerged as a key issue for radical and liberal feminists alike. At that point, hundreds of women a year were dying of botched abortions; illegal abortion accounted for 17 percent of all deaths attributed to pregnancy and childbirth in 1965—and those were just the official numbers. In some cities, there were entire hospital wards devoted to treating septic abortions. When news of the legislative hearing spread, several groups, including NOW, decided to go protest it.

Ellen and a group of five other liberationists went further than passive picketing: they resolved to loudly disrupt the hearing and submit their own testimony. Ellen, taken aback at her own initiative, offered to write up a leaflet. "In other political organizations I would have worried over a job like this for days and called a dozen people to ask what I should say," she recalled a few months later. "But this time I'm doing it for myself, writing from the memory of pregnancy scares, of the doctor who wouldn't prescribe pills for me because I was unmarried and underage and then bawled me out for wasting his time, of my friend screaming in the hospital. I'm writing from anger. Nobody needs to tell me a thing."

WHO ARE THE EXPERTS?

Today a panel of clergymen, doctors and other professional "experts"
is picking apart the abortion law. They will tell us, in their usual
daddy-knows-best manner, just how much control over our reproductive
processes we should be allowed to have.

We say:

THE ONLY REAL EXPERTS ON ABORTION ARE WOMEN!

Women who have known the pain, fear and socially-imposed guilt of
an illegal abortion. Women who have seen their friends dead or in agony
from a post-abortion infection. Women who have had children by the
wrong man, at the wrong time, because no doctor would help them.

Any woman can tell you:

Abortion laws are <u>sexist</u> laws, made by men to punish women.

LET THE EXPERTS TESTIFY.

SUPPORT CONSTANCE COOK'S BILL — REPEAL <u>ALL</u> ABORTION LAWS.

Women's Liberation Movement

On the day of the hearing, Ellen showed up in a black sheath dress, dark hair pulled back and parted down the middle, arms full of leaflets and her own private notes. She was nervous; she still had a deeply internalized aversion to seeming angry or conspicuous. After one of the witnesses, a judge, suggested that abortion be legal for women who had "done their social duty" by having at least four children, one of the organizers interjected from the audience and said, "Now let's hear from some *real* experts—the women." Ellen started telling the story of her scared friend in the emergency room, and she'd "never felt less inhibited." Another woman spoke: "We've waited and waited while you have held one hearing after another. Meanwhile, the baby I didn't want is two years old." And another: "Men don't get pregnant. Men don't rear children. They just make the laws."

The disruption was covered in the local papers with varying levels of seriousness. "Gals Squeal for Repeal," jeered a *Daily News* headline, recounting the "emotional outburst" of "angry females." Perhaps anticipating the hostile coverage, Ellen ignored journalistic scruples and reported the hearing herself in an unbylined "Talk of the Town" column in *The New Yorker*. She quoted the parting words of one woman (maybe herself?) who'd been at the hearing for more than seven hours: "Well, we're probably the first women ever to talk about our abortions in public. That's something, anyway."

The group of women who'd stormed the hearing gave themselves a name: Redstockings. After the success of the protest, they figured that a speak-out was a logical next step, a way to recognize that the pain and humiliation of trying to get an abortion was a social problem and not a personal one. Ellen hoped it would be interpreted as "politics rather than soap opera." Consciousness-raising groups were still new, and still beating back the condescending assumption that their discussions were just "group therapy." She wanted the public to put these women's private details in a larger political context.

The group managed to convince twelve women to talk about their abortions in front of three hundred people at a raucous event at Washington Square Methodist Church in late March. They made an audio recording of the event for posterity. At the speak-out, the "experts" told stories about times when a legal abortion wasn't possible, when they put their lives in the hands of quacks as a result. "Without anesthetic it's the most scary thing in the world," one woman in the audience said. "You're on the table and you feel the scraping and scraping." Another woman had to go to eleven hospitals before she could get an abortion at age twenty; the tenth had threatened to sterilize her.

A charming woman, whose impressive dramatic chops would fit in nicely with the cast of *The Marvelous Mrs. Maisel*, described how you couldn't just casually threaten suicide if you wanted a therapeutic abortion—you had to sound like you meant it. "You have to go and bring a razor, or whatever," she said, in a thick, old-timey New York accent. "'If you don't tell me I'm going to have an abortion right now, I'm going to go out and jump off the Verrazzano Bridge!'"

The woman ended up seeing two psychiatrists, who, to her relief, deemed her suicide threats real enough to be granted the procedure. The crowd clapped and roared at the absurdity of it all, until the woman explained that after her abortion, she was stuck in the maternity ward to recover, right next to crying babies. The crowd wasn't laughing anymore.

Susan Brownmiller, who covered the speak-out for *The Village Voice*, called the event "the politics of confrontation and catharsis." The aim was the former, but you can audibly hear the latter in the women's voices, even through the scratchy audio. They were finally able to talk freely, in front of people who understood exactly why their stories were important. "It's very, very frightening, and you're extremely alone," one woman piped up from the audience. "I don't know why friends don't help that much. . . . There's sort of really not anything much anyone can do. You feel extremely alone and you sort of drop out of life." There was a bit of relief in her voice: It was clear she didn't feel alone anymore.

• • •

My actual abortion was surprisingly awful; the only anesthetic I was instructed to take was some naproxen before the procedure, so I was moaning in pain while Dom stood across from me, watching splashes of red being vacuumed up a tube. I vomited violently once it was over, and I was out of commission for days afterward. But the unpleasantness was not what was on my mind in the aftermath. Instead, I kept thinking about the news. Iowa's supreme court had just struck down a heartbeat law that had been signed by Republican governor Kim Reynolds back in May. I lived in New York, whose governor signed a law codifying *Roe v. Wade* the same day the Iowa decision came down. But in some parallel heartbeat-law universe, I might have been racing against the clock, trying to find a provider who didn't require an ultrasound, or living in a state with only one abortion clinic, rather than simply making an appointment at my regular gyno.

I had an urge to share these thoughts, which seemed distinctly "politics rather than soap opera." I impulsively tweeted a thread:

So, I had an abortion the other day. Among other things, my experience made me realize just how supremely fucked up these fetal heartbeat bills really are.

I meticulously chart my cycles, so I knew I was pregnant right away. At 4.5 weeks I went to my gyno and was told it was TOO early for an abortion—they couldn't yet see anything on the ultrasound.

I was told to come back in a week. At 5.5 weeks pregnant, I was able to be scheduled for their first available procedure . . . 5 days away.

Finally I went in for my abortion at almost 6.5 weeks pregnant. A heartbeat can often be detected at 6 weeks. Under one of these laws, it could have been too late.

I live in abortion-friendly NYC, can afford it, and made my decision literally 1 day after my missed period. If I had to wait that long for an abortion, how the fuck are women supposed to plan for theirs under heartbeat laws???

These bills are cruel, disingenuous, evil mindfucks and are designed to send an ominous message, even if they do get struck down by federal judges. Iowa's did, but Florida and Ohio are next. The goal is the Supreme Court.

P.S. I feel a bit nervous and exposed tweeting about my abortion (which just shows how much I've internalized the hush-hush culture around it). But abortion is NORMAL. And restrictive laws like these ignore women's realities so thoroughly. #shoutyourabortion

• • •

Sometime in 1974, Ellen went on one of her ambiguous dates with Steve. They'd broken up the year before, but they would still meet up for dinner regularly. Occasionally those dinners would lead to a rehashing of why they broke up and end in tears or harsh, jealous words. Just as frequently, they would result in friendly, familiar sex. On this particular February night, horniness and nostalgia reigned. After a few drinks, the two made it back to Ellen's place on Second Street in Park Slope, the apartment the two had once shared. They forwent the diaphragm, not wanting to interrupt the closeness they felt that night.

When Ellen discovered she was pregnant, she and Steve briefly waxed poetic about what the kid would look like: her curly hair, his ginger coloring? She was thirty-three, and even though it would be several more years before *Washington Post* columnist Richard Cohen would invent the odious term "biological clock," the cultural concept existed in an ambient way. And she did want to have a child one day. Still, she knew what she needed to do. She cared for Steve but didn't want be forever tied to him in this way. They went to a clinic together on the Upper West Side, and my mother had the abortion.

I'd never heard this story until I spoke to Steve on the phone in December 2019. My mother and I had been nearly the same age when we had our abortions, albeit in vastly different cultural contexts. She might have been the perfect person to talk to during that awkward, hushed-toned waiting period, when most people around me seemed to have no idea what to say. Though she never mentioned her abortion, she did tell me about how she tried to get a diaphragm at nineteen, and how her doctor refused to prescribe one without her parents' consent. She probably channeled that rage she'd felt as a teen when she helped me get a morning-after pill in tenth grade, just a few months after I'd started having sex. Back then it was prescription-only. I spent hours racked by stress and bewilderment before I confessed to my mom what I needed. Ever respectful of my privacy, she didn't ask me what happened or who I was fucking; she just placed a call to her gyno, and two hours later I had the pills.

When I sifted through my mother's writings, I found a sole, blink-and-you-miss-it mention of the fact that she had indeed had an abortion. But no details, no elaboration, which seemed strange to me. My mother had often used her personal experiences to make political points, and she certainly wrote about abortion. By the time she needed one herself, society had never been more open about the issue. In 1974, reproductive rights activists were taking a victory lap amid a kind of honeymoon period of abortion history—after *Roe v. Wade* legalized it everywhere in the United States, but before the Hyde Amendment barred Medicaid from paying for abortions. New York, which began to repeal its laws criminalizing abortions in 1970, provided a glimpse into legalization's positive effects: Maternal mortality fell by 45 percent the year after the state legalized abortion in New York. By 1974, Planned Parenthood of New York City was performing twelve thousand safe abortions a year. Hospitals across the country closed their septic abortion wards. There were more than two thousand abortion providers in the United States just a year after *Roe v. Wade*. In many states, it was easier to get an abortion than it is today.

"In those early days, it was a very proud, happy time" for abortion providers, Dr. Suzanne T. Poppema recalled in a 2015 article in The Cut. Patients no longer had to risk their lives after an accidental pregnancy. "The main feeling I think we both had was a huge sense of relief that it was so easy and accessible," Steve told me.

Of course, America didn't magically become an abortion utopia. Access still lagged, and culture couldn't be changed overnight. Around this time, the Guttmacher Institute reported that although more than a million legal abortions had been performed in 1975, up to 42 percent of the people desiring them weren't able to get them. Abortion services were concentrated in liberal cities. Poor and rural women still struggled to get them, as did teenagers. Some women continued to seek out underground abortions because of time pressure, affordability, or a desire for secrecy. But abortion advocates were hopeful. Clinics were enjoying a new sense of freedom and expansion. There was barely a right-to-life movement back then, no protesters harassing clinics' patients or sending constant death threats to abortion doctors. For a brief moment in American history, my mother could get an abortion in a relatively depoliticized environment.

Almost immediately afterward, a rhetorical shift began to take place. Both the left and the right began to talk about abortion not in terms of the reality of women's lives, but in the far more abstract, speculative language of the "life" of the fetus—which was somehow being discussed entirely apart from the life of the person in which it resided. Meanwhile, legal access to abortion began to slip too. In one of the first victories for the burgeoning anti-abortion movement, Congress passed the Hyde Amendment, effectively shaving off access for low-income women.

As abortion rights faltered and pregnant people's realities became sidelined in the debate, people again saw the utility of personal abortion stories to make political points. In 1977, in McAllen,

Texas, twenty-seven-year-old Rosie Jimenez sought out a cheap, illegal abortion and died of a runaway bacterial infection the following week. Feminist groups held rallies and candlelight vigils and recounted her story again and again, positioning her death not simply as a senseless tragedy but as a direct consequence of the Hyde Amendment. With the help of Jimenez's family members and best friend, Diana Rivera, Jimenez's story was codified in an investigative book. One of the first abortion funds, created in 1978 in Central Texas to support low-income Texans, was established in her honor.

As the seventies moved into the Reagan Revolution, the religious right gained even more steam as evangelical Christians joined the Catholics in opposing abortion. Groups like Operation Rescue started forming human blockades in front of clinics. Extremists began assaulting, kidnapping, and murdering abortion providers. Meanwhile, more polite crusaders tinkered with state law, inserting changes like waiting periods and parental notification mandates that chipped away at access. Redstockings organized another speak-out for the twentieth anniversary of the original event, the same year a fire was started at the Feminist Health Center clinic in Concord, New Hampshire. The politics of "confrontation and catharsis" had renewed resonance. One of the audience members was civil rights activist Flo Kennedy, who'd cowritten a book with Diane Schulder in 1971 distilling the testimony of women who filed a lawsuit challenging the constitutionality of New York's abortion laws. She bemoaned the fact that the book was out of print at such a relevant time in history.

Decades later, the speak-out style is still a common strategy for bringing attention to any injustice, but particularly in the realm of abortion. The momentum for the Reproductive Health Act, new legislation passed in February 2019 that expanded New York's abortion rights, began with Erika Christensen, who told the story of her late-term abortion on Jezebel nearly three years before. Politicians like the former Texas candidate for governor Wendy Davis, Rep. Barbara Lee, Rep. Jackie Speier, Rep. Pramila Jayapal, and Rep. Cori Bush have spoken about their own abortions. Storytelling collectives like Shout Your Abortion, We Testify, and the Abortion Diary have posted countless stories online and in books.

I threw in the #ShoutYourAbortion hashtag out of a dim awareness that this storytelling movement existed, and with an assumption that my group of Twitter followers would understand the political point I was making. Hardly a social media strategist, I reasoned that a matter-of-fact approach was the best way to go about it (*"So, I had an abortion the other day . . ."*). My abortion went smoother than most, but I still found it galling that when it came to issues of sexuality—whether it's abortion, miscarriage, reproductive pain, rape, gay marriage, or trans rights—we often expected people to talk about private, sometimes traumatic experiences in public. So I pointedly did not mention the moaning, the vomiting, or the more private feelings it provoked.

The tweets quickly racked up tens of thousands of likes and retweets, and then my story was out of my hands. Many abortion-rights supporters appreciated my normalizing tone; opponents of abortion were horrified by my lack of emotion, calling me a "sociopath." Still others, including a close friend, essentially took the stance many homophobes take when it comes to gay people kissing in public: "Do what you want in private, but do you have to shove it in my face?" I was quickly discovering that public testimony requires walking a tightrope: Be honest and authentic, but not too emotional, lest your story be dismissed as purely confessional. Nobody wants to be accused of seeking attention with a sob story—but insufficient sobbing can attract ire, even among people you thought were on your side. No matter what I said, there was no way to win.

Or maybe, ultimately, there was. Amid the dissections of my tone and word choice, I received dozens of messages from women in this exact limbo, who were running out of time but couldn't find the funds or weren't sure of their options. Many of them confided in me that they wished they felt safe enough to tweet too. Some were currently pregnant, desperate for help, and just wanted someone to listen to them. They told me my tweets had made them feel less alone.

I realized it didn't really matter how I worded my tweets, or how anyone talked about their own abortions. The point was to talk. It has the potential to break the infuriating silence I felt during those few weeks before my abortion. As much as I valued privacy—the vague constitutional right *Roe v. Wade* was predicated on, much to some feminists' consternation—honesty and solidarity seemed more important.

A few months after Steve told me about my mother's 1974 abortion, a calm moment between two storms, I began to realize why she might not have been compelled to share her story with the world. It was a time when a woman could look up an abortion doctor in the phone book and visit a clinic without having to confront protesters blocking the entrance, wielding blown-up pictures of fetuses, or pointedly singing hymns. (Even in present-day New York, a version of this scene materializes regularly at the Planned Parenthood on Bleecker Street.) It was a time when abortion was so normalized that a feminist writer who'd helped organize the

1969 abortion speak-out did not feel the need to write about her experience.

When I floated my honeymoon-period abortion theory to Steve, he agreed that it was partly because at that time a legal abortion felt unexceptional. But he also suspected it might have been simpler than that: "because it was something of importance that was private and personal between the two of us." Indeed, it was partly events like the 1969 speak-out that allowed my mother to think of her own abortion in those terms. If I'd learned anything from the past few tumultuous years, it was that taking sexuality seriously, both collectively and in my own life, didn't just include talking bravely about pleasure. It also included talking about the confusing, painful outcomes of pleasure too.

On September 1, 2021, I was reminded yet again that silence and discomfort about these outcomes could cause tangible harm. It was the day the Supreme Court failed to block Texas's horrifying version of a heartbeat bill, which empowered private citizens to sue anyone who performs an abortion or "aids and abets" it.* I thought about the women waking up that morning unable to get their scheduled abortions, about the doctors and clinic workers who suddenly had a target on their backs. I blamed not only conservatives but every liberal public figure who'd squirmed or demurred about a very common, very safe procedure that was a part of many people's lives. I felt sure that being open about abortion in the short term would help to depoliticize it in the long term. It was precisely that openness that would paradoxically allow it, one day maybe, to be treated as something "private and personal."

---

*Lawsuits challenging the Texas Heartbeat Act (SB 8) were ongoing at the time of this writing.

11. Good Sex

It was toward the end of the summer in 2018 when I got the idea to go to an erotic massage therapist. It was a porny fantasy I'd had for a while, that an aboveboard massage would suddenly turn into a furtive hand job. Dom was cool with it, so I made an appointment with a dude who's known for providing sensual happy endings. A few hours before my appointment, I visited my friend Ruby's baby along with two other friends. I tenderly held her new son, just a week old, and took wholesome photos. As he dozed, I notified my girls of my plans later; they were intrigued but not scandalized. On my subway ride to the massage, Dom texted me a photo of a guy he was attracted to.

I felt unflappable going into the appointment, and thankful that all parts of my life could coexist harmoniously: *I'm going to get a happy ending,* I thought, *and everyone's okay with it!*

I got on the massage table. This man was skilled and perceptive.

Considering the circumstances, I was relaxed and turned on. He took his time "massaging" me, which really meant stroking my butt and breasts and, eventually, between my legs. His pussy-rubbing skills were legitimately advanced, and it was clear he was paying close attention, responding to every little moan I made and every time I pressed into his hand a bit more.

And yet I didn't come. I knew from the beginning I maybe wouldn't. My clitoris refused to cooperate, even when he understood (bless his heart) that his bare hand wasn't working and he employed a few vibrators—including the all-powerful Hitachi Magic Wand, the same toy that had made me come for minutes on end atop Rob's green couch. His methods were all fine and arousal inducing, but it felt empty, mechanical. The only time my brain fizzed with true excitement was when my arm grazed his hard-on. I began hearing a voice inside my head, a voice I recognized from back in the day: *Come on, concentrate. Don't hurt his feelings. Don't make it awkward.* I heard a newer voice, too, influenced by the wellness industrial complex's concept of "self-care": *Can't you just lie back, relax, and enjoy it? Can't you just do something for yourself, for once?*

I left feeling physically and emotionally chafed, not to mention a little embarrassed: I was an orgasmic underachiever, even when I was paying for it. I really think I need a good narrative honestly, I texted my friends from earlier. It felt like sort of glorified masturbation rather than a real scenario. I prefer another person getting pleasure and participating, and what I *really* wanted was a normal massage from a hot man to turn into something more organically and spontaneously. Like that's the fantasy but it's so unattainable! I ended with self-deprecation: I guess I'm just a tough nut to crack 😔

I'd assumed that when someone hires a stranger to get them off, there is not much at stake emotionally, allowing the client's true desires to be distilled. So what, exactly, had I desired from that encounter? It's not like I had a problem giving myself orgasms from masturbating (certainly not when I brought out the big guns like the Magic Wand)—so it couldn't have been the actual sensation I was after. There was part of me that figured getting "serviced," in a scenario where my pleasure was the only thing on the menu, could be a feminist rite of passage. And of course, I'd hoped the role-play could fulfill a longtime fantasy. But I think I also wanted to know if I was somehow missing out on some kind of "good sex" only an expert could provide. As with porn, I knew good sex when I saw it, but was it correlated with how many orgasms I had? What about the more nebulous "sexual satisfaction"? One thing was for sure: I had not found it on that massage table.

• • •

Before the eighteenth century in the Western world, female sexual pleasure was widely thought to be essential to reproduction. For thousands of years, women were assumed to have the same reproductive organs as men, just on the inside. The ancient Greeks, who likely bestowed on us the origin of the word *clitoris*, figured that if men had to come in order to make a baby, then their female partners must too. Methods for producing the female orgasm showed up in seventeenth-century midwifery manuals; without orgasm, a popular text declared, "the fair sex [would] neither desire nuptial embraces, nor have pleasure in them, nor conceive by them." Scientific communities knew of the clitoris since at least the second century, though it kept getting forgotten and rediscovered, like when an Italian anatomist, Realdo Colombo, triumphantly identified the clitoris as "the seat of woman's delight" in his 1559 medical treatise *De re anatomica*.

But around the time when doctors determined that ovulation was an automatic bodily process having nothing to do with orgasm, women's sexual pleasure was knocked off its pedestal. In accordance with Victorian values, the assumption was that women and men were opposites, including their libidos. Women were recast as pure and angelic, not sexually passionate (whereas a few years earlier, the opposite was believed to be true). Historian Thomas Laqueur points out that this culture shift probably had less to do with actual biological discoveries—sure, they knew ovulation was "spontaneous," but they didn't know much else until the 1930s—and more to do with a desire to shape science in the current culture's image. Basically, female orgasms became a casualty of societal prudery. More recent scholarship has even debunked the tantalizing theory that Victorian doctors and midwives regularly administered manual genital massages to calm down "hysterical" women (a party anecdote of mine that I sadly had to retire).

In the early 1900s, Sigmund Freud famously contributed to clitoral shit talking by classifying the vaginal orgasm as the only appropriate, healthy path to female pleasure. He deemed clitoral orgasms (or any orgasms between queer couples) immature and, if experienced by adults, outright disordered. It's hard to overstate how pervasive Freudian thinking on orgasms was for a long time afterward. Even feminist Simone de Beauvoir, not exactly faithful to orthodoxy, touted the vaginal orgasm as the only "normal satisfaction" in *The Second Sex*. Despite widely available evidence of female masturbation and lesbianism from Alfred Kinsey, whose 1953 study *Sexual Behavior in the Human Female* reported that "orgasm is a phenomenon which appears to be essentially the same in the human female and male," psychologists and mid-century marriage manuals continued to romanticize orgasms from vaginal intercourse.

Dutch gynecologist Theodoor Hendrik van de Velde's *Ideal Marriage*, which became a sensation in the United States in 1961, defined "normal sexual intercourse" as taking place between "two sexually mature individuals of opposite sexes" and "concludes with the ejaculation . . . of the semen into the vagina, at the nearly simultaneous culmination of sensation—or orgasm—of both partners." And of course, being in love was vital: "Only where Love is can the sexual pleasure be at its height, the orgasm ecstatic, the relief complete." Not only were women meant to chase an elusive orgasm several centimeters from their clits, but they had to time it exactly right with the ejaculation of their soul mates. (This wasn't a problem for the lucky ladies he interviews who climaxed "in response to the gush of semen.")

To be fair, van de Velde put just as much pressure on the husbands. The onus was on the man to set the pace, and to decide when foreplay would end and when penetration would begin. "Every considerable erotic stimulation of their wives that does not terminate in orgasm," he warns, could "lead to permanent—or very obstinate—damage to both body and soul."

Then, a perfect storm occurred. A media-friendly pair of researchers named William Masters and Virginia Johnson published *Human Sexual Response*, a tome that, among other things, showcased the clitoral orgasm and made clear that a woman did not need a man in order to come. The book, based on eleven years of research, was released in 1966, at a moment when, as Barbara Ehrenreich, Elizabeth Hess, and Gloria Jacobs put it in *Re-Making Love*, "expert theories of female sexuality ran increasingly counter to women's social experience." By the time early feminists were meeting in each other's living rooms and discussing their sexual discontents, Masters and Johnson had become international stars. Suddenly there was easily accessible physiological evidence to back up the theory that uninspiring, penis-centered sex had its roots in misogyny.

Anne Koedt's article "The Myth of the Vaginal Orgasm," published as a short piece in *Notes from the First Year* and expanded in the journal's next issue in 1970, was one of the first feminist documents to explicitly make this connection. The piece is a full-throated "fuck you" to Freud, who "did not base his theory upon a study of woman's anatomy, but rather upon his assumptions of woman as an inferior appendage to man." She decries Freudians' "elaborate mental gymnastics" to explain the so-called problem of mass frigidity, and instead shines a light on another mass problem: the relentless pursuit of a vaginal orgasm, a "charade" that only leads to misery. "Looking for a cure to a problem that has none can lead a woman on an endless path of self-hatred and insecurity," she wrote. Such a woman is told by her psychologist or her boyfriend to "be even more feminine, think more feminine, and reject her envy of men. That is, shuffle even harder, baby."

Men, for their part, "seem suspiciously aware of the clitoral powers" when they want to arouse a woman in preparation for intercourse. So why have men ignored the clitoris for so long? Because men are worried "they will become sexually expendable," she wrote. "Actually this has a great deal of validity if one considers only the anatomy."

Of course, considering only the anatomy was facetious; it didn't take into account the emotional desires of women who had sex with men, and nowhere does Koedt acknowledge that some people might actually like the sensation of penetration, regardless of orgasmic potential. But female desire's complexity was not on the minds of the mostly male, conservative critics of this new clit-focused mentality. Instead, they complained that this new emphasis on sexual technique was ruining the mood at best, and traditional marriage at worst. Some feminists like Germaine Greer also took issue, decrying "digital massage" as "pompous and deliberate." She warned that making the clitoris "the only site of [women's] pleasure" would render women "dominated by the performance ethic"—which, she points out, suppresses creativity and eerily mirrors Puritan, nose-to-the-grindstone values, converting sexual pleasure into a dutiful project. Or a bloodless formula: "The implication that there is a statistically ideal fuck which will always result in satisfaction if the right procedures are followed is depressing and misleading," she wrote.

Still, the consensus was that all this new information was a net gain for the movement. How could it not be? Women were exploring what felt good and asking for what they wanted in bed. Even if women weren't having unilaterally satisfying sex, they could at least recognize sexually stingy partners. Feminists started educating women across the country about their own bodies. A book compiled by the Boston Women's Health Book Collective, *Our Bodies, Ourselves*, offered women candid, scientifically sound, sex-positive information. Sex educator and writer Betty Dodson started running group masturbation workshops out of her Manhattan apartment. By the seventies, vaginal self-exams with a handheld mirror became par for the feminist course.

It would only be a few more years before the ones saying "Shuffle even harder, baby," were the feminists themselves.

As the orgasm equity battles of the seventies and eighties gave way to Third Wave notions of empowered sluthood, the right to an orgasm became not only a permanent tenet of feminism but somewhat of a requirement to being a successful, liberated woman. Growing up in the nineties and aughts, I distinctly remember the drumbeat of orgasm supremacy: the cheesy *Cosmo* headlines about the best positions for "the big O." The girl-power reminders that you "deserve" to come with your partner, and anything less is garbage sex, ladies. There were all kinds of orgasms you could have— breast orgasms, anal orgasms, blended orgasms, touch-free orgasms, squirting orgasms. The vaginal orgasm made a comeback by way of the G-spot. The opaque, more diffuse term "sexual satisfaction" had been largely replaced by that one explosive moment. Orgasms received "a starring role in women's aspirations for gender equality," critic Laura Kipnis wryly wrote in 2006. "The ascendant premise is that women aren't just sexual and social equals, we're the Sex Champs, or at least we *could* be champs *if* men would get with the program."

As expectations for sex and partnerships rose, our collective angst about sexual inadequacy and dysfunction remained stubbornly high. Women now knew they "deserved" pleasure, and yet many of them, particularly the heterosexual ones, were still sexually dissatisfied. Today, women's desire is lower than they want it to be; for many women, researcher Katherine Rowland discovered, "dwindling desire was an affront to identity" and "exposed the limits of what they had expected of themselves." A widely publicized 2017 survey of more than fifty thousand Americans, published in the journal *Archives of Sexual Behavior,* found that only 65 percent of straight women and 66 percent of bisexual women usually or always had orgasms during sex, as opposed to 95 percent of straight men and 86 percent of lesbians. (Other unsurprising findings: women were more likely to come if their last sex session included deep kissing, manual genital stimulation, and/or oral sex in addition to p-in-v intercourse.) People are split as to what's causing low libido, but most social scientists say it's culturally constructed—a result of women's crowded, multitasking lives; overfamiliarity with their live-in partners; or, frankly, a reasonable response to lackluster sex partner choices. There's more information out there than ever, and yet lots of women are still thinking, often silently: *What's wrong with me?*

All of this history followed me to the appointment with the happy-ending dude. It was impossible to parse out my own motivations from the din of characters in my head, ranging from girl-bossy pep talks to radical feminist rallying cries. But I wondered if any of it actually reflected my true desires. I knew orgasms were supposed to be good; self-centered or judgmental lovers, bad. The thing I still hadn't quite figured out, after twenty years of having sex, was how to identify my own path to sexual pleasure, separate from modern feminism's sky-high standards—which, despite good intentions, at times seemed just as impossible to meet as van de Velde's simultaneous matrimonial orgasm.

• • •

By the second half of middle school, I knew what horniness felt like. I remember observing a gush in my underwear during eighth-grade prom, when I close-talked with my crush, Nathan, as he grazed the swell of my cleavage heaving out of my pewter Wet Seal minidress. I started waking up panting from dreams about furtive make-outs or a hand feeling up my shirt. I had yet to have a full-on hookup, but I had desires, and they were distinctly carnal.

By ninth grade, I'd had a handful of sexual encounters, my favorite parts of which were my reveries afterward. "Maybe the next three days after I fooled around with a guy, at arbitrary times of the day, I'll think about him. Obsessively," I wrote. "I will replay the exact thing of what we did, the best parts. I'll close my eyes. And I make myself like mildly horny all over again."

Like many people with vulvas, I experienced sexual desire way before I ever experienced an orgasm. In the summer between ninth and tenth grade, I tried to masturbate, and it didn't go well. "I don't really know what to do because I've never had an orgasm. And all I get is sore," I groused:

> I can't get wet or anything from my own hands, I guess I am doing something wrong. I guess what I'm saying is that I'm sexually frustrated. I've never had one of those explosive orgasms from hooking up. I get mild shivers, but it just never seems worth it. I have never kissed a guy that I really like and am overpoweringly attracted to, and that I know it's the same with him. And that us hooking up isn't just about him—or to say that he got some play so as to not look pathetic, as a lot of guys do, I know it—but it is about us, and pleasing each other.

This North Star of mutual pleasure is sprinkled all throughout my diaries during high school. Only a few months after this entry, I began having sex with Noah—sex that I described in rapturous detail in my diary. "I don't even know if I've had an orgasm, because the whole thing seems like one big orgasm, with imploding warm shivers throughout the whole hour and some that we fuck each other basically every week." I had not, in fact, had an orgasm. Still, reading (and cringing) through these entries, I don't get the impression that Noah was unconcerned with my enjoyment, or that I felt cheated out of an orgasm.

I came closer to coming once I started having sex with my next boyfriend, Derek. I explained having "this sudden surge of amazing-ness through my body" twice in my diary, "only for a second but it was so incredible." It was obvious that I enjoyed sex with him, but I can now see the influence of competitive climax culture seeping through as I try to figure out whether I'd had an acceptable amount of orgasmic pleasure: "I have felt clitoral twinges (which have never actually finished), overall bursts (which is usually normal sex), and sudden amazingness-es like those two I described. Hmmm."

It feels significant to me that I can richly recall many hot moments of my teenage sex life, but I do not remember details of my first orgasm. I do know it was toward the end of high school, as a result of using a vibrator I had secretly purchased with a friend while on a summer-camp trip to Provincetown, and I do remember thinking, *Oh, THAT'S what everyone is talking about.* It was the start of many wonderful masturbation sessions. But the revelation of an orgasm didn't recolor all my worthwhile sexual experiences in the past, so much as create another, somewhat separate outlet for my memories of them.

For a while, orgasms were what I did in private, to the thoughts of what I'd done with another person. A memory of an encounter that produced great pleasure but not a contemporaneous climax didn't disappoint me; in fact it was a slow burn, a long game of how much residual pleasure I could squeeze out of one sex session. As long as it felt good and was sexy, I'd come from it eventually, even if it was days or months or years later.

I was, however, acutely aware that this wasn't good enough, that men thought it was hottest when a woman orgasmed in front of them during sex. So I resolved to learn how to do it, and in a timely way, so nobody got impatient. My first orgasm with an actual human happened when I was twenty-two, during oral sex with a crucial assist from his fingers—"multimedia to the max," I remember bragging to my friends. It was a welcome, if not game-changing, development. I eventually nailed down the tricks that worked: weed, fingering, grinding against my partner on top, sometimes with help from a vibrator. (And I zeroed in on factors that would definitely impede an orgasm, namely, having any more than two or three drinks.) Even during bad stretches of Aaron's and my sex life, I could come if I put my mind to it.

Despite these insights, I often ended up faking it anyway. I felt pressure, both from my partners and from myself, to put on a performance of pleasure even if I was drunk, or tired, or the stars didn't align. It was that same neoliberal metric of empowerment I'd reached for when my best friend, Sarah, and I preemptively sidestepped slut-shaming by wielding our agency. It was a way to stay in control in the face of the many climax-killing variables, one of which was the expectation itself. Men would get this expectant look on their faces while they tried to pleasure me—a look that said, *Like that? How 'bout that? Ooh, how 'bout there, does that feel good?* I got the funny feeling that they were concerned about something other than my pleasure.

Simone de Beauvoir's elevation of the vaginal orgasm sounds old-fashioned now, but there's some truth to how she describes a magnanimous man using his hands to produce a clitoral climax instead: "If woman suffers from the egoism of men intent only upon their own relief," she wrote in *The Second Sex*, "she is also offended by a too obvious effort to give her pleasure." She then quotes psychologist Wilhelm Stekel: "To make the other feel pleasure means to dominate the other; to give oneself to someone is to abdicate one's will."

The concept of "giving" someone an orgasm has a tinge of condescension, as if an outside force can know your own body better than you can, but the concept is especially dubious when it is "given" by a gender who dominates another culturally. This had been a trope since the early days of the sexual revolution, when men "spoke of ecstasy but fucked with their egos," as my mother recalled. "Can't you just smell the male chauvinism all over that?" said a woman in Shulamith Firestone's reconstruction of a 1968 consciousness-raising session. "Man, the great lover, playing on woman like a violin—woman the sensitive instrument. . . . They don't produce our orgasms too, you know." There's truly nothing more annoying than a dude trying to get you off in order to boost his own self-esteem.

As for me, not only were orgasms not my goal when I had sex, but being told I needed to chase them really stressed me out. I worried that my partners would get bored by the pause in momentum, but more to the point, that *I* would. Receiving oral sex, especially, became an anxiety-producing event. I'd try to explain that even though I liked it, it probably wouldn't make me come. Men acted cool about this, but their faces belied bewilderment: *Hadn't they always been told that pussy eating is the key to a woman's heart and orgasm?*

When I did come from partnered sex, it didn't always feel victorious. Sometimes I'd feel connected to a person who was hitting my spot just right, but just as often I'd feel a million miles away, employing his body in a very specific way to catapult myself into a different realm. Those moments could be hot, and even sorta role-play-ish—*Use my dick, baby*—but they weren't ranked above the moments when I wasn't coming. Masturbating to a memory, and then letting my partner know that I did so, often did a better job of sealing a connection that was already there precisely because I had been present during sex, not fretting over my climax.

All of this secretly disturbed me for years. Wasn't the holy grail of female empowerment having an orgasm during sex, "owning" your pleasure? Why didn't I care all that much about it? I could see the sex therapists' smirks in my brain, implying that I wasn't being vulnerable enough, or that I didn't think I truly deserved pleasure, or that I should be worried if I had to concentrate *that* much to come during sex, or that I prioritized men's more easily accessible pleasure over my own. Remembering the knowing comments from Leila and other queer women, I wondered: Was my disinterest in cunnilingus just the way my body worked, or had I just not found someone who was good enough at it?

Later, in the time of Rob and Mor, all the way up to Dom, I learned to relax more during sex, which led to both more orgasms and less faking. I was genuinely grateful for both developments: The bliss-producing hormones released by those orgasms fueled our closeness. Being able to come more comfortably was nothing but good news. And yet, this period of sexual awakening taught me about not the centrality of orgasm but rather the holistic function of sex. The revelation came from acknowledging that I liked sex for all kinds of reasons *besides* getting off: the closeness and the chemical cocktail, the skin touch and the admiration, the thrill of pursuit, the playground of power dynamics. I can recall lots of times I tangled myself in Dom's body after a period of physical or emotional distance, and in those moments I didn't want to leave him, even to focus on orgasm. I wanted to look him in the eye, stroke his hair, grab his skin, rather than worry about positioning his fingers or tongue just so. Ironically, once I learned to have orgasms with partners more consistently, I could know for sure that their existence during sex was not essential, and in fact not usually the point.

Not that I didn't feel the specter of the pleasure gap hovering over my sex. There were still things I couldn't bring myself to ask for, a hesitance that felt distinctly gendered. I remained reluctant to ask my partners to simply luxuriate in my body and gift me an exploratory patience without runaway momentum taking over. Dom's and my sex, especially, had always been so driven by a concentrated hunger for each other—and by our mutual, sincere love of intercourse—that it took us a couple of years to truly slow down and have the kind of aimless, meandering sex sessions that lead to surprises or a deeper sense of closeness. But even with those times, it was less about orgasms, per se, than about savoring all the millions of feelings and sensations during sex, which could power my fantasy life later.

It was a relief, after years of faking and worrying, to make peace with my unique relationship to sexual pleasure, to recognize what genuinely turned me on and what didn't. When I looked at my desires with clear eyes, though, one question lingered: Why did I feel agnostic about my own orgasms, yet so adamant about producing them in men?

• • •

A few months after visiting the happy-ending guy, I became fascinated by the women who sought out male sex workers. Learning more about these escorts and the women who hired them wasn't an easy task. Although male escorts who service women are on the rise, they're still a teensy portion of the estimated forty-two million sex workers worldwide. And thanks to the 2018 FOSTA/SESTA laws, which made websites liable for what users say and do on their platforms, American sex workers can no longer advertise on Craigslist or Backpage. Sex workers who advertise any kind of service keep being kicked off platforms that once afforded them independence and safety.

Eventually, though, I was able to find about a dozen very lovely men around the world who sell pleasure and companionship, many of whom connected me with their female clients. I quickly discovered that, for many women, paying someone to fulfill your sexual desires is no casual whim. Women I spoke to often agonized over the decision. Emails, phone calls, and even nonsexual meetings happened before any actual sex. Many of these women were at the tail end of a vulnerable life experience. Some of them were coming out of an abusive relationship, and some of them had never had sex.

One thirty-nine-year-old woman I spoke to, Ange, had severe cerebral palsy and lost her fiancé years ago in a terrible accident. The man she eventually hired, a Sydney-based male escort and sex work advocate named John Oh, was the first man to penetrate her, perform oral sex on her, and witness her orgasm. "Having sex with John for the first time was awesome," Ange wrote me in one of several emails, which she composed through eye-gaze technology that enables her to type by training her eyes on specific symbols. "I was so happy and excited that he had made me a proper woman."

John Oh told me most of his clients took between two and six months to decide whether to book him. "The lack of normalization, the personal insecurity they feel about their bodies—there's so many things pushing back against women seeing sex workers," he said. So by the time women actually decide to book him, "it's a big deal. . . . They've made an enormous emotional investment already. They want someone to validate them." I had been wrong to presume that hiring a sex worker was emotionally low stakes. For many women, that couldn't be further from the truth.

Before the term *slut-shaming*, there was a concept in feminist theory meant to nullify the moral wedge artificially put between women who sell sex and women who don't: "whore stigma." If women break from what sex work scholar Jill Nagle calls "compulsory virtue," they risk being marginalized. It doesn't apply just to women whose sexual services are literally for sale; any woman who steps outside the bounds of the "good girl" role can be punished for it. It seems that "whore stigma" is what stops most women from buying sex with men, even though they'd be the customer, not the worker. For a woman living in a society that assumes she's the gatekeeper of sex, there's an added feeling of shame. For many women I spoke to, their desire to pay for sex initially made them feel deficient or like failures.

All of this is to say that the women who hire men to please them have done something particularly brave: they've prioritized their desires over avoiding some very potent cultural taboos. As one woman put it: "It actually felt pretty good to feel selfish."

The woman I interviewed who felt the least ambivalent about hiring a male escort was a former sex worker herself. Jan was in her fifties and happily married to a former client on the West Coast, but lately she hadn't been able to have sex with her husband because of his health issues. With his blessing, she'd seen five or six male sex workers by the time we spoke, an "elegant solution" because of the built-in boundaries.

But even Jan, who talks about these sessions like they're the most normal things in the world, bumped up against internalized ideas of how a woman should be during sex. "I really want to be very present," she said. "I don't want to feel rushed, fake anything, feel forced."

I ended up telling Jan about the happy-endings guy, about how my favorite part was when I noticed *his* erection. She understood. Women's "own arousal is often so plugged into feeling desired, not just desiring," she said. Because of a combination of biology and cultural dynamics, it could really hurt a woman's feelings if a male escort isn't visibly turned on. She has worried whether all these extremely hot and much younger men she hires find her attractive. Even though her first session with a young, gorgeous "Greek god" turned out to be "passionate," and "wonderful," Jan has had to peel back "layers upon layers of programming" and do away with "all these ten thousand little ways that I'm going to make [a man] feel comfortable." It was hard for her to learn how to have sex "just for me"—which is ostensibly what hiring an escort purely for pleasure should be all about.

My two months of immersive research had left me in awe of these women. It became clear that their paid pursuit of pleasure was nothing less than an announcement of erotic autonomy and full-on sexual rebellion, a way to forge that expectation-free path I had struggled with so much. But if I was honest, I couldn't relate to this idea of "selfish sex." It was why I couldn't come on that massage table: I powerfully did *not* want the focus to be just on me. Since I first started having sex, I've loved mutual acts like kissing and intercourse. I also enjoy giving pleasure. Savoring every moment of a tender blow job has long been a reliable way to get me aroused. And high on my list of why I enjoy sex with cis men is cum—the physical demonstration of an orgasm, which features in many of my fantasies. It thrills me to have a role in its creation.

Here came another thing to worry about: What did it say about me that my pleasure was tied to whether the man was having a good time? It seemed impossible to know whether I'm simply a person who naturally gets off by giving, or whether I'm a victim of the patriarchy, a cliché of a woman who prioritized male pleasure and approval rather than orgasms of my own. Elements of both were probably true, but it also frustrated me that men who relished eating pussy and facilitating their partners' pleasure would be celebrated for their generosity, while my preferences might be questioned by feminist orgasm cheerleaders. And it frustrated me further that I indulged this defensive line of thinking in the first place—couldn't I just have the sex I wanted to have, without feeling bad or guilty or like a shitty feminist? Without having to think at all? I felt grateful for the radical feminism that encouraged shame-free sexual exploration, but I resented its high bar too.

Therein lay the kinship between me and the women who hired sex workers, even if our sexual predilections were miles apart: Their declarations of sexual freedom were in constant tension with unattainable, contradictory expectations of what women were supposed to want. Even in moments of high satisfaction, pleasure, and orgasm, extracting what I actually desired from a mess of cultural and political influences—including feminist ones—was still an active effort, a dangling carrot, ever so slightly out of my reach.

● ● ●

In the last few years, pleasure rhetoric has shifted slightly to a less blatantly prescriptive (but still marketable) message. Emphasis on multiple orgasms has morphed into calls for "realness," "self-care," and "self-love" by sexual wellness companies—it's not about finding a partner to give you orgasms, but rather about being responsible for your *own* pleasure. We're trading in the idea of "foreplay" for less hierarchal, linear ways to think about the sexual act, which is no longer just a buildup to hetero intercourse. The new ideal is "embodied sex," fully present sex, authentic sex, mindful sex. The ascendant field of somatic sex therapy often helps clients heal from sexual trauma not by climaxing, but by breathing and feeling every sensation in their bodies.

Of course, mindfulness itself has already started to become another sexual Mount Everest we feel we must climb, and "self-care" is often code for more shit you need to buy, from luxury vibrators to orgasmic meditation classes to CBD-infused lube. But in this new language, I detect a bit of acknowledgment from empowerment capitalism that even the most ruthless among us are getting kinda sick of the sex goddess Olympics.

It's easy to figure out why: Hewing to any kind of orthodoxy is exhausting, and eventually alienating. For me and my mother and so many others, movements like feminism have provided sweet relief at the consciousness stage—like a patient who finally receives a doctor's diagnosis for mysterious symptoms. It's wonderful to be part of a bigger story, to be accepted by a group, to feel like you're not alone. I found that feeling in the "club" of friends who stepped off the conveyer belt. I felt it during cultural flashpoints like #MeToo and the rise of "yes means yes," and when I read about the lightbulb moments of radicals throughout history. This feeling helped me identify and reject the things I didn't want, like bad sex or being held hostage to oppressive cultural norms. But at some point I always land on the lonely thought that there will be no collective epiphany, especially if the ultimate goal is freedom—that no ideology, not even a feminist one, can deliver the key to my deepest desires.

Deciphering such a thing requires a scarier, more solitary journey, past Emma Goldman's soapbox and late-sixties speak-outs, past the neatly packaged gestures of vulnerability and bravery and anger that we all scroll through daily. Seen one way, it's all a little deflating: I went through a whole-ass feminist awakening only to discover that I'm ultimately on my own, on a seemingly futile search for erotic enlightenment. What kind of sad sexual quixotry is that? It gives me a twinge in my stomach to face that this kind of freedom neatly dovetails with American individualism, the value at the center of self-interested neoliberal feminism, and a value that will always be in conflict with my strongly held beliefs of community and shared political identity. An atomized quest for happiness is a classic threat to collective action.

Then there are times when I remember that freedom and loneliness don't have to go hand in hand. I think of the consciousness-raising session that so dismayed one woman, who observed that the group's problems and desires all contradicted one another. And then another woman's clarifying reply: "Maybe that's what liberation really is"—saying different things, but together and to one another, without worrying if they matched up with the person next to them.

But that still didn't solve the problem, because even if I could freely express my desires, how could I tell they were really mine? Recently, several hours after midnight, I searched for the phrase *good sex* in *The Essential Ellen Willis*, hoping once again that my mom could provide some answers to this conundrum. It led me to an unusually pessimistic passage of a 1981 essay in which she addresses the Sisyphean task of discovering how one really feels. "Women's sexual feelings have been stifled and distorted not only by men and men's ideas but by our own desperate strategies for living in and with a sexist, sexually repressive culture," she wrote. "Our most passionate convictions about sex do not necessarily reflect our real desires; they are as likely to be aimed at repressing the pain of desires we long ago decided were too dangerous to acknowledge, even to ourselves."

We shouldn't assess whether desires are good or bad, in other words, but we should also not assume they can ever be context-free. When exploring her enduring attraction to the forbidden, adrienne maree brown concedes that her fantasies are partly a result of "conditioning, being raised in a culture of repression, sex shaming, patriarchy and danger." In the end, she settles on acceptance: "But it's also how my desire is wired, even after decades of therapy and somatics." That's how I feel about my penchant for blow jobs, my agnosticism toward orgasms, and possibly my heterosexuality itself. These preferences don't mean I'm a failed feminist, but they do mean *something*—possibly that I've converted the pain of misogyny into pleasure, or more simply that the prevailing culture has nested itself into my imagination. Or maybe I'd still prefer those things if I were living ten thousand years ago—there is really no way to know. As Tracy Clark-Flory wrote in her memoir, *Want Me*, "There is no pre-cultural self to which we can return."

My foray into buying sex hadn't given me the answers to my authentic desires. In fact, it served as a mildly humiliating detour amid my never-ending effort to understand my own sexuality. Still, my impulse to purchase erotic agency also revealed an urge for a bubble devoid of judgment, far away from the world, so I could be free from the pressure of having my desires line up with some hazy feminist or feminine ideal, so I could free my male partners from pressures that hurt them too. Of course, this bubble does not exist. That's the prime letdown of utopia: it's the good place, but it's also no place at all.

Actually, the elusive quality of sex may be ultimately what I like best about it. Lately I've been appreciating its oxygenated elasticity, how it refuses to be reduced to a sharp, finite peak of pleasure or a neat set of tenets. Instead it writhes and hides, expands and contracts, hitchhikes on history like barnacles while also shading the contours of our own tiny lives. Sex can strip us down to a raw nub of honesty or it can be a thrilling escapist performance (and the latter can also lead to the former). One's access to sexual self-awareness can go in and out; it can be retrospective or anticipatory. Sex can mean everything to us, or nothing at all. Desire is so amorphous, so maddening, so surprising—so utterly predetermined and individual at the exact same time.

In the end, the very nature of sex eschews happily ever after, and so does love, despite its wildly unearned reputation as a fixed destination. The timeline of this book concludes with me in a relationship with a man, but one of the central principles of my partnership with Dom is the acceptance of unknowability, a standard that has proved to be both terrifying and gratifying. When we were still a very new couple, before we could fathom the existence of incoming curveballs, I bought him Rebecca Solnit's *A Field Guide to Getting Lost* as a present ahead of a trip he was taking alone. It was one of the books I brought with me on my own solo getaway, that infamous trip to Monoblet, France, in 2013. Dom was struck by a passage about growth, a passage I only faintly remembered reading four years before. Solnit writes, "Many love stories are like the shells of hermit crabs," which spend their lives outgrowing shells and finding new ones. Others, she observes, "are more like chambered nautiluses, whose architecture grows with the inhabitant and whose abandoned smaller chambers are lighter than water and let them float into the sea." Its outgrown past doesn't disappear or sink the nautilus—it buoys it.

This concept has become a touchstone in my romantic relationship, but also in my relationship with sex, and the relationship we all have to sexuality's history. Finally pinning down our own bespoke versions of good sex will never be possible, because context and motivations and priorities will always change. I barely recognize the woman who went to France and made a pros and cons list about her marriage and scribbled out the most important part, but I see her as on the continuum of all the stories that keep me afloat through revelation. The unsteady conclusions of liberationists that ended up inspiring me more than any righteous slogan. My parents' love story, flecked with the muck of patriarchy and yet luminous, durable. My mother's words, of which there are so many, and also never enough. I'm grateful for the chambers of air they all created.

ACKNOWLEDGMENTS

Thank you to my agent, Samantha Shea, who has excellent taste, if I do say so myself, and who gave this book its title. Thank you to my editor, Maya Ziv, for instantly loving and encouraging this project, even before I finished the proposal. Thank you to Lux Alptraum, Tracy Clark-Flory, Moira Donegan, Kate Dries, Rachel Dry, Emma Eisenberg, Ann Friedman, Jenn Gann, Melissa Giannini, Amanda Hess, Briallen Hopper, Michelle Legro, Alana Levinson, Glynnis MacNicol, Collier Meyerson, Haley Mlotek, Rachel Monroe, Samhita Mukhopadyay, Geraldine Sealey, Charlotte Shane, Alix Kates Shulman, Dodai Stewart, Kat Stoeffel, Joyce Tang, Rebecca Traister, Jessica Valenti, Alicia Wittmeyer, and Jenny Zhang for being my editors, advocates, and book-advice fairy godparents. Thanks to Samhita Mukhopadhyay, Aerial East, Brigid Dunn, Cille Songhai, Reina Gattuso, and D. Ann Williams for your feedback on versions of this book. Thanks to Cashen

Acknowledgments

Conroy for a truly obsessive fact-check, in the best way. Thank you to Carrie Frye for your preternatural insight and gentle pep talks, and for helping me find the "magic lassos" of these chapters.

Thank you to the Radcliffe Institute's Schlesinger Library for your impeccably organized archives. Thank you to the Jentel Foundation for providing me with a special month in an unspeakably gorgeous space that inspired major, vital revisions to this book. Thank you to Bob Christgau for digging up a treasure trove of my mother's letters and making copies for me, just in the nick of time. Thank you to the scholars who generously sent me books and PDFs when libraries were COVID-closed: Jean Silver-Isenstadt, Patricia Cline Cohen, John Spurlock, Cherríe Moraga, Jessica Marie Johnson, and Laina Bay-Cheng.

Thank you to all my sweet friends for putting up with my bouts of book jail. Thank you to my mother, whose love and wisdom are the backbone of this book. Thank you to my father, my first teacher in class and race consciousness, who peacefully left this world in his sleep only days after I put this book to bed. And thank you to Domenick Bauer, for your endless puree.

BAD SEX ESSENTIALS:
A SELECTED BIBLIOGRAPHY

These are all sources that greatly shaped the DNA of *Bad Sex*; either I turned to them again and again or they provided epiphanies that were crucial to the hearts of these chapters.

BOOKS

Allyn, David. *Make Love, Not War: The Sexual Revolution: An Unfettered History*. Boston: Little, Brown, 2000.

Angel, Katherine. *Tomorrow Sex Will Be Good Again: Women and Desire in the Age of Consent*. Brooklyn, NY: Verso, 2021.

Aronowitz, Stanley. *False Promises: The Shaping of American Working Class Consciousness*. New York: McGraw-Hill, 1973.

Beauvoir, Simone de. *The Second Sex*. London: Vintage, 1997.

Bracewell, Lorna N. *Why We Lost the Sex Wars: Sexual Freedom in the #MeToo Era*. Minneapolis: University of Minnesota Press, 2021.

brown, adrienne maree. *Pleasure Activism: The Politics of Feeling Good*. Chico, CA: AK Press, 2019.

Brown, Helen Gurley. *Sex and the Single Girl: The Unmarried Woman's Guide to Men*. New York: Random House, 1962.

Brown, Rita Mae. *Rubyfruit Jungle*. New York: Bantam Books, 1977.

Brownmiller, Susan. *Against Our Will: Men, Women, and Rape*. New York: Simon & Schuster, 1975.

Chen, Angela. *Ace: What Asexuality Reveals about Desire, Society, and the Meaning of Sex*. Boston: Beacon Press, 2020.

Coontz, Stephanie. *Marriage, a History: From Obedience to Intimacy or How Love Conquered Marriage*. New York: Viking, 2005.

———. *The Way We Never Were: American Families and the Nostalgia Trap*. New York: Basic Books, 1992.

Cooper, Brittney C. *Beyond Respectability: The Intellectual Thought of Race Women*. Urbana: University of Illinois Press, 2017.

Cott, Nancy F. *Public Vows: A History of Marriage and the Nation*. Cambridge, MA: Harvard University Press, 2000.

Echols, Alice. *Daring to Be Bad: Radical Feminism in America, 1967–1975*. Minneapolis: University of Minnesota Press, 1989.

Ehrenreich, Barbara. *The Hearts of Men: American Dreams and the Flight from Commitment*. New York: Anchor Books, 1983.

Ehrenreich, Barbara, Elizabeth Hess, and Gloria Jacobs. *Re-Making Love: The Feminization of Sex*. Garden City, NY: Anchor Press/Doubleday, 1986.

Falk, Candace. *Love, Anarchy, and Emma Goldman: A Biography*. New Brunswick, NJ: Rutgers University Press, 1990.

Farrell, Warren. *The Liberated Man: Beyond Masculinity: Freeing Men and Their Relationships with Women*. New York: Random House, 1974.

Fasteau, Marc Feigen. *The Male Machine*. New York: McGraw-Hill, 1974.

Fateman, Joanna, and Amy Scholder, eds. *Last Days at Hot Slit: The Radical Feminism of Andrea Dworkin*. South Pasadena, CA: Semiotext(e), 2019.

Firestone, Shulamith. *The Dialectic of Sex: The Case for Feminist Revolution*. New York: Bantam Books, 1972.

Friedman, Jaclyn, and Jessica Valenti, eds. *Yes Means Yes: Visions of Female Sexual Power and a World without Rape*. New York: Seal Press, 2019.

Giddings, Paula. *When and Where I Enter: The Impact of Black Women on Race and Sex in America*. New York: William Morrow, 1988.

Goldman, Emma. *Anarchism and Other Essays*. New York: Dover Publications, 1969.

———. *Living My Life*. New York: Alfred A. Knopf, 1931. Digitized by Anarchist Library, https://theanarchistlibrary.org/library/emma-goldman-living-my-life.

Hartman, Saidiya. *Wayward Lives, Beautiful Experiments: Intimate Histories of Social Upheaval*. New York: W. W. Norton, 2019.

Heyn, Dalma. *The Erotic Silence of the American Wife*. New York: Turtle Bay Books, 1992.

Hite, Shere. *The Hite Report: A Nationwide Study on Female Sexuality*. New York: Macmillan, 1976.

———. *The Hite Report on Male Sexuality*. New York: Alfred A. Knopf, 1981.

Hunter, Tera W. *Bound in Wedlock: Slave and Free Black Marriage in the Nineteenth Century*. Cambridge, MA: The Belknap Press of Harvard University Press, 2017.

Hutchins, Loraine, and Lani Ka'ahumanu, eds. *Bi Any Other Name: Bisexual People Speak Out*. Boston: Alyson Publications, 1991.

Levine, Judith. *My Enemy, My Love: Women, Men, and the Dilemmas of Gender*. New York: Anchor Books/Doubleday, 1993.

Lorde, Audre. *Sister Outsider: Essays and Speeches*. Trumansburg, NY: Crossing Press, 1984.

Machado, Carmen Maria. *In the Dream House: A Memoir*. Minneapolis, MN: Graywolf Press, 2019.

Moraga, Cherríe, and Gloria Anzaldúa, eds. *This Bridge Called My Back: Writings by Radical Women of Color*. New York: Kitchen Table, Women of Color Press, 1983.

Morgan, Joan. *When Chickenheads Come Home to Roost: A Hip Hop Feminist Breaks It Down*. New York: Simon & Schuster, 2000.

Nagle, Jill, ed. *Whores and Other Feminists*. New York: Routledge, 1997.

Perel, Esther. *Mating in Captivity: Unlocking Erotic Intelligence*. New York: HarperCollins, 2007.

———. *The State of Affairs: Rethinking Infidelity*. New York: HarperCollins, 2017.

Radicalesbians. "The Woman-Identified Woman." In *Out of the Closets: Voices of Gay Liberation*, edited by Karla Jay and Allen Young, 172–77. New York: Douglas Book Corp., 1972.

Rowland, Katherine. *The Pleasure Gap: American Women and the Unfinished Sexual Revolution*. New York: Seal Press, 2020.

Sarachild, Kathie, ed. *Feminist Revolution*. New York: Random House, 1978.

Shulman, Alix Kates. *A Marriage Agreement and Other Essays: Four Decades of Feminist Writing*. New York: Open Road, 2012.

Silver-Isenstadt, Jean L. *Shameless: The Visionary Life of Mary Gove Nichols*. Baltimore: Johns Hopkins University Press, 2002.

Vance, Carole S., ed. *Pleasure and Danger: Exploring Female Sexuality*. Boston: Routledge & Kegan Paul, 1984.

Wallace, Michele. *Black Macho and the Myth of the Superwoman*. New York: Dial Press, 1979.

Ward, Jane. *The Tragedy of Heterosexuality*. New York: New York University Press, 2020.

Willis, Ellen. *No More Nice Girls: Countercultural Essays*. Hanover, NH: University Press of New England, 1992.

Willis Aronowitz, Nona, ed. *The Essential Ellen Willis*. Minneapolis: University of Minnesota Press, 2014.

ARTICLES

Bay-Cheng, Laina Y. "The Agency Line: A Neoliberal Metric for Appraising Young Women's Sexuality." *Sex Roles* 73 (2015): 279–91.

Boo, Katherine. "The Marriage Cure." *The New Yorker*, August 10, 2003. https://www.newyorker.com/magazine/2003/08/18/the-marriage-cure.

Brownmiller, Susan. "'Sisterhood Is Powerful': A Member of the Women's Liberation Movement Explains What It's All About." *New York Times*, March 15, 1970. https://www.nytimes.com/1970/03/15/archives/sisterhood-is-powerful-a-member-of-the-womens-liberation-movement.html.

Combahee River Collective. "The Combahee River Collective Statement." Black Past, 1977. https://www.blackpast.org/african-american-history/combahee-river-collective-statement-1977.

Densmore, Dana. "On Celibacy." *No More Fun and Games: A Journal of Female Liberation* 1, no. 1 (October 1968): 23–26.

Dominus, Susan. "Is an Open Marriage a Happier Marriage?" *New York Times*, May 11, 2017. https://www.nytimes.com/2017/05/11/magazine/is-an-open-marriage-a-happier-marriage.html.

Firestone, Shulamith. "Women Rap about Sex." *Notes from the First Year: Women's Liberation* (1968): 8–11.

Franke, Katherine M. "Marriage Is a Mixed Blessing." *New York Times*, June 23, 2011. https://www.nytimes.com/2011/06/24/opinion/24franke.html.

Hopper, Briallen. "On Spinsters." *Los Angeles Review of Books*, July 12, 2015. https://lareviewofbooks.org/article/on-spinsters.

Koedt, Anne. "The Myth of the Vaginal Orgasm." *Notes from the Second Year: Women's Liberation* (1969): 37–41.

Lindsey, Treva B., and Jessica Marie Johnson. "Searching for Climax: Black Erotic Lives in Slavery and Freedom." *Meridians* 12, no. 2 (2014): 169–95.

Massey, Alana. "Against Chill." *Matter*, April 1, 2015. https://medium.com/matter/against-chill-930dfb60a577.

Morgan, Joan. "Why We Get Off: Moving Towards a Black Feminist Politics of Pleasure." *Black Scholar* 45, no. 4 (2015): 36–46.

Rich, Adrienne. "Compulsory Heterosexuality and Lesbian Existence." *Signs* 5, no. 4 (Summer 1980): 631–60. http://www.jstor.org/stable/3173834.

Seresin, Asa. "On Heteropessimism." *New Inquiry*, October 9, 2019. https://thenewinquiry.com/on-heteropessimism.

Shulman, Alix Kates. "Sex and Power: Sexual Bases of Radical Feminism." *Signs* 5, no. 4 (Summer 1980): 590–604. https://www.jstor.org/stable/3173832.

ARCHIVAL MATERIAL

Ellen Willis fonds. Schlesinger Library at the Radcliffe Institute. Cambridge, Massachusetts.

Letters from Ellen Willis to Robert Christgau. 1969–1970.

"Tell It Like It Is: A Transcript of the First Abortion Speakout." Transcribed by Georgia Christgau for the speak-out's fiftieth-anniversary event, New York City, March 23, 2019.

NOTES

INTRODUCTION

4 **"It was the best"**: Ellen Willis, "Coming Down Again: After the Age of Excess," in *The Essential Ellen Willis*, ed. Nona Willis Aronowitz (Minneapolis: University of Minnesota Press, 2014), 282.

CHAPTER 1: BAD SEX

5 **"tell the truth"**: Alix Kates Shulman, "Sex and Power: Sexual Bases of Radical Feminism," *Signs* 5, no. 4 (Summer 1980): 594.

12 **In the fall of 1967**: The history of early feminism and consciousness-raising in this section (unless otherwise specified) was reconstructed from Alice Echols, *Daring to Be Bad: Radical Feminism in America, 1967–1975* (Minneapolis: University of Minnesota Press, 1989); Joy Press, "The Life and Death of a Radical Sisterhood," The Cut, November 2017, https://www.thecut.com/2017/11/an-oral-history-of-feminist-group -new-york-radical-women.html; and *She's Beautiful When She's Angry*, directed by Mary Dore (New York, 2014).

13 **"sexual garbage cans"**: Francine Silbar, "Women and the Draft Movement," *New Left Notes* 2, no. 12 (1967): 11.

13 **"Speak pain to recall pain"**: Susan Brownmiller, "'Sisterhood Is Powerful': A Member of the Women's Liberation Movement Explains What It's All About," *New York Times*, March 15, 1970, https://www.nytimes.com/1970/03/15/archives /sisterhood-is-powerful-a-member-of-the-womens-liberation-movement.html.

14 **"Sex was a central"**: Shulman, "Sex and Power," 594, 592.

14 **came out as lesbians:** June Arnold, "Consciousness-Raising," in *Radical Feminism: A Documentary Reader*, ed. Barbara A. Crow (New York: New York University Press, 2000), 285.

14 **a mass admission of faked orgasms:** Shulman, "Sex and Power," 593.

15 **"The guys fucked like rabbits"**: David Allyn, *Make Love, Not War: The Sexual Revolution: An Unfettered History* (Boston: Little, Brown, 2000), 103.

16 **a satirical "funeral oration"**: Kathie Amatniek, "Funeral Oration for the Burial of Traditional Womanhood," *Notes from the First Year: Women's Liberation* (1968): 20, https://idn.duke.edu/ark:/87924/r3k10d.

16 **that caused men to come:** Anne Koedt, "The Myth of the Vaginal Orgasm," *Notes from the First Year*, 11.

16 **"not just grease between men"**: Shulamith Firestone, "Abortion Rally Speech," *Notes from the First Year*, 25.

16 **"simply because we WANT to"**: Shulamith Firestone, "Women Rap about Sex," *Notes from the First Year*, 8.

17 **"what liberation really is"**: Arnold, "Consciousness-Raising," 285.

17 **"in the papers for fighting"**: Ellen Willis, "Up from Radicalism: A Feminist Journal," in *The Essential Ellen Willis*, ed. Nona Willis Aronowitz (Minneapolis: University of Minnesota Press, 2014), 11.

18 **"off the hook too easily"**: Willis, "Up from Radicalism," 11.

19 **"real wifely bit"**: Judy Oppenheimer, interview with the author, January 30, 2020.

19 **A "very cocky" guy:** Willis, "Up from Radicalism," 9.

19 **"other women, except friendlier"**: Willis, "Up from Radicalism," 12.

20 **"It makes you more conscious"**: Willis, "Up from Radicalism," 17.

20 **"my private life"**: Willis, "Up from Radicalism," 18.

21 **"ten months of feminist nagging"**: Robert Christgau to Ellen Willis, one of three letters written on October 17, 1969.

21 **"I no longer dig your lust"**: Christgau to Willis.

21 **"I trusted you to be kind"**: Christgau to Willis.

21 **"new kind of consciousness"**: Christgau to Willis.

21 **"doubt myself again"**: Ellen Willis to Robert Christgau, undated, circa fall 1969.

22 **"essentially male supremacist phenomena"**: Ellen Willis to Robert Christgau, October 25, 1969.

22 **"supercharged emotional excitement"**: Willis to Christgau, October 25, 1969.

22 **deeply ingrained gender roles:** Willis to Christgau, undated, circa fall 1969.

22 **"missing sense of yourself"**: Robert Christgau to Ellen Willis, October 20, 1969.

22 **"perhaps external pressures"**: Willis to Christgau, October 25, 1969.

22 **"very specific ways"**: Ellen Willis to Robert Christgau, October 31, 1969.

22 **"how tight the shoe is"**: Willis to Christgau, October 31, 1969.

23 **"not qualified to interfere with"**: Willis to Christgau, undated, circa fall 1969.

23 **"isolation, dependency, honeymoonisoverness"**: Ellen Willis to Robert Christgau, November 20, 1970.

24 **"be by herself"**: Steve Dyer, interview with the author, December 15, 2019.

29 **"what I could hold out for"**: Ellen Willis, "The Family: Love It or Leave It," in Aronowitz, *The Essential Ellen Willis*, 101.

32 **"moral coercion is oppressive"**: Willis, "The Family," 102, 106.

CHAPTER 2: STATUS BUMP

33 **"I believe marriage"**: Phyllis Rose, *Parallel Lives: Five Victorian Marriages* (New York: Alfred A. Knopf, 1983), 7.

37 **At a Christmas party**: This section on Mary Gove Nichols, the free love movement, and marriage's role in abolition (unless otherwise specified) was reconstructed from John C. Spurlock, "Mary Gove Nichols," in *Women in World History: A Biographical Encyclopedia* (Waterford, CT: Yorkin Publications), 766–71; Jean Silver-Isenstadt, *Shameless: The Visionary Life of Mary Gove* (Baltimore: Johns Hopkins University Press, 2002); Holly Jackson, *American Radicals: How Nineteenth-Century Protest Shaped the Nation* (New York: Crown, 2019), 133–38; Joanne E. Passet, *Sex Radicals and the Quest for Women's Equality* (Champaign: University of Illinois Press, 2003), 23–26; Stephanie Coontz, *The Way We Never Were: American Families and the Nostalgia Trap* (New York: Basic Books, 1992): 3–5; Tera W. Hunter, *Bound in Wedlock: Slave and Free Black Marriage in the Nineteenth Century* (Cambridge, MA: The Belknap Press of Harvard University Press, 2017), 40–42; and Nancy F. Cott, *Public Vows: A History of Marriage and the Nation* (Cambridge, MA: Harvard University Press, 2000).

38 **"as beautiful as rare"**: Mary Gove Nichols, *Mary Lyndon; or, Revelations of a Life. An Autobiography* (New York: Stringer and Townsend, 1855), 358.

38 **"burning prairie"**: Jean Silver-Isenstadt, "Mary S. Gove Nichols: Making the Personal Political," in *Ordinary Women, Extraordinary Lives: Women in American History*, ed. Kristen Lindenmeyer (Wilmington, DE: SR Books, 2000), 73.

39 **"I must go"**: Patricia Cline Cohen, "The 'Anti-Marriage Theory' of Thomas and Mary Gove Nichols: A Radical Critique of Monogamy," *Journal of the Early Republic in the 1850s* 34, no. 1 (Spring 2014): 5, https://www.jstor.org/stable/24486929.

41 **"thrust their immoralities"**: Cott, *Public Vows*, 69.

41 **"love every day if I please"**: Victoria Woodhull, "And the Truth Shall Make You Free: A Speech on the Principles of Social Freedom," Steinway Hall, New York,

November 21, 1871 (New York: Woodhull, Claflin & Co., 1871), https://www.loc.gov/item/09008216/.

41 **"Abolish all marriage this day":** Thomas Nichols and Mary Gove Nichols, *Marriage: Its History, Character, and Results* (New York: T.L. Nichols, 1854), 114.

42 **"the coarsest lust":** "A Bad Book Gibbeted," *New York Times*, August 17, 1855, https://timesmachine.nytimes.com/timesmachine/1855/08/17/80268603.html.

42 **"changeless, stagnant condition":** Francis Barry, "Marriage—Defining Positions," *Nichols' Monthly: A Magazine of Social Science and Progressive Literature*, n.s., 1 (January 1855): 32.

42 **"patron of slavery":** Thomas Nichols, "Marriage—Defining Positions," *Nichols' Monthly: A Magazine of Social Science and Progressive Literature*, n.s., 1 (January 1855): 31.

43 **trivializing slavery as a result:** See Ana Stevenson, *The Woman as Slave in Nineteenth-Century American Social Movements* (London: Palgrave Macmillan, 2019), for an excellent, exhaustive study of the slavery-marriage parallel.

44 **"positively beat their wives":** Dorothy Sterling, *We Are Your Sisters: Black Women in the Nineteenth Century* (New York: W.W. Norton, 1984), 340, 405.

44 **she deemed slavery the most:** Stevenson, *The Woman as Slave*, 241.

44 **"rape and lifelong slavery":** Sara Davidson, "An 'Oppressed Majority' Demands Its Rights," *Life*, December 12, 1969, https://www.maryellenmark.com/bibliography/magazines/article/life/an-oppressed-majority-demands-its-rights/L.

45 **"decided to re-examine":** Alix Kates Shulman, *A Marriage Agreement and Other Essays: Four Decades of Feminist Writing* (New York: Open Road, 2012), 8.

45 **The divorce rate:** Alexander A. Plateris, "Divorces and Divorce Rates, United States," *Vital and Health Statistics* 21, no. 29 (April 1980), https://www.cdc.gov/nchs/data/series/sr_21/sr21_029.pdf; Sheela Kennedy and Steven Ruggles, "Breaking Up Is Hard to Count: The Rise of Divorce in the United States, 1980–2010," *Demography* 51, no. 2 (2014): 587–98, https://doi.org/10.1007/s13524-013-0270-9.

45 **One out of every three marriages:** Stephanie Coontz, *Marriage, a History: From Obedience to Intimacy or How Love Conquered Marriage* (New York: Viking, 2005), 252.

45 **"autonomy and love too":** Ellen Willis, "The Family: Love It or Leave It," in *The Essential Ellen Willis*, ed. Nona Willis Aronowitz (Minneapolis: University of Minnesota Press, 2014), 109.

46 **"What a big fish":** Judy Oppenheimer, interview with the author, January 30, 2020.

47 **"no irresistible economic or social pressure":** Ellen Willis, "Say It Loud: Out of Wedlock and Proud," in Aronowitz, *The Essential Ellen Willis*, 368.

47 **"women's dependence on marriage":** Willis, "Say It Loud," 369.

47 **"very existence and survival":** *Loving v. Virginia*, 388 U.S. 1 (1967).

48 **"fulfillment for themselves":** *Obergefell v. Hodges*, 576 US _ (2015).

48 **"emotional and material labor"**: Briallen Hopper, "On Spinsters," *Los Angeles Review of Books*, July 12, 2015, https://lareviewofbooks.org/article/on-spinsters.

49 **"hardly something to celebrate"**: Katherine M. Franke, "Marriage Is a Mixed Blessing," *New York Times*, June 23, 2011, https://www.nytimes.com/2011/06/24/opinion/24franke.html.

49 **The average age of first marriage**: U.S. Census Bureau, "Historical Marital Status Tables," December 2020, figure MS-2, "Median Age at First Marriage, 1890 to Present," accessed September 1, 2021, https://www.census.gov/content/dam/Census/library/visualizations/time-series/demo/families-and-households/ms-2.pdf.

50 **Emily Witt called "neo-marriages"**: Emily Witt, *Future Sex* (New York: Farrar, Straus and Giroux, 2016), 156.

51 **twice as many servants**: Coontz, *The Way We Never Were*, loc. 5, Kindle.

51 **"no fear of leaving him"**: Mary White Ovington, *Half a Man: The Status of the Negro* (Norwood, MA: Plimpton Press, 1911), 141, Project Gutenberg ebook.

51 **"propensity for being poor"**: Jane Austen to Fanny Knight, March 13, 1817, https://pemberley.com/janeinfo/brablt15.html#letter83.

52 **almost 60 percent of the population**: Coontz, *The Way We Never Were*, 23.

52 **nearly two-thirds of American families**: U.S. Census Bureau, "Tracking the American Dream—Fifty Years of Housing Changes," April 1994, accessed February 13, 2021, https://www.census.gov/prod/1/statbrief/sb94_8.pdf.

52 **less than 10 percent of Americans**: Coontz, *The Way We Never Were*, 24.

52 **the median age at first marriage**: U.S. Census Bureau, "Historical Marital Status Tables," figure MS-2.

52 **"the world of alienated work"**: bell hooks, *Feminist Theory: From Margin to Center* (London: Pluto Press, 1984), 134.

52 **Nowadays, the college educated**: Kim Parker and Renee Stepler, "As U.S. Marriage Rate Hovers at 50%, Education Gap in Marital Status Widens," Pew Research Center, 2017, https://www.pewresearch.org/fact-tank/2017/09/14/as-u-s-marriage-rate-hovers-at-50-education-gap-in-marital-status-widens/; Wendy Wang, "The Link between a College Education and a Lasting Marriage," Pew Research Center, 2015, https://www.pewresearch.org/fact-tank/2015/12/04/education-and-marriage/.

53 **A 2013 study**: Sarah Corse, "Intimate Inequalities: Love and Work in a Post-Industrial Landscape" (presentation, American Sociological Association, New York, August 2013).

53 **"sharing resources with a partner"**: Amanda Hess, "Marriage Is the New Middle-Class Luxury Item," *Slate*, August 13, 2013, https://slate.com/human-interest/2013/08/marriage-wage-gap-post-recession-only-middle-class-americans-can-afford-to-get-married.html.

53 **"materially and emotionally for others"**: Corse, "Intimate Inequalities."

53 **"she has not even tried"**: Ovington, *Half a Man*, 168–69.

54 **state-sponsored marriage seminar**: Katherine Boo, "The Marriage Cure," *New Yorker*, August 10, 2003, https://www.newyorker.com/magazine/2003/08/18/the -marriage-cure.

54 **one-third of Black women**: Kelly Raley, Megan M. Sweeney, and Danielle Wondra, "The Growing Racial and Ethnic Divide in U.S. Marriage Patterns," *Future of Children* 25, no. 2 (Fall 2015), https://www.ncbi.nlm.nih.gov/pmc/articles/PMC4850739.

54 **"Assimilating was part of my survival"**: Sadye (last name withheld), interview with the author, July 12, 2020.

56 **excoriated and misunderstood**: Silver-Isenstadt, "Mary S. Gove Nichols," 86; Jean Silver-Isenstadt, *Shameless: The Visionary Life of Mary Gove* (Baltimore: Johns Hopkins University Press, 2002), 227.

56 **"took marriage seriously"**: Patricia Cline-Cohen, email to the author, May 10, 2020.

59 **A woman's earning power**: Sascha O. Becker et al., "Discrimination in Hiring Based on Potential and Realized Fertility: Evidence from a Large-Scale Field Experiment," *Institute of Labor Economics*, no. 12308 (2019): 2.

CHAPTER 3: I WANT THIS

61 **"Desire so often"**: Brandy Jensen, "How to Poach an Egg and Leave a Marriage," MyRecipes.com, March 29, 2018, https://www.myrecipes.com/extracrispy/how-to -poach-an-egg-and-leave-a-marriage.

64 **"repressive rampages"**: Stanley Aronowitz, *False Promises: The Shaping of American Working Class Consciousness* (New York: McGraw-Hill, 1973), 339.

65 **"reproduced the prevailing"**: Aronowitz, *False Promises*, 353.

65 **"bills, work, and alienated leisure"**: Aronowitz, *False Promises*, 353.

65 **"having to support a family"**: Aronowitz, *False Promises*, 355.

66 **"valuable suggestions"**: Aronowitz, *False Promises*, viii.

68 **"dry the dishes"**: Ellen Willis, "Up from Radicalism," in *The Essential Ellen Willis*, ed. Nona Willis Aronowitz (Minneapolis: University of Minnesota Press, 2014), 5.

70 **"Karl is working"**: Gloria Steinem, "Introduction," in Marc Feigen Fasteau, *The Male Machine* (New York: McGraw-Hill, 1974), xiii.

71 **"defining our fate"**: Ellen Willis, "Coming Down Again: After the Age of Excess," in Aronowitz, *The Essential Ellen Willis*, 281.

72 **"Lies are boring"**: Kathie Sarachild, "Going for What You Really Want," in *Women and Romance: A Reader*, ed. Susan Ostrov Weisser (New York: New York University Press, 2001), 135.

72 **"with a channel"**: Quoted in Alice Echols, "Taming of the Id," in *Pleasure and Danger: Exploring Female Sexuality*, ed. Carole Vance (Boston: Routledge & Kegan Paul, 1984), 57.

72 **"replenishing and provocative force"**: Audre Lorde, *Sister Outsider: Essays and Speeches* (Trumansburg, NY: Crossing Press, 1984), 54.

72 **"self-effacement, depression, self-denial"**: Lorde, *Sister Outsider*, 57–58.

75 **on the acceptability scale:** "Americans Hold Record Liberal Views on Most Moral Issues," Gallup, May 11, 2017, accessed September 17, 2020, https://news.gallup.com /poll/210542/americans-hold-record-liberal-views-moral-issues.aspx.

75 *more* **likely to have affairs:** Wendy Wang, "Who Cheats More? The Demographics of Infidelity in America," Institute for Family Studies, January 10, 2018, https://if studies.org/blog/who-cheats-more-the-demographics-of-cheating-in-america.

77 **"selflessness and obligations"**: Dalma Heyn, *The Erotic Silence of the American Wife* (New York: Turtle Bay Books, 1992), 188.

77 **"take care of anyone else"**: Esther Perel, *The State of Affairs: Rethinking Infidelity* (New York: Harper, 2017), 185.

79 **"all my experience"**: Lorde, *Sister Outsider*, 57.

79 **"emerged from a trance"**: Heyn, *The Erotic Silence of the American Wife*, 188.

CHAPTER 4: THE VULNERABILITY PARADOX

88 **"at their mercy"**: Katherine Angel, *Tomorrow Sex Will Be Good Again: Women and Desire in the Age of Consent* (Brooklyn, NY: Verso, 2021), 99.

89 **"no end to desire?"**: Carole S. Vance, "Pleasure and Danger: Toward a Politics of Sexuality," in *Pleasure and Danger: Exploring Female Sexuality*, ed. Carole S. Vance (Boston: Routledge & Kegan Paul, 1984), 5.

89 **"Her body wants to"**: Helen Gurley Brown, *Sex and the Single Girl: The Unmarried Woman's Guide to Men* (New York: Random House, 1962), 226.

89 **"unwracked by guilt"**: Brown, *Sex and the Single Girl*, 228.

89 **"most emotional problems"**: Brown, *Sex and the Single Girl*, 229.

89 **her own needs:** Brown, *Sex and the Single Girl*, 227.

90 **"what makes a man happy"**: Brown, *Sex and the Single Girl*, 71, 73.

90 **"a little dead"**: Karen Durbin, "Casualties of the Sex War: A Women's Lib Dropout," *Village Voice*, April 6, 1972, https://www.villagevoice.com/2011/02/10/casualties-of -the-sex-war-a-womens-lib-dropout.

90 **"really like each other!"**: Shere Hite, *The Hite Report: A Nationwide Study on Female Sexuality* (New York: Macmillan, 1976), 328.

91 **"the total separation"**: Hite, *The Hite Report*, 331.

91 **"people who are emotionally inadequate"**: Hite, *The Hite Report*, 331.

91 **"holding something back"**: Ellen Willis, "Coming Down Again," in *The Essential Ellen Willis*, ed. Nona Willis Aronowitz (Minneapolis: University of Minnesota Press, 2014), 284.

91 **"leave me alone"**: Hite, *The Hite Report*, 315.

92 **"in a state of fear"**: Susan Brownmiller, *Against Our Will: Men, Women, and Rape* (New York: Simon & Schuster, 1975), 14–15.

93 **isn't compatible with male aggression:** Johanna Fateman and Amy Scholder, eds., *Last Days at Hot Slit: The Radical Feminism of Andrea Dworkin* (South Pasadena, CA: Semiotext(e), 2019), 69, 220, 170, 135, 203.

93 **"women feel 'unfeminine' and unworthy"**: Ellen Willis, "Lust Horizons: Is the Women's Movement Pro-Sex?," in Aronowitz, *The Essential Ellen Willis*, 204.

94 **"we just can't control him"**: Ellen Willis, "Feminism, Moralism, and Pornography," in Aronowitz, *The Essential Ellen Willis*, 94.

94 **"not ladyhood, not anything"**: Toni Morrison, "What the Black Woman Thinks about Women's Lib," *New York Times*, August 22, 1971, https://www.nytimes.com /1971/08/22/archives/what-the-black-woman-thinks-about-womens-lib-the-black -woman-and.html.

95 **"depicted as shit"**: Alice Walker, "Coming Apart," in *Take Back the Night: Women on Pornography*, ed. Laura Lederer (New York: William Morrow, 1980), 103.

95 **"invisible empire of womankind"**: Hortense J. Spillers, "Interstices: A Small Drama of Words," in Vance, *Pleasure and Danger*, 74.

95 **"explain my sexuality"**: Lorna N. Bracewell, *Why We Lost the Sex Wars: Sexual Freedom in the #MeToo Era* (Minneapolis: University of Minnesota Press, 2021), 170.

95 **vivid images of sexual desire:** "Passage," Cherríe Moraga, in Vance, *Pleasure and Danger*, 422; Cherríe Moraga, "La Dulce Culpa," in Vance, *Pleasure and Danger*, 417.

95 **"a white woman's thing"**: Cherríe Moraga, interview with the author, November 16, 2020.

95 **"slow to appear?"**: Bracewell, *Why We Lost the Sex Wars*, 177.

97 **"they must be weak"**: Paula Kamen, *Her Way: Young Women Remake the Sexual Revolution* (New York: New York University Press, 2000), 234.

97 **hypersexual and unflappable:** Joan Morgan, interview with the author, September 1, 2020.

97 **"complete sense of power"**: Clover Hope, "The Meaning of Lil' Kim" (book excerpt), *Pitchfork*, January 25, 2021, https://pitchfork.com/thepitch/the-meaning -of-lil-kim-motherlode-book.

98 **"not to peek"**: Ellen Willis, untitled article on teen sex, circa 1989, Ellen Willis fonds, Schlesinger Library at the Radcliffe Institute, Cambridge, Massachusetts.

99 the **"agency line"**: Laina Y. Bay-Cheng, "The Agency Line: A Neoliberal Metric for Appraising Young Women's Sexuality," *Sex Roles* 73 (2015): 279–91.

102 **mine was a mix of both:** Bay-Cheng, "The Agency Line," 282.

102 **"a funny reversal"**: Angela Chen, *Ace: What Asexuality Reveals about Desire, Society, and the Meaning of Sex* (Boston: Beacon Press, 2020), 63.

103 **"came out fine"**: Nona Willis Aronowitz, "Come Home with Me, Baby!" *New York Observer*, February 19, 2007, https://observer.com/2007/02/come-home-with -me-baby.

103 **"bullet proof glass"**: Rachel Simmons, "Why the Hook Up Culture Is Hurting Girls," RachelSimmons.com, February 2010, https://www.rachelsimmons.com /why-the-hook-up-culture-is-hurting-girls.

103 **"that shit sucks"**: Nona Willis Aronowitz, "Thoughts on 'Hook Up Culture,' or What I Learned from My High School Diary," *Women's Media Center*, February 28, 2010, https://www.womensmediacenter.com/fbomb/thoughts-on-hook-up-culture -or-what-i-learned-from-my-high-school-diary.

103 **"Girls deserve to discover themselves"**: Aronowitz, "Thoughts on 'Hook Up Culture.'"

104 **a magical manifesto**: Alana Massey, "Against Chill," *Matter*, April 1, 2015, https:// medium.com/matter/against-chill-930dfb60a577.

106 **to be trusted with others' vulnerability**: Jaclyn Friedman, "Sex & Consent: It's Time to Go Beyond the Rules," *Refinery29*, September 6, 2018, https://www .refinery29.com/en-us/sex-consent-laws-yes-means-yes-jaclyn-friedman.

106 **this "humanizing ethic" in action**: Nona Willis Aronowitz, "'Yes Means Yes': Can Teaching Good Sex Prevent Rape on Campus?," NBC News, October 16, 2014, https://www.nbcnews.com/news/education/yes-means-yes-can-teaching-good-sex -prevent-rape-campus-n226416.

114 **surprise vulnerabilities may lie in wait**: For further discussion of this concept, including how the unknown is both necessary and makes room for coercion, see the "Vulnerability" chapter in Katherine Angel's *Tomorrow Sex Will Be Good Again*.

CHAPTER 5: THE VULNERABILITY GRADIENT

115 **"Pleasure warred with common sense"**: Saidiya Hartman, *Wayward Lives, Beautiful Experiments: Intimate Histories of Social Upheaval* (New York: W.W. Norton, 2019), 220.

117 **Then there are women of color**: For more on the history of stereotypes about women of color's sexuality, see Melissa V. Harris-Perry, *Sister Citizen: Shame, Stereotypes, and Black Women in America* (New Haven, CT: Yale University Press, 2013); Myra Mendible, ed., *From Bananas to Buttocks: The Latina Body in Popular Film and Culture* (Austin: University of Texas Press, 2007), 8–9; Patricia Park, "The Madame Butterfly Effect: Tracing the History of a Fetish," Bitch, July 30, 2014, https://www.bitchmedia .org/article/the-madame-butterfly-effect-asian-fetish-history-pop-culture; and Leila Ettachfini, "The Women Fighting Sexist, Racist Stereotypes around 'Belly Dancing,'" *Vice*, July 11, 2017, https://www.vice.com/en/article/43dajq/the-arab-women -fighting-sexist-racist-stereotypes-around-belly-dancing.

118 **"the brown girl's paradox":** Fariha Roisin, "The Brown Girl's Paradox: We're Both Invisible and Sexualized," *Splinter*, January 12, 2016, https://splinternews.com/the-brown-girls-paradox-were-both-invisible-and-sexual-1793854038.

118 **Selah's grandmother:** The family history in this section and the personal history of Selah (a pseudonym) in the following sections are based on several interviews with Selah conducted by the author in July 2020 and August 2021.

120 **"history in sexual soil":** Joane Nagel, *Race, Ethnicity, and Sexuality: Intimate Intersections, Forbidden Frontiers* (Oxford: Oxford University Press, 2003), 125.

120 **"mistresses, whores, or breeders":** Paula Giddings, *When and Where I Enter: The Impact of Black Women on Race and Sex in America* (New York: William Morrow, 1988), 43.

120 **"than any other girls":** Hartman, *Wayward Lives*, 220.

121 **not to judge her too harshly:** Harriet Jacobs, *Incidents in the Life of a Slave Girl* (Chapel Hill: University of North Carolina Press, 2003), 86, ebook, https://docsouth.unc.edu/fpn/jacobs/jacobs.html.

121 **"destroy her image of herself":** Michele Wallace, *Black Macho and the Myth of the Superwoman* (New York: Dial Press, 1979), 144.

121 **"law court and custom":** Chester J. Fontenot, Sarah Gardner, and Mary Alice Morgan, eds., *W.E.B. Du Bois and Race: Essays Celebrating the Centennial Publication of "The Souls of Black Folk"* (Macon, GA: Mercer University Press, 2001), 161.

121 **"black women who got pregnant":** David Allyn, *Make Love, Not War: The Sexual Revolution: An Unfettered History* (Boston: Little, Brown, 2000), 88–89.

122 **"dresses down, and legs closed":** Shayne Lee, *Erotic Revolutionaries: Black Women, Sexuality, and Popular Culture* (Lanham, MD: Hamilton Books, 2010), viii.

122 **Black women are less likely:** Lisa Wade, *American Hookup: The New Culture of Sex on Campus* (New York: W.W. Norton, 2017), 93.

122 **less likely to have oral sex:** Beth A. Auslander, Frank M. Biro, Paul A. Succop, Mary B. Short, and Susan L. Rosenthal, "Racial/Ethnic Differences in Patterns of Sexual Behavior and STI Risk among Sexually Experienced Adolescent Girls," *Journal of Pediatric Adolescent Gynecology* 22, no. 1 (February 2009): 33–39, https://doi.org/10.1016/j.jpag.2008.01.075.

122 **being perceived by adults:** Rebecca Epstein, Jamilia Blake, and Thalia González, "Girlhood Interrupted: The Erasure of Black Girls' Childhood" (Georgetown Law Center on Poverty and Inequality, June 27, 2017), http://dx.doi.org/10.2139/ssrn.3000695.

122 **"gits real hot":** Alice Walker, *The Color Purple* (New York: Washington Square Press, 1982), 79.

123 **this impossible choice:** Joan Morgan, interview with the author, September 1, 2020.

123 **Strong Black Woman "in recovery":** Joan Morgan, *When Chickenheads Come Home to Roost: A Hip Hop Feminist Breaks It Down* (New York: Simon & Schuster, 2000), 109.

123 **"the 'right way'?":** Morgan, *When Chickenheads Come Home to Roost*, 188.

123 **"might drop the ball":** Morgan, *When Chickenheads Come Home to Roost*, 146.

128 **A couple of miles south:** The quotes from the following two paragraphs are found in Hartman, *Wayward Lives,* 123–53.

129 **"The violence of the archive":** Saidiya Hartman, "Venus in Two Acts," *Small Axe* 12, no. 2 (2008): 1–14, muse.jhu.edu/article/241115.

129 **"archival silence":** Lauren F. Klein, "The Image of Absence: Archival Silence, Data Visualization, and James Hemings," *American Literature* 85, no. 4 (2013): 661–88.

129 **"pale imitation of the ghetto girl":** Hartman, *Wayward Lives*, xiv.

129 **"evidence of wrongdoing":** Hartman, *Wayward Lives*, 241.

129 **"a minor figure":** Hartman, *Wayward Lives*, 225.

129 **"unmade men and women":** Hartman, *Wayward Lives*, 323.

130 **out of reach for them:** Catherine Damman, "Saidiya Hartman," *Art Forum*, July 14, 2020, https://www.artforum.com/interviews/saidiya-hartman-on-insurgent-histories-and-the-abolitionist-imaginary-83579.

130 **"open rebellion":** Hartman, *Wayward Lives*, xiii.

130 **"experience something else?":** Damman, "Saidiya Hartman."

130 **"irresistible to me":** adrienne maree brown, *Pleasure Activism: The Politics of Feeling Good* (Chico, CA: AK Press, 2019), 24.

130 **"male models of power":** Audre Lorde, *Sister Outsider: Essays and Speeches* (Trumansburg, NY: Crossing Press, 1984), 53.

130 **"personal expression and pleasure":** Stephanie Camp, *Closer to Freedom: Enslaved Women and Everyday Resistance in the Plantation South* (Chapel Hill: University of North Carolina Press, 2004), 68, 83.

131 **"twinned with our pain":** Joan Morgan, "Why We Get Off: Moving Towards a Black Feminist Politics of Pleasure," *Black Scholar* 45, no. 4 (2015): 36, https://doi.org/10.1080/00064246.2015.1080915.

131 **"the sanctity of dogma":** Morgan, "Why We Get Off," 38.

131 **analyzing and plotting:** Joan Morgan, interview with the author, September 1, 2020.

131 **BDSM can be a powerful:** See Ariane Cruz, *The Color of Kink: Black Women, BDSM, and Pornography* (New York: New York University Press, 2016).

131 **intentional and subversive:** Brittney C. Cooper, *Beyond Respectability: The Intellectual Thought of Race Women* (Urbana: University of Illinois Press, 2017), 74.

132 **"lives to our detriment":** Treva B. Lindsey and Jessica Marie Johnson, "Searching for Climax: Black Erotic Lives in Slavery and Freedom," *Meridians* 12, no. 2 (2014): 169–95.

132 **"can be created"**: Lindsey and Johnson, "Searching for Climax."

132 **"Damn the law"**: Hartman, *Wayward Lives*, 147.

CHAPTER 6: AN OLD MALE REVOLT IN A NEW DISGUISE

135 **"That neat, angel-devil"**: Sophie Kupetz, "'That Neat, Angel-Devil Theory Was No Longer Useful': Prisoners against Rape, the D.C. Rape Crisis Center and the Partnership That Transcended the Prison Walls and Critiqued the Society That Built Them" (bachelor's thesis, Brown University, 2019), 73.

135 **In January 1969**: The inauguration incident is reconstructed from Ellen Willis, "Up from Radicalism: A Feminist Journal," in *The Essential Ellen Willis*, ed. Nona Willis Aronowitz (Minneapolis: University of Minnesota Press, 2014), 15; Alice Echols, *Daring to Be Bad: Radical Feminism in America, 1967–1975* (Minneapolis: University of Minnesota Press, 1989), 113–117; Marilyn Webb, interview with the author, January 11, 2019; and Susan Faludi, "Death of a Revolutionary," *New Yorker*, April 8, 2013, https://www.newyorker.com/magazine/2013/04/15/death-of-a-revolutionary.

136 **"the mildest speech"**: Faludi, "Death of a Revolutionary."

137 **"through independence and solidarity"**: Willis, "Up from Radicalism," 15.

137 **"The system is like a woman"**: Echols, *Daring to Be Bad*, 144.

137 **"illuminated [their] economic construct"**: Shulamith Firestone, *The Dialectic of Sex: The Case for Feminist Revolution* (New York: Bantam Books, 1972), 5.

137 **"Che Guevara with breasts"**: Michele Wallace, *Black Macho and the Myth of the Superwoman* (New York: Dial Press, 1979), 13.

138 **"a farcical gyration of dykes"**: Shere Hite, *The Hite Report on Male Sexuality* (New York: Alfred A. Knopf, 1981), 312.

139 **"more fun to be with"**: Hite, *The Hite Report on Male Sexuality*, 316.

139 **"easier to offend people"**: Hite, *The Hite Report on Male Sexuality*, 317.

139 **"and more love"**: Hite, *The Hite Report on Male Sexuality*, 310.

139 **"make me nervous and uncomfortable"**: Hite, *The Hite Report on Male Sexuality*, 112.

139 **"I was lucky to have"**: Erica Jong, email to the author, January 10, 2019.

140 **"rug out from under me"**: Vivian Gornick, interview with the author, January 10, 2019.

140 **"looking for a scab"**: Robert Christgau to Ellen Willis, October 17, 1969.

140 **"unfathomable and unchangeable"**: Daphne Davies, "Falling in Love Again," *Red Rag*, no. 13 (1978): 14.

141 **"delighted and excited for Ellen"**: Alix Kates Shulman, email to the author, July 31, 2021.

141 **"support to be more independent"**: Bonnie Bellow, interview with the author, August 3, 2021.

141 "combat in practice": Davies, "Falling in Love Again," 14.

142 the bad-faith motto: Joanna Russ, *On Strike Against God* (Brooklyn, NY: Out & Out Books, 1980), 33.

143 "It coexists, never peacefully": Judith Levine, *My Enemy, My Love: Women, Men, and the Dilemmas of Gender* (New York: Anchor Books/Doubleday, 1993), 3.

147 Riot grrrl icon Kathleen Hanna: Kathleen Hanna, email interview with the author, September 23, 2016.

150 "washes the dishes": Judy Jarvis, "New Rules in the Mating Game," *Esquire*, July 4, 1978, https://classic.esquire.com/article/1978/7/4/new-rules-in-the-mating-game.

150 "yes to sex more frequently": Hite, *The Hite Report on Male Sexuality*, 309.

151 "their ability to be human": Jack Sawyer, "On Male Liberation," *Liberation* 15, nos. 6–8 (August–October 1970): 32.

151 a feature on men's liberation: Barry Farrell, "You've Come a Long Way, Buddy," *Life*, August 27, 1971, 50–59.

152 "we're talking about feelings": Lisa Hammel, "Men's Lib—Almost Underground, but a Growing Movement," *New York Times*, August 9, 1972, https://www.nytimes.com/1972/08/09/archives/mens-lib-almost-underground-but-a-growing-movement.html.

152 "phony parts of masculinity": Hammel, "Men's Lib—Almost Underground."

152 On the phone, he was: Warren Farrell, interview with the author, December 11, 2018.

153 "a male mystique": Warren Farrell, *The Liberated Man: Beyond Masculinity; Freeing Men and Their Relationships with Women* (New York: Random House, 1974), 69.

153 "success objects": Farrell, *The Liberated Man*, 83, 347.

153 "a view of personality": Marc Feigen Fasteau, *The Male Machine* (New York: McGraw-Hill, 1974), 196.

153 *People* magazine profiled: May Vespa, "Woman's Lib Marries Man's Lib: A Real-life 'Adam's Rib,'" *People*, December 9, 1974, https://people.com/archive/womans-lib-marries-mans-lib-a-real-life-adams-rib-vol-2-no-24.

153 "a spy in the ranks": Gloria Steinem, "Introduction," in Fasteau, *The Male Machine*, xiv.

154 "control her husband": Warren T. Farrell, "The Human Lib Movement: II," *New York Times*, June 18, 1971, https://www.nytimes.com/1971/06/18/archives/the-human-lib-movement-ii.html.

154 "Men may be even *more*": Farrell, *The Liberated Man*, 98.

154 "less vulnerable to guilt": Herb Goldberg, *The Hazards of Being Male: Surviving the Myth of Masculine Privilege* (New York: New American Library, 1977), 170.

154 the Gray Flannel Dissidents: Barbara Ehrenreich, *The Hearts of Men: American Dreams and the Flight from Commitment* (New York: Anchor Books, 1983), loc. 553, Kindle.

154 "something was wrong": Ehrenreich, *The Hearts of Men*, loc. 553–66, Kindle.

154 **"the great sentimental lie"**: Richard Yates, *Revolutionary Road* (New York: Vintage Books, 2008), 117.

155 **"new disguise"**: Ehrenreich, *The Hearts of Men*, loc. 2085–2100, Kindle.

155 **"respond to feminism"**: Ehrenreich, *The Hearts of Men*, loc. 2085, Kindle.

155 **"sounded spiteful or misogynist"**: Ehrenreich, *The Hearts of Men*, loc. 2100, Kindle.

155 **"great hope for men's groups"**: Ellen Willis to Robert Christgau, March 13, 1970.

155 **"whining about being"**: Carol Hanisch, "Men's Liberation," in *Feminist Revolution*, ed. Kathie Sarachild (New York: Random House, 1978), 75–76.

156 **"those who have the luxury"**: Warren Farrell, email to the author, August 1, 2021.

156 **"a self-conscious quest for manhood"**: Paula Giddings, *When and Where I Enter: The Impact of Black Women on Race and Sex in America* (New York: William Morrow, 1988), 60.

156 **some scholars believe machismo**: Alfredo Mirande, *Hombres y Machos: Masculinity and Latino Culture* (London: Routledge, 2018), 36, 45.

156 **"The official ideology"**: Ehrenreich, *The Hearts of Men*, loc. 2366, Kindle.

157 **"embarrassing vanguard"**: Farrell, "You've Come a Long Way, Buddy," 55.

157 **A 1975 *New York Times* review**: Larry McMurtry, "Why Can't a Man Be More Like a Woman?," *New York Times*, January 5, 1975, https://www.nytimes.com/1975/01/05/archives/why-cant-a-man-be-more-like-a-woman.html.

157 **"On some level every man"**: Farrell interview.

157 **"Obviously I would rather"**: Farrell, *The Liberated Man*, 62.

158 **is it worth listening to?**: Farrell interview.

160 **I still remembered a story**: This story is reconstructed from Loretta Ross, interview by Joyce Follet, Northampton, Massachusetts, November 2004–February 2005, transcript, Voices of Feminism Oral History Project, https://www.smith.edu/libraries/libs/ssc/vof/transcripts/Ross.pdf; Kupetz, "'That Neat, Angel-Devil Theory Was No Longer Useful.'"

160 **She shared her own experiences**: Loretta Ross, "I'm a Black Feminist. I Think Call-Out Culture Is Toxic," *New York Times*, August 17, 2019, https://www.nytimes.com/2019/08/17/opinion/sunday/cancel-culture-call-out.html.

161 **"being resentful, and so on"**: Ellen Willis, "Coming Down Again: After the Age of Excess," in Aronowitz, *The Essential Ellen Willis*, 285.

CHAPTER 7: IN IT FOR THE DICK

167 **ever wry and ever optimistic**: See Jane Ward, *The Tragedy of Heterosexuality* (New York: New York University Press, 2020), for a complete discussion of this "collective performance of resilience."

170 **Polina's growing lust for Molly:** Rita Mae Brown, *Rubyfruit Jungle* (New York: Bantam Books, 1977), 198–201.

171 **"pretty Emilio Pucci dresses":** Rita Mae Brown, *Rita Will: Memoir of a Literary Rabble-Rouser* (New York: Bantam Books, 1997), 224.

171 **"the act of women":** Brown, *Rita Will*, 225.

171 **"I'm a lesbian":** Brown, *Rita Will*, 228.

172 **"a gay woman's life":** Brown, *Rita Will*, 234.

173 **"male-defined response patterns":** Radicalesbians, "The Woman-Identified Woman," in *Out of the Closets: Voices of Gay Liberation*, ed. Karla Jay and Allen Young (New York: Douglas Book Corp., 1972), 174–75.

173 **"the key to liberation":** Charlotte Bunch, "Lesbians in Revolt," in *Radical Feminism: A Documentary Reader*, ed. Barbara A. Crow (New York: New York University Press, 2000), 336.

173 **the term "lesbian chauvinist":** Jill Johnston, *Lesbian Nation: The Feminist Solution* (New York: Simon & Schuster, 1973), 148, 153.

174 **"build a politic":** Combahee River Collective, "The Combahee River Collective Statement," 1977, Black Past, https://www.blackpast.org/african-american-history/combahee-river-collective-statement-1977.

174 **"The T-line to Black Roxbury":** Cherríe Moraga and Gloria Anzaldúa, eds., *This Bridge Called My Back: Writings by Radical Women of Color* (New York: Kitchen Table, Women of Color Press, 1983), xiii.

174 **"Being lesbian and raised Catholic":** Gloria Anzaldúa, *Borderlands/La Frontera: The New Mestiza* (San Francisco: Aunt Lute Book Company, 1987), 19.

174 **"an act of resistance":** Cheryl Clarke, "Lesbianism: An Act of Resistance," in Moraga and Anzaldúa, *This Bridge Called My Back*, 128.

174 **"I name myself 'lesbian'":** Cheryl Clarke, "New Notes on Lesbianism," in *The Days of Good Looks: The Prose and Poetry of Cheryl Clarke, 1980 to 2005* (Boston: Da Capo, 2006), 81.

175 **dismissed bi women:** Sharon Dale Stone, "Bisexual Women and the 'Threat' to Lesbian Space: Or What If All the Lesbians Leave?" *Frontiers: A Journal of Women Studies* 16, no. 1 (1996): 108, https://doi.org/10.2307/3346927.

175 **"at the cost of my own":** Lani Ka'ahumanu, "The Bisexual Community: Are We Visible Yet?," *The 1987 March on Washington for Lesbian and Gay Rights Civil Disobedience Handbook*, October 8–13, 1987, https://www.lanikaahumanu.com/OUT%20OUT RAGED.pdf.

175 **influential 1971 essay:** Sue Katz, "Smash Phallic Imperialism," in Jay and Young, *Out of the Closets*, 259–61.

175 **"Every woman here knows":** Robin Morgan, *Going Too Far: The Personal Chronicle of a Feminist* (New York: Vintage Books, 1978), 181.

176 **"come very loudly"**: Lorna N. Bracewell, *Why We Lost the Sex Wars: Sexual Freedom in the #MeToo Era* (Minneapolis: University of Minnesota Press, 2021), 166.

176 **"wanted to fuck"**: Cherríe Moraga, interview with the author, November 16, 2020.

176 **"pure as snow"**: Susan Helenius, "Returning the Dyke to the Dutch," *Everywoman*, July 9, 1971, n.p.

176 **"both black people *and* lesbians"**: Dajenya, "Sisterhood Crosses Gender Preference Lines," in *Bi Any Other Name: Bisexual People Speak Out*, ed. Loraine Hutchins and Lani Ka'ahumanu (Boston: Alyson Publications, 1991), 249.

177 **"they taste good"**: Brown, *Rubyfruit Jungle*, 203.

178 **"on that account, too"**: Brown, *Rubyfruit Jungle*, 201.

179 **"fuck me / til dawn"**: Denise F. Fitzer, "Audre Lorde's Expansive Influence on Black Lesbians: Jewelle Gomez, Cheryl Clarke, and Kate Rushin" (master's thesis, Eastern Illinois University, 2000), 36, https://thekeep.eiu.edu/theses/1611.

179 **"I want age, knowledge"**: Cherríe Moraga, "The Slow Dance," in *Loving in the War Years* (Boston: South End, 1983), 26.

179 **"prey before her hunter"**: Cherríe Moraga, "Where Beauty Resides," in *The Last Generation: Prose and Poetry* (Boston: South End Press, 1993), 182.

180 **"maintained by force"**: Adrienne Rich, "Compulsory Heterosexuality and Lesbian Existence," *Signs* 5, no. 4 (1980): 648, http://www.jstor.org/stable/3173834.

180 **"freely and powerfully assumed"**: Rich, "Compulsory Heterosexuality and Lesbian Existence," 657.

180 **"My commitment to heterosexual sex"**: Ellen Willis, "Up from Radicalism: A Feminist Journal," in *The Essential Ellen Willis*, ed. Nona Willis Aronowitz (Minneapolis: University of Minnesota Press, 2014), 18.

183 **"dimly good"**: Brown, *Rubyfruit Jungle*, 69.

184 **"performative disidentification"**: Asa Seresin, "On Heteropessimism," *New Inquiry*, October 9, 2019, https://thenewinquiry.com/on-heteropessimism.

184 **study after study**: Justin R. Garcia et al., "Variation in Orgasm Occurrence by Sexual Orientation in a Sample of U.S. Singles," *Journal of Sexual Medicine* 11, no. 11 (2014): 2645–52, https://doi.org/10.1111/jsm.12669; David A. Frederick et al., "Differences in Orgasm Frequency among Gay, Lesbian, Bisexual, and Heterosexual Men and Women in a U.S. National Sample," *Archives of Sexual Behavior* 47 (2018): 273–88; Katherine Rowland, "What I Learned Talking to 120 Women about Their Sex Lives and Desires," *Guardian*, February 5, 2020, https://www.theguardian.com/lifeandstyle/2020/feb/05/katherine-rowland-the-pleasure-gap-women-sex-lives-desire.

188 **"complexities of every kind"**: Carmen Maria Machado, *In the Dream House: A Memoir* (Minneapolis, MN: Graywolf Press, 2019), 48.

188 **"less charitable, arrogance"**: Machado, *In the Dream House*, 109.

188 **writes about how she hung out**: Carol A. Queen, "The Queer in Me," in Hutchins and Ka'ahumanu, *Bi Any Other Name*, 18–20.

189 **"straight culture for the better"**: Seresin, "On Heteropessimism."

189 **"renewed investigation"**: Jane Ward, *The Tragedy of Heterosexuality* (New York: New York University Press, 2020), loc. 74, Kindle.

190 **"but heterosexual misery"**: Ward, *The Tragedy of Heterosexuality*, loc. 2933, Kindle.

190 **"Deep heterosexuality proclaims"**: Ward, *The Tragedy of Heterosexuality*, loc. 2700, Kindle.

191 **pegging, BDSM, or polyamory**: Ward, *The Tragedy of Heterosexuality*, loc. 2646, Kindle.

191 **"your communal living space"**: Yasmin Nair, "Your Sex Is Not Radical," Yasmin Nair.com, June 28, 2015, https://yasminnair.com/your-sex-is-not-radical.

191 **"despite all the difficulty?"**: Ward, *The Tragedy of Heterosexuality*, loc. 2733, Kindle.

192 **"not just blindly"**: Jane Ward, interview with the author, October 21, 2020.

192 **"a place of desire"**: Ward interview.

192 **"silence articulations of women's desire"**: Seresin, "On Heteropessimism."

192 **"I found its consequences"**: Harron Walker, "The Moment I Stopped Knowing How to Label My Sexuality," *W*, February 16, 2021, https://www.wmagazine.com/life/harron-walker-sexuality-column.

193 **identification fosters eroticism**: Ward, *The Tragedy of Heterosexuality*, loc. 2857–69, Kindle.

194 **"I like men, and that's that"**: Walker, "The Moment I Stopped Knowing How to Label My Sexuality."

CHAPTER 8: THE FALLOW PERIOD

195 **"refuge of the mindless"**: Valerie Solanas, *SCUM Manifesto* (Oakland, CA: AK Press, 2013), 36.

197 **In the summer of 1968**: The story of Cell 16's formation was reconstructed from Dana Densmore, "A Year of Living Dangerously: 1968," in *The Feminist Memoir Project: Voices from Women's Liberation*, ed. Rachel Blau DuPlessis and Ann Snitow (New York: Three Rivers Press, 1998); Alice Echols, *Daring to Be Bad: Radical Feminism in America, 1967–1975* (Minneapolis: University of Minnesota Press, 1989); and Dana Densmore, interview with the author, October 22, 2020.

197 **"completely cool and cerebral"**: Solanas, *SCUM Manifesto*, 36.

198 **now-classic piece on celibacy**: Dana Densmore, "On Celibacy," *No More Fun and Games: A Journal of Female Liberation* 1, no. 1 (October 1968): 23–26.

199 **another essay in the same journal**: Dana Densmore, "Sexuality," *No More Fun and Games* 1, no. 1 (October 1968): 54.

199 **"the most lucid person"**: Roxanne Dunbar, "Asexuality," *No More Fun and Games* 1, no. 1 (October 1968): 52.

200 **"committed a crime"**: Judith Levine, *My Enemy, My Love: Women, Men, and the Dilemmas of Gender* (New York: Anchor Books/Doubleday, 1993), 2.

200 **"insufficient unto herself"**: Simone de Beauvoir, *The Second Sex* (London: Vintage, 1997), 679.

200 **"What is love but the payoff"**: Ti-Grace Atkinson, *Amazon Odyssey: The First Collection of Writings by the Political Pioneer of the Women's Movement* (New York: Links Books, 1974), 7.

200 **"a cultural tool of male power"**: Shulamith Firestone, *The Dialectic of Sex: The Case for Feminist Revolution* (New York: Bantam Books, 1971), 147.

200 **"total emotional vulnerability"**: Firestone, *The Dialectic of Sex*, 128.

200 **"logic in the bedroom?"**: Firestone, *The Dialectic of Sex*, 126.

201 **"passion we felt"**: Shere Hite, *The Hite Report: A Nationwide Study on Female Sexuality* (New York: Macmillan, 1976), 338.

201 **"new things can grow"**: Hite, *The Hite Report*, 341–42.

202 **"deny sex to the other"**: Robert Christgau, *Going into the City: Portrait of a Critic as a Young Man* (New York: Dey Street, 2015), 164–65.

202 **"a rest from sex"**: Ellen Willis to Robert Christgau, undated, circa fall 1969.

203 **"sexual love in its most passionate sense"**: Ellen Willis, "The Family: Love It or Leave It," in *The Essential Ellen Willis*, ed. Nona Willis Aronowitz (Minneapolis: University of Minnesota Press, 2014), 106.

203 **"surrendering detachment and control"**: Willis, "The Family," 107.

203 **"our biggest weapon"**: Ellen Willis, "Radical Feminism and Feminist Radicalism," in Aronowitz, *The Essential Ellen Willis*, 241.

204 **"boy crazy"**: Rosalyn Baxandall, email to the author, September 14, 2012.

204 **"our troops couldn't"**: Levine, *My Enemy, My Love*, 2.

204 **"you have to promise"**: Echols, *Daring to Be Bad*, 111.

205 **"from bad relationships"**: Dana Densmore, interview with the author, October 22, 2020.

205 **"I feel a heavy social pressure"**: Hite, *The Hite Report*, 336–37.

205 **"nice but it's not everything!"**: Hite, *The Hite Report*, 336.

206 **Kate Julian wrote of the "sex recession"**: Kate Julian, "Why Are Young People Having So Little Sex?," *Atlantic*, December 2018, https://www.theatlantic.com/magazine/archive/2018/12/the-sex-recession/573949.

207 **"Recognition is a human need"**: Brittney Cooper, *Eloquent Rage: A Black Feminist Discovers Her Superpower* (New York: St. Martin's, 2018), 233.

207 **"I refuse to subject myself"**: Samhita Mukhopadhyay, interview with the author, January 13, 2021.

208 **"not be repressed"**: Angela Chen, *Ace: What Asexuality Reveals about Desire, Society, and the Meaning of Sex* (Boston: Beacon Press, 2020), 49.

208 **"is embarrassing"**: Chen, *Ace*, 50.

208 **"what I mean by real choice"**: Chen, *Ace*, 66.

CHAPTER 9: FIRE NEEDS AIR

211 **"Yes, love is free"**: Emma Goldman, *Anarchism: And Other Essays* (New York: Dover Publications, 1969), 236.

211 **"Your promiscuity tears"**: Candace Falk, *Love, Anarchy, and Emma Goldman: A Biography* (New Brunswick, NJ: Rutgers University Press, 1990), loc. 1071, Kindle.

217 **"'Smashing monogamy' is nothing new"**: Barbara Leon, "The Male Supremacist Attack on Monogamy," in *Feminist Revolution*, ed. Kathie Sarachild (New York: Random House, 1978), 128.

217 **"Until there is genuine equality"**: Ellen Willis, "The Trouble with Marriage," *Newsday* (Nassau edition), October 15, 1972, 111.

217 **"these women's true desires"**: Ellen Willis, "Radical Feminism and Feminist Radicalism," in *The Essential Ellen Willis*, ed. Nona Willis Aronowitz (Minneapolis: University of Minnesota Press, 2014), 232.

217 **The famed pre-AIDS gay bathhouses:** Allan Bérubé, "The History of Gay Bathhouses," *Journal of Homosexuality* 44 (2003): 3–4, 33–53, https://doi.org/10.1300/J082v44n03_03.

218 **"Places devoted to sex"**: Gayle Rubin, "The Catacombs: A Temple of the Butthole," in *Leatherfolk: Radical Sex, People, Politics, and Practice*, ed. Mark Thompson (Boston: Alyson Publications, 1992), 139.

218 **A popular lesbian button:** Lillian Faderman, *Odd Girls and Twilight Lovers: A History of Lesbian Life in Twentieth-Century America* (New York: Penguin, 1992), 232.

219 **"If you want your sex life"**: Brandy Jensen (@BrandyLJensen), "if you want your sex life to heavily rely on google cal i frankly do not care but please don't pretend you are Being Leftist," Twitter, July 28, 2019, 7:20 p.m., https://twitter.com/BrandyLJensen/status/1155619117220712449.

221 **"For the philosophically polyamorous"**: Susan Dominus, "Is An Open Marriage a Happier Marriage?," *New York Times*, May 11, 2017, https://www.nytimes.com/2017/05/11/magazine/is-an-open-marriage-a-happier-marriage.html.

221 **It was the beginning:** The biographical details about Emma Goldman in this passage and the rest of this chapter, unless otherwise indicated, can be found in Emma Goldman, *Living My Life* (New York: Alfred A. Knopf, 1931), digitized by the Anarchist Library, https://theanarchistlibrary.org/library/emma-goldman-living-my-life; Alice Wexler, *Emma Goldman: An Intimate Life* (New York: Pantheon Books, 1984); and Falk, *Love, Anarchy, and Emma Goldman*.

222 **"The new commandment is"**: John C. Spurlock, *Free Love: Marriage and Middle-Class Radicalism in America, 1825–1860* (New York: New York University Press, 1990), 80–81.

222 **Not one man did**: Details about the Greenwich Village scene, Emma Goldman and Mabel Dodge's friendship, and Goldman's first night at the salon can be found in Andrea Barnet, *All-Night Party: The Women of Bohemian Greenwich Village and Harlem, 1913–1930* (Chapel Hill, NC: Algonquin Books of Chapel Hill, 2004).

223 **"their lure remained strong"**: Goldman, *Living My Life*.

224 **"utter despair"**: Goldman, *Living My Life*.

224 **"the stomach, the brain"**: Wexler, *Emma Goldman*, 92.

224 **"as many as she pleases"**: Wexler, *Emma Goldman*, 94.

225 **"that poor little State"**: Goldman, *Anarchism*, 236.

225 **"Can there be anything more outrageous"**: Goldman, *Anarchism*, 231.

225 **She also condemned**: The quotes and facts in this paragraph can be found in Alix Kates Shulman, ed., *Red Emma Speaks: An Emma Goldman Reader* (New York: Open Road Media, 2012), loc. 3019–3124, Kindle.

225 **right to be a "varietist"**: Wexler, *Emma Goldman*, 93.

226 **"nothing but dead leaves remain"**: Shulman, *Red Emma Speaks*, loc. 3124, Kindle.

226 **"a disciple of Emma"**: Wexler, *Emma Goldman*, 142.

227 **"washed for some time"**: Goldman, *Living My Life*.

227 **"exerted such fascination"**: Goldman, *Living My Life*.

227 **"blue-eyed Mommy"**: Falk, *Love, Anarchy, and Emma Goldman*, loc. 4786, Kindle.

227 **"opened up"**: Wexler, *Emma Goldman*, 147.

227 **"your precious head"**: Falk, *Love, Anarchy, and Emma Goldman*, loc. 1027, 1034, Kindle.

228 **"no rebel spirit"**: Falk, *Love, Anarchy, and Emma Goldman*, loc. 1095, Kindle.

228 **"and dismally disagreeable"**: Falk, *Love, Anarchy, and Emma Goldman*, loc. 1098, Kindle.

228 **"foreign to myself"**: Falk, *Love, Anarchy, and Emma Goldman*, loc. 1070, Kindle.

229 **had even finished speaking**: John Boudreau, "All About Emma," *Los Angeles Times*, July 31, 1992, https://www.latimes.com/archives/la-xpm-1992-07-31-vw-4326 -story.html.

229 **"two to harmonize?"**: Falk, *Love, Anarchy, and Emma Goldman*, loc., 1335, Kindle.

229 **"Maybe while I suffer"**: Falk, *Love, Anarchy, and Emma Goldman*, loc. 1003, Kindle.

229 **"for that, hobo mine"**: Falk, *Love, Anarchy, and Emma Goldman*, loc. 1089, Kindle.

230 **"hateful to me"**: Falk, *Love, Anarchy, and Emma Goldman*, loc. 1367, 1361, Kindle.

230 **"on a foaming ocean"**: Falk, *Love, Anarchy, and Emma Goldman*, loc. 190, Kindle.

230 **"I can't do it!"**: Falk, *Love, Anarchy, and Emma Goldman*, loc. 47, Kindle.

230 **"required reading"**: Falk, *Love, Anarchy, and Emma Goldman*, loc. 30, Kindle.

230 **"peacefully in her life"**: Falk, *Love, Anarchy, and Emma Goldman*, loc. 1024, Kindle.

231 **"mired in trivia"**: "Love, Anarchy, and Emma Goldman," *Kirkus Reviews*, August 15, 1984, https://www.kirkusreviews.com/book-reviews/a/candace-falk/love -anarchy-and-emma-goldman/.

231 **"most enduring passion"**: Alice Wexler, letter to the editor, *New York Times*, March 31, 1985, https://www.nytimes.com/1985/03/31/books/l-love-and-emma-goldman -129865.html.

231 **"what love was"**: Candace Falk, voicemail to the author, April 7, 2021.

231 **"the model of the superwoman"**: Alix Kates Shulman, "Emma Goldman's Feminism: A Reappraisal," in Shulman, *Red Emma Speaks*, loc. 206, Kindle.

232 **"Better not to try anything"**: Kate Millett, *Flying* (New York: Alfred A. Knopf, 1974), 16.

232 **"I suspect that"**: Ellen Willis, "The Family: Love It or Leave It," in Aronowitz, *The Essential Ellen Willis*, 107.

232 **"really believe that possessiveness"**: Ellen Willis to Robert Christgau, October 25, 1969.

233 **"hadn't quite taken hold"**: Ellen Willis to Robert Christgau, undated, circa fall 1969.

233 **"born again, into"**: Ellen Willis, "Coming Down Again," in Aronowitz, *The Essential Ellen Willis*, 281.

233 **"And, in a sense, win"**: Willis, "Coming Down Again."

234 WHEN THERE'S A BAD VIBE: Ellen Willis, untitled diary entry, circa 1982, Ellen Willis fonds, Schlesinger Library at the Radcliffe Institute, Cambridge, Massachusetts.

235 WHEN ALL IS REVEALED: Ellen Willis, untitled diary entry, circa 1983/early 1984, Ellen Willis fonds, Schlesinger Library at the Radcliffe Institute, Cambridge, Massachusetts.

236 MY DAD'S AFFAIR: Ellen Willis, fictionalized memoir, circa 2004, Ellen Willis fonds, Schlesinger Library at the Radcliffe Institute, Cambridge, Massachusetts. Note: it is the author's personal judgment that the account is fictionalized memoir.

241 **Fire needs air**: Esther Perel, "The Secret to Desire in a Long-Term Relationship," filmed February 2013 in New York, TED video, 18:51, https://www.ted.com/talks /esther_perel_the_secret_to_desire_in_a_long_term_relationship.

241 **"their separateness is unassailable"**: Esther Perel, *Mating in Captivity: Unlocking Erotic Intelligence* (New York: Harper, 2007), 211.

245 **"delighting each other"**: Dominus, "Is an Open Marriage a Happier Marriage?"

CHAPTER 10: THE REAL EXPERTS

250 **"more closeted than gay people"**: Maya Dusenbery, "Speaking of Abortion," Feministing, September 9, 2009, http://feministing.com/2009/09/09/speaking -of-abortion.

251 **In April 1968**: The story from the following two paragraphs can be found in Ellen Willis "Up from Radicalism," in *The Essential Ellen Willis*, ed. Nona Willis Aronowitz (Minneapolis: University of Minnesota Press, 2014), 10–11.

252 **Only ten months**: Additional details of these early abortion protests, besides where specified, were sourced from Alice Echols, *Daring to Be Bad: Radical Feminism in America, 1967–1975* (Minneapolis: University of Minnesota Press, 1989), 141.

252 **hundreds of women**: Rachel Benson Gold, "Lessons from before Roe: Will Past Be Prologue?," *Guttmacher Policy Review* 6, no. 1 (2003), https://www.guttmacher.org /gpr/2003/03/lessons-roe-will-past-be-prologue.

252 **"tell me a thing"**: Willis, "Up from Radicalism," 16.

254 **"*real* experts—the women"**: Echols, *Daring to Be Bad*, 141.

254 **"never felt less inhibited"**: Willis, "Up from Radicalism," 16.

254 **"two years old"**: Edith Evans Asbury, "Women Break Up Abortion Hearing; Shouts for Repeal of Law Force Panel to Move," *New York Times*, February 14, 1969, https: //www.nytimes.com/1969/02/14/archives/women-break-up-abortion-hearing -shouts-for-repeal-of-law-force.html.

254 **"Men don't get pregnant"**: Ellen Willis, "Hearing," *New Yorker*, February 14, 1969, https://www.newyorker.com/magazine/1969/02/22/hearing.

254 **"angry females"**: Alfred Miele, "Gals Squeal for Repeal, Abort State Hearing," *Daily News*, February 14, 1969, 5.

254 **"That's something, anyway"**: Willis, "Hearing."

254 **"politics rather than"**: Willis, "Up from Radicalism," 16.

255 **"scraping and scraping"**: Susan Brownmiller, "Everywoman's Abortions: 'The Oppressor Is Man,'" *Village Voice*, March 27, 1969, https://womenwhatistobedone.files .wordpress.com/2013/09/1968-03-27-village-voice-full.pdf.

255 **"jump off the Verrazzano Bridge!"**: "Tell It Like It Is: A Transcript of the First Abortion Speakout," transcribed by Georgia Christgau for the speak-out's fiftieth-anniversary event, New York City, March 23, 2019, 9–10.

256 **"confrontation and catharsis"**: Brownmiller, "Everywoman's Abortions."

256 **"drop out of life"**: "Tell It Like It Is," 18.

257 **"So, I had an abortion"**: Nona Willis Aronowitz (@nona), "So, I had an abortion the other day. Among other things, my experience made me realize just how supremely fucked up these fetal heartbeat bills really are," Twitter, January 28, 2019, 12:32 p.m., https://twitter.com/nona/status/1089939181848141825?lang=en.

258 **the odious term "biological clock"**: Richard Cohen, "The Clock Is Ticking for the Career Woman," *Washington Post*, March 16, 1978, https://www.washingtonpost .com/archive/local/1978/03/16/the-clock-is-ticking-for-the-career-woman /bd566aa8-fd7d-43da-9be9-ad025759d0a4/.

259 **indeed had an abortion**: Ellen Willis, "Putting Women Back in the Abortion Debate," in *No More Nice Girls: Countercultural Essays* (Hanover, NH: University Press of New England, 1992), 80.

259 **Maternal mortality**: Katha Pollitt, "Abortion in American History," *Atlantic*, May 1997, https://www.theatlantic.com/magazine/archive/1997/05/abortion-in -american-history/376851/.

259 **twelve thousand safe abortions**: Nadine Brozan, "There's Far More to Abortion Than Finding the Best Price," *New York Times*, August 10, 1974, 34.

259 **two thousand abortion providers**: Edward Weinstock et al., "Abortion Need and Services in the United States, 1974–1975," *Family Planning Perspectives* 8, no. 2 (1976): 58, https://doi.org/10.2307/2133988.

259 **"proud, happy time"**: Alex Ronan, "The First Legal Abortion Providers Tell Their Stories," The Cut, October 13, 2015, https://www.thecut.com/2015/10/first-legal -abortionists-tell-their-stories.html.

260 **"The main feeling"**: Steve Dyer, interview with the author, December 15, 2019.

260 **42 percent of the people**: Weinstock et al., "Abortion Need and Services," 58.

260 **in liberal cities**: Weinstock et al., "Abortion Need and Services," 59.

260 **Poor and rural women**: Weinstock et al., "Abortion Need and Services."

260 **desire for secrecy**: Brozan, "There's Far More," 34.

261 **an investigative book**: See Ellen Frankfort with Frances Kissling, *Rosie: The Investigation of a Wrongful Death* (New York: Dial Press, 1979).

261 **in her honor**: For more on Rosie Jimenez, see Alexa Garcia-Ditta, "Reckoning with Rosie," *Texas Observer*, November 3, 2015, https://www.texasobserver.org/rosie -jimenez-abortion-medicaid.

261 **She bemoaned the fact that the book**: Redstockings 20th Anniversary of 1969 Abortion Speakout, March 3, 1989, New York City, Archive.org, accessed August 5, 2020, https://archive.org/details/Redstockings20thAnniversaryAbortionSpeakout NYC1989.

262 **late-term abortion on Jezebel**: Jia Tolentino, "Interview with a Woman Who Recently Had an Abortion at 32 Weeks," *Jezebel*, June 15, 2016, https://jezebel.com /interview-with-a-woman-who-recently-had-an-abortion-at-1781972395.

264 **"something of importance"**: Steve Dyer, email to the author, March 25, 2021.

CHAPTER 11: GOOD SEX

267 **Before the eighteenth:** Additional details about the history of orgasms and female pleasure, besides the quotes specified, were sourced from Katherine Rowland, *The Pleasure Gap: American Women and an Unfinished Revolution* (New York: Seal Press, 2020), 19–21.

267 **"conceive by them":** Thomas Laqueur, *Making Sex: Body and Gender from the Greeks to Freud* (Cambridge, MA: Harvard University Press, 1992), 2–3.

267 **"the seat of woman's delight":** Jonathan Margolis, *O: The Intimate History of the Orgasm* (New York: Grove Press, 2004), 240.

268 **Historian Thomas Laqueur points out:** Laqueur, *Making Sex*, 8–10.

268 **More recent scholarship has even:** Hallie Lieberman and Eric Schatzberg, "A Failure of Academic Quality Control: The Technology of Orgasm," *Journal of Positive Sexuality* 4, no. 2 (2018): 24–47.

268 **"normal satisfaction":** Simone de Beauvoir, *The Second Sex* (New York: Vintage Books, 1989), 392.

268 **"orgasm is a phenomenon":** Alfred Kinsey, *Sexual Behavior in the Human Female* (Philadelphia: Saunders, 1953), 640.

269 **"normal sexual intercourse":** Theodoor Hendrik van de Velde, *Ideal Marriage: Its Physiology and Technique* (New York: Random House, 1962), 145.

269 **"Only where Love":** Van de Velde, *Ideal Marriage*, 176.

269 **"gush of semen":** Van de Velde, *Ideal Marriage*, 184.

269 **"damage to both body and soul":** Van de Velde, *Ideal Marriage*, 189.

269 **"expert theories of female sexuality":** Barbara Ehrenreich, Elizabeth Hess, and Gloria Jacobs, *Re-Making Love: The Feminization of Sex* (Garden City, NY: Anchor Press/Doubleday, 1986), 65.

270 **Anne Koedt's article:** Anne Koedt, "The Myth of the Vaginal Orgasm," *Notes from the Second Year: Women's Liberation* (1970): 37–41, https://repository.duke.edu/dc/wlmpc/wlmms01039.

271 **Germaine Greer also took issue:** Germaine Greer, *The Female Eunuch* (New York: McGraw-Hill, 1971), 32–35.

272 **"a starring role":** Laura Kipnis, *The Female Thing: Dirt, Sex, Envy, Vulnerability* (New York: Vintage Books, 2007), 43.

272 **"expected of themselves":** Katherine Rowland, "What I Learned Talking to 120 Women about Their Sex Lives and Desires," *Guardian*, February 5, 2020, https://www.theguardian.com/lifeandstyle/2020/feb/05/katherine-rowland-the-pleasure-gap-women-sex-lives-desire.

272 **A widely publicized 2017 survey:** David A. Frederick et al, "Differences in Orgasm Frequency among Gay, Lesbian, Bisexual, and Heterosexual Men and Women in a U.S. National Sample," *Archives of Sexual Behavior* 47 (2018): 273–88.

273 **a reasonable response:** Rowland, "What I Learned."

276 **"If woman suffers":** Beauvoir, *The Second Sex*, 392.

277 **"fucked with their egos":** Ellen Willis, "Coming Down Again," in *The Essential Ellen Willis*, ed. Nona Willis Aronowitz (Minneapolis: University of Minnesota Press, 2014), 282.

277 **"Can't you just smell":** Shulamith Firestone, "Women Rap about Sex," *Notes from the First Year: Women's Liberation* (1968): 9.

280 **"Having sex with John":** Ange (last name withheld), emails to the author, December 20, 2018; January 9, 2019; and February 15, 2019.

281 **"someone to validate them":** John Oh, interview with the author, December 14, 2018.

281 **"whore stigma":** Carol Queen, "Sex Radical Politics, Sex-Positive Feminist Thought, and Whore Stigma," in *Whores and Other Feminists*, ed. Jill Nagle (New York: Routledge, 1997), 125.

281 **"compulsory virtue":** Jill Nagle, ed., *Whores and Other Feminists* (New York: Routledge, 1997), 5.

281 **The woman I interviewed:** "Jan," interview with the author, December 15, 2018.

285 **neoliberal feminism:** See Catherine Rottenberg, *The Rise of Neoliberal Feminism* (Oxford: Oxford University Press, 2018).

285 **"liberation really is":** June Arnold, "Consciousness-Raising," in *Radical Feminism: A Documentary Reader*, ed. Barbara A. Crow (New York: New York University Press, 2000), 285.

286 **"Our most passionate convictions":** Ellen Willis, "Lust Horizons: Is the Women's Movement Pro-Sex?," in Aronowitz, *The Essential Ellen Willis*, 201.

286 **"therapy and somatics":** adrienne maree brown, *Pleasure Activism: The Politics of Feeling Good* (Chico, CA: AK Press, 2019), 183.

286 **"There is no pre-cultural":** Tracy Clark-Flory, *Want Me: A Sex Writer's Journey into the Heart of Desire* (New York: Penguin Books, 2021), 191.

288 **"float into the sea":** Rebecca Solnit, *A Field Guide to Getting Lost* (New York: Penguin, 2006), 141–42.

ABOUT THE AUTHOR

NONA WILLIS ARONOWITZ is the sex and love columnist for *Teen Vogue*. Her essays and reporting have been published in *The New York Times*, *The Cut*, *Elle*, *Vice*, and *Playboy*, among many others. She is the coauthor of *Girldrive: Criss-Crossing America, Redefining Feminism*. She is also the editor of an award-winning anthology of her mother Ellen Willis's rock criticism, called *Out of the Vinyl Deeps*, as well as a comprehensive collection of Willis's work, *The Essential Ellen Willis*, which won the National Book Critics Circle Award for Criticism. She splits her time between Brooklyn and upstate New York.